A Late
Dinner

Discovering the Food
of Spain

Paul Richardson

SCRIBNER

New York   London   Toronto   Sydney

SCRIBNER

A Division of Simon & Schuster, Inc.
1230 Avenue of the Americas
New York, NY 10020

First Scribner hardcover edition August 2007

SCRIBNER and design are trademarks of
Macmillan Library Reference USA, Inc., used under license
by Simon & Schuster, the publisher of this work.

For information about special discounts for bulk purchases,
please contact Simon & Schuster Special Sales:
1-800-456-6798 or business@simonandschuster.com

Book design by Ellen R. Sasahara
Text set in Aldine 401 BT

Manufactured in the United States of America

1   3   5   7   9   10   8   6   4   2

Library of Congress Cataloging-in-Publication Data

Richardson, Paul, date.
A late dinner / Paul Richardson.
p.   cm.
1. Spain—Description and travel. 2. Cookery, Spanish.
3. Food habits—Spain. I. Title.

DP43.2.R43 2007
914.6044092—dc22   2007002417
[B]

ISBN-13: 978-0-7432-8493-6

Photo credits: Heinz Hebeisen/Iberimage: p. 37;
Miguel Raurich/Iberimage: p. 185

*"Cuisine may be generally regarded as a part of a people's culture.
The quality of the fare, the manner in which it is prepared,
the time devoted to its ingestion, the conventions of the dinner table:
these are intimately related to, and frequently reflect,
a people's aesthetic development."*

—Angelo Pellegrini, *The Unprejudiced Palate* (1948)

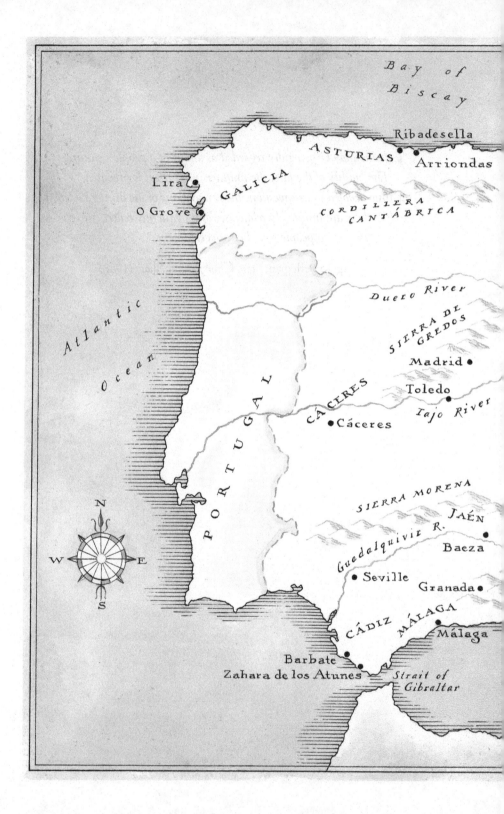

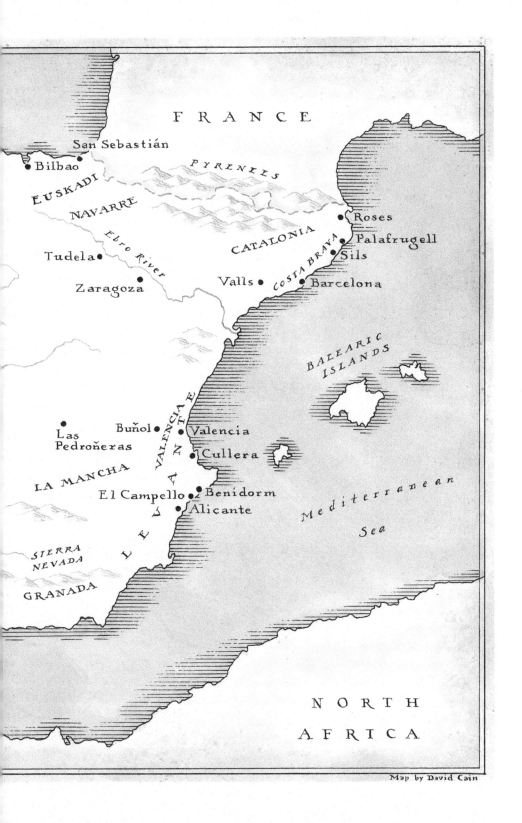

Map by David Cain

Contents

❧

Introduction

RAVEL BROADENS THE MIND; that's true enough. But a whistle-stop on the grand tour, or a weekend break on a low-budget airline, won't widen it very much. Real understanding of a country and its culture takes longer: years and years must go by, practically a lifetime.

The surfaces are what impress us first; they are tastable, curious, striking, or at least inoffensive; they either confirm our prejudices, or ask a bigger question, leading us in. So we nibble away at the edges of a place, telling ourselves with every mouthful that the center will taste roughly similar—anything to insure ourselves against the thousand natural shocks of foreignness. But little by little, perhaps, we begin to acquire the taste. The phrase is precise and oddly profound; it implies that the experience of food is more than a spectacle, something external to ourselves, which can eventually be interiorized and possessed, coming to form part of who we are. Manuel Vicent, the Spanish novelist, says that eating is a mystical act—it converts what you consume into yourself.

When, as a teenager, I crossed the border at Port Bou on the night train from Paris, I had never been to Spain before. As a middle-class family from a well-to-do county of southern England, we generally took our vacations in Italy or France. Spain was not much favored by those of our social group. Whereas Italy and France had bourgeois social stability and a solid infrastructure, Spain seemed somehow rickety, with cheap package hotels lining the coast, and the interior as scary as Africa. In short, it had a dubious reputation. Perhaps that was what attracted me to it.

My formative experience of Spain, my earliest gingerly taste of the way it lived and ate, was a two-month stint one summer on the Inter-rail—that great early experiment in European relations. Interrail was travel on the cheap at a time when there were no budget airlines, no mobile phones, and no e-mail for keeping in touch with home. You carried your life in a belt around your midriff, and if you ran out of money you were in trouble, because the cash machine was not yet a feature of life in southern Europe—and as a callow nineteen-year-old, I was not yet of an age to be trusted with credit cards. Mostly I sur-vived on cheapo bar food: tortilla de patatas, meatballs from tins, patatas bravas laced with spicy sauce, the student standby, and what I call public-transportation bocadillos—chunks of bread with some-thing laid inside them: cheese, ham, or chorizo, but never any olive oil, no tomato, nothing to mitigate their ascetic dryness.

What I knew about Spanish food as a teenager were the standard tourist clichés: paella and gazpacho, gazpacho and paella. My knowl-edge of Spanish ingredients could be scribbled on the writing side of a postcard, one of those kitsch tourist postcards with the flamenco dancer's dress standing out from the photo. Olives, oranges, saffron, garlic . . . what else? I was unfamiliar with the excellence of Spanish ham—unsurprisingly, I now know, since after an outbreak of swine fever in the early 1980s none reached the outside world for almost a decade. I must have heard of manchego cheese, but I could hardly imagine there were any others. Spanish wine was rioja or sherry, sherry or rioja.

My introduction to the Spanish culinary universe was largely con-ditioned by my limited vocabulary: I knew only certain words, and I was too embarrassed to order unfamiliar dishes. My backpacker's budget was dreadfully meager, but I still liked to mark the close of day with a glass of sherry and a plate of almonds. I must have imagined this was a profoundly Spanish thing to do, though, given my age and sta-tus, and the aperitif's inelegant backdrop of station bars and hotel cafeterias, a beer and a packet of potato chips might have been more appropriate.

Nonetheless, there were meals I have never quite forgotten. In late summer, at a little pensión in the Majorcan town of Deià, on a terrace smelling of pinewood and sea air, I was served a fragrant rice dish—my first true Spanish rice, made in the paella with chicken and saffron and peppers, golden and glowing and pungent with saffron; and I drank a bottle of iced rosado all by myself and gazed down at the dark sea in a euphoric, alcoholic blur.

It was August, and Spain was in its usual summer limbo, the cities like ghost towns, the beaches pullulating, the signs in the windows of shops and restaurants bidding their clients farewell until September. Armed with a motley list of contacts, I roamed the country on the cheapest, slowest trains. Spain was in the throes of a democratic revolution, did I but know it. Even in 1982 it felt underdeveloped, and pungently exotic.

The trains were stinky old slam-door carriages with compartments and windows you could pull down and lean out of, and soap in the toilets that you ground into your hand in a powder like pepper from a pepper mill. It was entirely normal, at that innocent time, for rail travelers to offer their food to those sitting around them. One time, on the night train from Paris, a Spanish family took me under their wing and invited me to share their midnight feast: cold breaded lamb chops, tortilla sandwiches, thin-sliced jamón serrano wrapped in aluminum foil, and gazpacho poured into plastic cups from a thermos bottle. The next morning, with an hour to go for Barcelona, out came the picnic box again, and there were sweet María biscuits and café con leche. I was struck by the way the family all dunked their biscuits in the coffee with gusto, raising the cup the better to convey each coffee-soaked biscuit to the mouth. It was my first contact with the sensible Spanish tendency to use solids as a vehicle for liquids: sauce is automatically mopped up with bread, sponge cakes are made "drunken" with sweet wine, and hot chocolate is used as a dip for piping-hot lengths of crisp, oily churros.

I was keen to avoid the expense of staying in hotels, so my route was determined by the dates when I knew my acquaintances would be at home. After Majorca I headed inland to Madrid, where I had the address of a school friend. There was no answer at his family's apartment in the posh Salamanca neighborhood; the concierge told me they'd gone for the summer to their seaside home in Santander. It was a big house with a big garden, right on the seafront at Sardinero beach, I couldn't miss it. So I caught the train north, found the house, and spent a week with the jeunesse dorée of Santander, roaring around town at night with the rich kids in their flashy cars.

On my last night we all went out for a late dinner. I had never before eaten supper at midnight, and found the idea madly decadent. We ate at the fishing dock where canteen-like restaurants dished up plates of seafood for the crowds that came in ravenous from their day on the beach. Tin platters of prawns a la plancha, squid in its own ink, crisp fried battered rings of calamares, juicy steamed mussels, clams a la marinera with parsley and white wine, huge boiled crabs, heaps of little black winkles seemed to emerge from nowhere and land chaotically on a white paper tablecloth that quickly became a stained and crumpled mess. A heady atmosphere flooded the room as a hundred happy eaters shouted their heads off between mouthfuls. There was a squeezing of lemons, a sucking of shells, a cracking of claws, a dunking of bread in the slopping juices, a swigging of Duralex jugsful of sticky sangría packed with ice. This was nothing less than a full-on Spanish feast, loudly vocal, apparently anarchic but actually quite under control. The platters kept on coming and we kept on eating, late into the night. It was all a revelation to me, in my cloistered, cut-and-dried Englishness. I had no idea that it was possible to have so much fun.

THE YEARS WENT BY. There was the university, then a life in London. After spells as a waiter and wine merchant's apprentice I landed an editor's job on a publication with the brave, but in retrospect embarrassing, name of *Taste,* run on a shoestring in a former garage near the old docks at Fulham.

The truly pivotal moments in life are those that happen, as John Lennon once said, when you are busy doing other things. I was clearing my desk on a Friday night in May when the phone rang: it was a woman from the food export department at the Spanish embassy in London. Breathlessly she gave me the lowdown: there was a food fair in Madrid this weekend at which all of the important Spanish chefs of the moment would be present. Someone from the press had dropped out at the last minute: could I go instead? It would mean taking the first flight on Saturday morning. Everything was paid for: I would be the honored guest of the Spanish government.

For a few seconds I hesitated. I had nothing very important planned for the weekend, and the proposal did sound intriguing. But in the late 1980s in London, the very idea of a Spanish chef sounded at least unusual, if not actually oxymoronic. In the wake of the nouvelle cuisine, creativity in restaurant cooking was still essentially the domain of the French, while the rustic cooking most valued at the time was undoubtedly Italian, and the gastronomic avant-garde was most active in California. Spain simply didn't figure.

That May weekend proved to be a watershed in at least two ways. On the Saturday I went to a birthday party at a lake and met the person with whom I was to share my life. Nacho was an agronomist with the ministry of agriculture who specialized in the genetics of seeds and knew more about the growing of vegetables, grains, and fruits than anyone else I have met before or since. It was with Nacho that I first set up house in Spain, on the island of Ibiza, and with him that I still live, on a farm in Extremadura where the two of us produce most of our own food, drawing on Nacho's expertise and my own decade and a half of agricultural experiments.

Nacho had grown up in a family of seven children in which life was a vortex of noise and emotion. In charge of the family kitchen was Nacho's mother, María Teresa, a remarkable cook and woman who, over the years, has become one of my guiding lights in the simple yet variegated art of Spanish home cooking. For almost half a century she has cooked two meals a day of two and sometimes three dishes each, catering to a public that fluctuates wildly depending on which of her children and their spouses, offspring, and friends happens to be passing through her small apartment in Alicante.

María Teresa cannot be persuaded to think there is anything especially remarkable about the food she prepares. But for me, the remarkable fact about her cooking is precisely what she thinks unworthy of mention—her innate understanding that the food you make to please and nourish a family is less about fireworks or fancy produce and more about the quiet rhythm of balanced eating, meal after meal. Her cooking is careful, economical, and flavorful. She is not given to extravagance, except on a few particular occasions, notably Christmas. The type of cuisine she practices, if one could characterize it in a few words, is a Spanish domestic cookery that cuts across regional differences—though her rice dishes, her skill with vegetables like artichokes and cardoons, and her Levantine specialities like pelotas de pava (meatballs made from turkey, with pine nuts and lemon) reflect her roots in the communities of the southeast coast, Alicante and Murcia. Her family, though originally from Asturias in the north, came down in 1910 to run the salt flats at Santa Pola, and never went back.

If that Saturday in Madrid was a red-letter day in my sentimental education, the following day at the food fair was when I realized for the first time that something remarkable was going on in the world of Spanish cuisine. Cooks had come from all over the country to represent their regions in a contest of culinary ambition. They were mostly men and women of my own age, working away with enormous seriousness at field kitchens set up around the fair, producing sophisticated dishes that used Spanish ingredients in radically new ways. The language may have been beyond me, but there was no doubting the sensory impact of beet gazpacho with saffron foam; rice with goat cheese, octopus, asparagus, and paprika; or essence of fresh peas with jellied barnacles and salted butter toffee. On this late spring day flooded with sunshine, there were warmth and color in everything I saw, everything I tasted. There was a stand where fine jamón serrano was being sliced and served—the deepest-flavored ham I had ever tasted, making Parma seem sweetly innocuous. There was a multiplicity of cheeses, wines, sausages, and preserves. All of it seemed to suggest what I had never considered before—that in the matter of ingredients, and in the richness of its regional culinary tradition, Spanish food was worthy to be compared to the famous cuisines of Italy and France. I remember that weekend as a blaze of newness, marking out paths in my life which I am still traveling, a decade and a half after the event.

In 1991 I left London in a brown Mini, as economic recession turned my homeland a shade of ashen gray, and a year's sabbatical turned into a new life.

Over the years, cooking in the Spanish manner became second nature to me; its techniques and rhythms became a part of my life. When I wasn't traveling around the country, meeting fishermen and farmers, cheese makers and chefs, I was cooking for friends, talking about Spanish food, or eating it. My larder filled up with Spanish ingredients, my library with Spanish cookbooks.

In the early years of the twenty-first century, Spain was at a crossroads. It maintained the old and new, the solidly traditional and madly futuristic, in a delicate balance. On one level the country seemed uninterested in its own past: the peseta had been discarded; the new euro currency had been embraced without a whimper of nostalgia. Yet history was clearly still embedded in the culture, in individual lives, in families and communities, in the form of tradition. The observance of time-honored modes of behavior, ethical, linguistic, celebratory, religious, agricultural, architectural, or culinary, was still central to the Spanish modus vivendi. But for how long could the balance last?

Little by little I conjured up a grand design: a yearlong journey that would take me to the heart of the Spanish culinary universe. I would work from the outside in, as I had gotten to know the country in the first place, drawing on formative experiences of Spanish food and life, hunting down the people and landscapes that had shaped the eating habits of the nation. In the course of the year I would spend time seeking out the traditions of the rural interior, and the creative cooking of the modern Spanish city. But for one summer at least, I would stick to the costas, the coasts. I would start with the tourist heartland of Alicante, site of my own particular landfall as a child, then move northward to Valencia, the place which indirectly defines the outside world's perception of Spanish food, providing it with its defining symbol, its "signature dish," the paella. Up north on the Costa Brava, beside the French border, there would be tourist food in its most shameless form, but also alta cocina at the most exalted level. In the coastal communities of the far south, richly traditional but deeply colonized by tourism, I might find that providing for visitors and catering for locals are not so very different. But the Spanish coast is not only the Mediterranean. There is also the Atlantic, and a very different culinary culture, which, nonetheless, has certain crucial elements in common with that other ocean. There was a famous seafood festival I had been wanting to get to for years, up on the far western coast of Galicia. If I wasn't fed up with fish by the time autumn came around, this would be where you'd find me.

It was mid-June, a time of year that in northern climes would be hot enough for high summer, but in Spain is merely the first agreeable stage of summer's four-month journey into Hades. I loaded up the car with maps and restaurant guides; books on history, geography, and the traditional food of the regions; and notebooks full of every contact I had ever made, every new friend whose number I had ever scribbled down in a drunken haze in some late-night bar. I got myself a mobile phone, an iPod full of music, and a box of heartburn pills for when the going got tough. And I did what thousands of European vacationers were doing at this very moment: I slapped on the sun cream and headed for Benidorm.

Coast

1

Levante

T HE SPANISH HAVE A PHRASE, leyenda negra, to indicate a bad
reputation so obstinately perdurable that it takes on the quality of myth. And there have been few legends blacker, if you
discount the Inquisition, the expulsion of the Jews by the Catholic
kings, and the atrocities of the Spanish empire in the New World, than
the abominable food supposedly served in the fondas and posadas of
Spain. What was attractive about this country to foreign writers and
artists was the exotic archaism of a place out of step with the rest of
Europe, its wild and little-visited landscapes, its immense wealth of

architectural and artistic treasures, but never or almost never the quality of its food.

Generally speaking, when writers on Spain have turned their attention to the national cuisine, it has been to cast aspersions. Literary travelers of all eras turn up the same catalog of shocking hygiene, primitive installations, and general ignorance of the culinary arts. Spanish food was thought to be monotonous, poorly prepared in foul conditions, swimming in rancid oil, and stinking of garlic.

The French, while thrilling to the passionate wildness of their southern neighbor, have traditionally turned up their noses at Spanish cuisine. A saying popular in nineteenth-century France declared of Spain: *Des milliers de prêtres, et pas un cuisinier* ("Thousands of priests, and not a single cook"). One of the earliest literary incursions by a Frenchman in the field of Spanish gastronomy is an account by Jean Muret, priest and diplomat, of dinner at a posada in Tolosa in 1666. The meal is presented as tragicomical: it begins with a bowl of thin soup which is intended not to be drunk but to have bread dunked in it. On so doing, the priest burns his mouth. The second course is a salad of "grasses" with oil and vinegar, followed by a piece of goat which needs to be chewed for half an hour in order to be swallowed.

The account of a visit to Spain, a few years later, by the comtesse d'Aulnoy, a lady of mode, exercised a powerful influence on subsequent writers on the subject—despite the distinct possibility that she may not actually have traveled to many of the places she described—contributing in large measure to the popularity of Spain and Spanishness among several generations of French romantics. The countess found *la cuisine espagnole* so repulsive, so excessively flavored with saffron, garlic, and spices, that, she said, she would have died of hunger were it not for the French cook she brought along with her. She did approve of the fruit, especially the figs; she adored the muscat wine; and she thought Spanish lettuces sweet and refreshing. The favorite meal of her trip was a collation offered by an upper-class household in Madrid, at which she happily nibbled at fruit conserves served on gold paper, and drank hot chocolate with milk and egg yolks. With almost everything else, however, the comtesse found fault. In Spain, she pronounced, the roast partridge was "usually" burned to a cinder. The lamb was tender enough (the quality of local lamb is often mentioned by early travel writers), but ruined by being fried in filthy oil. Spanish table manners, or the lack of them, horrified the comtesse: in some establishments she found no cutlery or napkins, her fellow diners burped openly at the table, and their custom of picking their teeth with a stick seemed to her beneath contempt.

Taken as a whole, the image of Spanish food over the centuries is rather like that of the country itself: primitive, crude, and so strongly flavored as to be shocking to delicate palates. Even Richard Ford, whose *Handbook for Spain* (1845) is possibly the best-researched (as well as the most opinionated) travelers' guide to the country ever written, describes the national cuisine as "by no means despicable." The worst stumbling block, for Ford, as for most of the early travelers in Spain, is a somewhat too liberal infusion of garlic. "From the quantity eaten in all southern countries, where it is considered to be fragrant, palatable, stomachic, and invigorating," he writes, "we must assume that it is suited to local tastes and constitutions. Wherever any particular herb grows, there lives the ass who is to eat it."

It is true that, as the author and gastronome Rafael Núñez remarks in his curious study of foreign attitudes toward Spanish cooking, *Con la Salsa de su Hambre* (literally "With the Sauce of Their Hunger"), for much of its history Spain presented serious natural disadvantages to the visitor from northern Europe, unused to the country's extremes of heat and cold, its forbidding terrain, and its unfathomable bureaucracy. To cover the large distances between cities where there was, from the point of view of the nineteenth-century cultural tourist, something to see, required considerable fortitude in the traveler, as well as plenty of money. (The trip from Madrid to Cádiz by stagecoach cost an astronomic 3,000 reales in 1844, three times a schoolmaster's annual salary.) The awfulness of Spanish hotels became one of the great clichés of travel literature—a much-repeated joke divided them into three categories: bad, worse, and worst—and writers fell over each other to regale readers with bug-infested beds, towels the size of handkerchiefs, and sanitary arrangements that were an affront to civilization. Visitors were often advised to bring their own sustenance, because the food provided was supposed to be inedible.

All the same, can the food these travelers were served really have been quite so extravagantly bad? As Rafael Núñez wistfully inquires, how much of what they found in Spain was simply what they expected to find? Spanish food was so routinely disparaged, just as the dreadfulness of Spanish roads and accommodations was so ghoulishly dwelled on, that one wonders whether readers didn't come to expect the thrill of horror these accounts so faithfully provided. It may be that, for early writers traveling in the peninsula, Spanish culinary habits were another fine example of that savage exoticism, that primitive brutishness, which formed the basis of the romantic image of Spain.

THE SUMMER BEFORE I went to the university, my family broke with the habits of a lifetime and took a holiday apartment in Jávea, on the Costa Blanca. We had little money to spend on what we were used to thinking of as luxuries, like groaning platters of fresh seafood. Our meals were taken at the apartment, with its perfectly awful view of a building site, and we kept to the English timetable and mostly to the English culinary repertoire.

During the day we lay on the beach, but when the weather turned cloudy we got into the car and drove along the traffic-clogged roads to take a look at the other resorts strung out along the coast.

So I had been to Benidorm before. To the snobbish middle-class juvenile that I was, Benidorm seemed the epitome of all that was vulgar and plebeian about vacations abroad. I remember the day we went there to laugh in the red, booze-shiny face of mass tourism. In the event, the soaring towers of this Manhattan-on-Sea amazed and rather shocked us; the sheer scale of the operation silenced our snickering. There is something about the sight and sound of 20,000 people having fun in the sun that renders meaningless such elitist concepts as taste and authenticity.

At the beginning of the twenty-first century, Benidorm was still in rude good health. In early June the place was full to the gunwales, and the Playa de Levante, Benidorm's spectacular arc of sand, was a panorama of pink flesh with a flotsam of sunshades above.

Environment, life, and food: all are interconnected. If you drive into Benidorm, what you see of the countryside is almost entirely new; the urbanizaciones have appeared as if by magic in the midst of a landscape as dusty and unforgiving as the moon. Olive trees that once provided oil for food and light now serve as decoration, islands in a bright green sea of irrigated grass. Carob trees whose long brown pods were once used as animal feed, and even kept human beings alive in times of scarcity, have long since been retired from a life of utility.

I parked behind the beach and walked along the Playa de Levante, dodging a succession of pale-skinned families in various states of undress. A background babble of European languages: French, Dutch, German, English, and what sounded like Finnish. A bar on the promenade offered a complete list of the elements likely to appeal to the Anglo-Saxon male on his vacation abroad:

> Sky Sports
>
> Bar Snacks
>
> Live Football
>
> English Beers
>
> Live Racing
>
> Hot Meals

There was a surreal, postmodern quality about Benidorm's food, like something out of the twisted, out-of-kilter, sci-fi worlds of J. G. Ballard. There were pizzerias and pasta joints, English pubs and French bistros, Chinese and Indians and Moroccans and Thais. The menu at one bar zigzagged from spaghetti bolognese and prawn cocktail to French omelette, Hungarian goulash, and arroz a la cubana—the homespun Spanish dish of plain rice, fried egg, fried banana, and tomato sauce, supposedly invented in the 1920s by a Cuban exile in Madrid. Only in a place like this might you find a hybrid of Norwegian tavern and Spanish bar, El Quijote Nordiska Krogen, serving, on the day I put my head around the door, a choice of "beef cordon blue and chips," or "stroggenoff."

In a documentary I once saw on the BBC about British expatriates in Spain, there was an unforgettable image—a corpulent Englishwoman in the tiny kitchen of her restaurant on the Costa Blanca, serving up English dinners with roast beef, gravy, three veg, and Yorkshire pudding, the poor woman pink and sweating in the heat of a Spanish summer. It is not that there is anything wrong with good old-fashioned British fare, especially on a good old-fashioned British winter day, with a cold drizzle falling from a gray sky. But here, under a blistering sun that cracks pavements and strips paint off walls, it is as incongruous as a bullfight in the snow.

Everywhere you looked in the restaurants of Benidorm, there were photographs of food: color snapshots provided to indicate what would arrive on your plate, should you decide to order it. This entirely functional form of food photography is very much a part of Spanish life, and not just in tourist establishments. You see these photos in the kind of restaurant that serves up platos combinados, the "combined plates" numbered one, two, three, in their various permutations of fried egg, bacon, pork chop, fried green pepper, tortilla, tomato, and french fries. These images have canonized a certain type of proletarian cuisine, now going out of fashion as fast as the kitschy images themselves. I find them strangely poignant, and often wonder about the anonymous photographer who must have taken them, probably back in the 1970s. At the café by the church, where a balustrade looks out over Benidorm's two magnificent beaches, one on each side of the peninsula, the photographs of ice cream sundaes and banana splits were now almost completely undistinguishable, their once lurid colors bleached white by a decade of Costa Blanca summers.

The gastronomic history of Benidorm is not well documented, but you can get some idea from the general history of the place and its sudden transformation from rustic village to tourist megapolis. Although the soil of this barren coast is poor, chalky, and lacking in minerals, the village of Beni-Dorm ("son of Dahrim") had always found a way of producing decent harvests of wheat, barley, maize, figs, and carob beans.

In 1926, when the population of the village was 2,160, its main occupations were agriculture and fishing. Benidorm had no proper harbor, but the boats were drawn up on the beach. In 1944, at the height of its importance as a fishing port, no less than 500 tons came in on Benidorm's fleet. By the start of the 1950s, however, it began to be clear that there were easier ways of making money, and the fishing industry foundered.

At the dawn of the tourist era Benidorm tried hard to sell itself, if not quite as a gastronomic paradise, then at least as a place where the diet was healthful and affordable. A press advertisement for the "Grand Sea Bathing Establishment of the Virgin of Suffrage in the Village of Benidorm, property of Don Francisco Ronda y Galindo," assured those readers tempted by the idea of a summer residence by the seaside, that "nowhere else will they find a more benign climate, more delicious beaches, healthier or cheaper food, or a bathing establishment with better conditions for the bather than that which Don Francisco Ronda has the pleasure of offering to the public." A note at the bottom of the advertisement draws our attention to various prices: a kilogram (or kilo) of lamb (1 peseta), a pound of beef (1.75 pesetas), chickens (1.50 each), and boiling fowls (interestingly, hens, at 3 pesetas each, were twice the price of chickens). Red mullet and hake were priced at 1 peseta per kilo. Grapes, melons, pears, apples, peaches, and figs were 10 céntimos a kilo. Vegetables were simply baratísimas: "very cheap." Most of this produce would have come straight from the gardens that stood behind the Playa de Levante, where forests of high-rises now crowd the shoreline.

Leaving Nacho at home to look after the farm, I drove across the country to stay with his mother and father at their place in Alicante. The morning after my arrival we sat on the veranda, with its distant view of the Mediterranean, drinking coffee in the early sunshine. When I told Nacho's father, Manuel, that I was off to Benidorm, he cast his mind back to the days of his youth, when the resort was just a scruffy village surrounded by almond orchards and dry stone walls.

"I knew Benidorm when there was nothing. Nada. Just the village and the beach. What was it like then? It was precioso. Well, the whole coast was lovely," he said mournfully.

"It was just a white village. There were fishing boats, pulled up on the sand. . . . We used to go there on excursions, myself and a few friends. I used to know the man who went around the village with a horse and cart, selling vegetables. The beach had fields behind it, with fig trees. There was never anyone on it. At one end was a chiringuito, a beach shack built of bamboo, where you could have something to eat. It was very simple. I went there once with María Teresa, when we were courting. I think we ate tortilla. María Teresa, do you remember that day?" He called to his wife, who was busy in the kitchen, "Didn't we have tortilla?"

"How should I remember what we ate?" she replied laughingly, bringing in more coffee. "Honestly, Manolo, it was nearly sixty years ago!"

Nothing remains of that time, and few people now remember it.

The dizzying changes Benidorm has undergone during the last half century have given the place an entirely new identity. The town's population has grown tenfold in forty years, from 6,202 in 1961 to 67,573 in 2004. Twenty-eight percent of its inhabitants are English, French, Dutch, German, Moroccan, Ecuadoran, Swedish, or Norwegian. Of the town's 330 restaurants, according to official bulletins, around fifty are "foreign."

James A. Michener, in his odyssey *Iberia,* writes memorably, if fancifully, that when he first came to Spain, around 1932, the traveler arriving near Valencia by boat could smell the orange groves even before he made landfall, as the perfume of their blossoms was carried out to sea on the ocean breezes. More than three-quarters of a century later, the distant fragrance of orange flowers has its modern equivalent in the reek of frying oil, bubbling in a thousand deep-fat fryers in restaurants along the Spanish Mediterranean coast.

By midday I had walked the whole length of the Playa de Levante, and the tourists were already sitting down to their steak pies and stroganoffs. Wedged between a French patisserie and a Spanish pizzeria was an unassuming bar specializing in the cuisine of the neighboring region of Murcia. Spread out on the countertop were baskets of green peppers, artichokes, tomatoes, and broad beans. The huerta, the fertile well-watered region that cradles the city of Murcia, has inculcated a profound respect for vegetables that amounts almost to dependency. Some of the great dishes in the Murcian repertoire are entirely vegetarian. The murcianos' love of broad beans is proverbial, and it's not uncommon to see them munching their way through piles of raw beans, either as a bar snack in a heap beside the plate or along with the main meal. They remove the pods with a stroke of the thumb to devour the tender beans within.

"There used to be a walk along the river, when we visited Murcia," Manuel had reminisced that morning, "where we would all go to walk in the afternoon. In the summer, there used to be a stand selling lettuces, and people would buy one and walk along the river. It was funny to see all these young folk like us strolling along the river, munching these lettuces as if they were ice cream. But actually they were delicious, and a very refreshing food for a summer afternoon."

Only in Murcia could lettuce be conceived of as a fast food.

I sat down gratefully at a table on the terrace and ordered a plate of snails, a handful of fried almonds, and a large Estrella Levante, the excellent local beer of Murcia. The snails—another great levantine favorite, cooked in a sauce with a slight kick of chili heat—arrived with a glassful of toothpicks for wiggling the creatures out of their shells. They tasted so good, and the beer was slipping down so nicely, that I decided to stay put and forget about a proper lunch. The bartender brought me a plate of michirones, the classic murciano stew made with dried broad beans; a plate of zorongollo, a variation of scrambled eggs with onion and zucchini; another large beer; and a couple of juicy salted anchovies with toast and olive oil, and before long I was beginning to feel the relief and satisfaction that come when you realize you have made the right choice about a place to eat. It may have been the purest fluke, but I had managed it. And in a place like Benidorm, the odds were not exactly in my favor.

THAT AFTERNOON I set out on foot from Manuel and María Teresa's house along the beach, the towers of Benidorm gleaming in the distance like a futuristic vision. Between Alicante and Benidorm is a string of minor towns that never quite made it to Benidorm's fame and fortune, but were happy to chug along gently in its wake, often preserving something of their original character. The Playa de San Juan, just to the south, is a magnificent, wide swath of sand, whereas El Campello has an ugly, stony beach, making it imperative for the town to possess some industry other than tourism. That is why it has clung with such tenacity to its little fishing fleet, and still has a proper fish market where the general public can go on most days and buy fish straight off the boats, without any of the intermediaries who cut fishermen's profits and push up prices at the larger Mediterranean ports.

In the early evening sun, after a long hot day, commerce and society spring back to life. Down on the beach at El Campello a game of pétanque was in progress, and a group of old men in shorts and sandals looked on, calling encouragement in Catalan and Spanish. Up on the harborside stood the lonja, a newish brick construction with the kind of all-purpose municipal modern look that could just as well have been a primary school or a library as a fish market.

When I got there the market was about to start. Two boats, tied up in the harbor outside, had just came in from the day's work; their nets lay in a heap on deck, and the blue plastic boxes of fish were being unloaded from the deck to the harborside, and from there to the back door of the lonja. From production to consumption in the shortest possible time, in the shortest possible distance. A crowd was gathering in the interior of the market, watching the fish come in from the boats in lots of a kilogram or sometimes more, each lot on its own white tray.

The slab was filling up: I saw conger eels, flatfish, red mullet, and escórpora, the ugly spiny orange scorpion fish that (as rascasse) is a main ingredient of the French bouillabaisse and bourride. I wandered away from the action to look at the photographs around the walls, which showed El Campello as it used to be in the 1950s. A line of dark little boats along the beach, with a row of low houses behind them. Women and children in rough black dresses, their hair pinned back, each sitting on a nest of nets like a giant spider in a web. The fleet's various boats with their picturesque names: *Marufina, Lolica, Fina Tendero de Terol*. The *Toñi Carmen*, tragically shipwrecked in 1954.

A man in a white coat with a head mike, the auctioneer, was strutting about, explaining the process to his attentive audience. Housewife-cooks of a certain age, in flowery summer dresses with robust arms protruding from their short sleeves. One woman wore the bata de casa, a blue-and-white pinafore that is practically the uniform of the Spanish housewife. The big-bellied man who schmoozed with the auctioneer was clearly a restaurateur. As at any kind of auction, the public fell into two types: buyers and nonbuyers. The latter looked on in curiosity, with the quick superficial gaze of the tourist; the former focused intensely on particular items, their eyes as beady as those of the specimens they examined so expertly.

The merchandise slapped and flapped in its white trays. First up was a flying fish: a novelty item. The auctioneer held it up for all to see, a boxlike creature like one of the Wright brothers' early machines, pushing open tiny concertina wings. The bids went on and on, but the fish failed to take wing in a commercial sense and it was shunted away sadly, unsold and unloved. The unglamorous lots, the ugly and unfashionable fish, went for so little money one wondered whether they were worth anyone's while. An ashen-gray conger eel went for one euro and fifty cents. A kilo of dogfish could be yours for a euro.

One woman made off with a large lampuga (the common dolphin

fish), then came back for three kilos of red mullet: "Do that on the plancha, flip flip, bit of olive oil, bit of lemon, and you've got yourself a nice lunch," spieled the auctioneer. And now we came to the rock-fish, the bony little fish which are essential for a good fish stock, such as that needed for the fish-and-rice caldero typically eaten for Sunday lunch in El Campello. And of course it was a Friday evening, and the whole town was thinking about the weekend. Now suddenly there was a flurry of interest. Hands were going up all over the place. Each tray held three or four of these diminutive monsters—the man called them morralla. Caught up in the bidding fever, I bid three euros for a kilo, proudly taking them to the counter to be weighed and paid for. I would take them back for María Teresa, and beg her to make me a proper caldero for lunch the next day.

A moray eel in an elegant mottled yellow-and-tan design. "That's also a good one for stock," confided the woman in the blue pinafore, who was now standing next to me. Then came a tray of small pargos, with a huge tiger prawn that had somehow gotten in among the fish. And a greasy-looking dogfish, looking more like a catfish. The auctioneer held out the tray so the fish's toothy muzzle faced the audience, and frightened a little boy in the front row.

And now, señoras y señores, for the stars of the show. The dorada or gilthead bream has long been one of Spain's absolutely favorite fish. But the dorada has been so ruthlessly overfished in the Mediterranean that it is rarely seen in public these days, and depends on an army of lookalike farmed doradas—at half the price and half the flavor—to keep alive its reputation. The single real, wild gilthead bream at today's auction went for twenty-one euros to the big-bellied restaurateur. When the price was announced, the woman in the pinafore poked me sharply in the ribs.

IN THE SUMMER of 1991, with Britain in the throes of an economic recession and Peter Mayle's *A Year in Provence* reminding its millions of readers that life was easier in the south, I quit my job at the magazine and moved to the island of Ibiza. For the next ten years I lived with Nacho in a house within sight of the Mediterranean Sea, on a stretch of coastline that had somehow escaped the rampant development which has pulverized the rest.

The island was a microcosm of Spanish food in the sense that it could be divided into the coastal zone, where the cooking was mainly marinera; and the inland uplands, where a different kind of cuisine had developed, based more on meats, the products of the matanza (the annual pig slaughter), and vegetables from the huerta. The remarkable thing was the way that, on a scrap of land just forty by twenty kilometers, there could be such a world of difference between the two. But there was. In the center of the island, where elderly peasants lived who had seldom been to the seaside, you might be served up a sofrit pagès, a popular dish of mixed meats first simmered, then sautéed with garlic and vegetables. On the coast, there were fish soup-stews like bullit de peix and skate wings with potatoes.

Misery and starvation were just around the corner, historically speaking, because this island society, thanks to mass tourism, had become extremely rich in a very short time. For centuries the people had been paupers; now they were millionaires. One understood, partly by intuition, that they had by no means always had it so good. Hair-raising tales were told of the civil war years, when the Republican militiamen commandeered any food they could lay hands on, to the extent of robbing grain from underground stores, and the rural populace subsisted on carob pods. The tourist boom had been a blessing (though it may ultimately prove to be a deadly curse). Now the islanders could shop at supermarkets like everyone else. They could buy smoked salmon, if they could afford it, and greenhouse tomatoes and Roquefort cheese.

Our village had been a fishing community, and it still bore the marks of centuries of dependence on the sea. The sandy bay where a couple of hotels now cater to tourism was still known as es port. On weekends, teenage boys from the village went out in dinghies from es port to fish for lobster and grouper, which they sold to the restaurants scattered along the seafront. The menu at these simple places was the epitome of cocina marinera as practiced all along the Spanish Mediterranean coast, a nearly unvarying repertoire of rice dishes with fish and shellfish, whole bream or bass baked a la sal, calamares a la romana, and cuttlefish a la plancha with parsley and garlic, as well as a few local specialities.

But that was restaurant cooking. In the daily lives of the locals, the "cooking of the sea" was a simpler, saltier affair, based on whatever

could be gleaned from the ocean in the immediate vicinity of the village. Every few days a man with a white van would appear in the village square selling gerrets, a small fish caught locally by amateurs,
probably illegally. They were dirt cheap: a kilo of gerrets could be had
for the price of a bocadillo. But it was their versatility that made them
popular—you could do what you liked with them. Fried, grilled over
coals, or cooked up with rice, they always tasted good; their white
flesh was flavorsome in a rough-hewn sort of way, like sardines without the oiliness or the pungent smell.

Felipe Fernández-Armesto, in his history of food, claims that the
appeal of fish as food is explained not so much by contemporary ideals
of healthy eating as by its romantic status as the last important foodstuff obtained by something that resembles hunting. Certainly the
seafood the villagers enjoyed was not the kind of thing you would find
in a fish store. One old man went fishing for moray eels down at a
deserted cove, bringing them back slimy and squirming in a bucket,
for his wife to cook in a saffron-scented stew for their supper. One
moonlit night in high summer we went out fishing for squid in a llaut,
a little wooden boat with a square sail. The llaut belonged to Juan
Antonio, a friend whose grandfather had built it with his own hands at
a time when building his own boat was thought entirely right and
proper for a young man in a Spanish fishing village. We rowed out
from the miniature harbor at the end of the beach, stopping within
sight of the shoreline where the water was calm and deep. Shreds of
laughter and guitar music drifted from the beach bar, a whitewashed
shack that had once been a fisherman's hovel. Juan Antonio showed
us how to drop the thick nylon line with sardine bits attached to big
hooks. From the rim of the boat hung two old flashlights upside
down, for attracting the squid to the surface. When we pulled in the
lines they loomed up like ghosts through the blackness.

Nights on the water, days on the rocks. On summer afternoons we
hiked down to a string of little bays along the coastline where no one
else went, since access was only on foot down a long mountain path.
We collected sea snails and urchins—I learned that the purple and
brown ones were finer-flavored, though harder to find, than the black.

The fun was in the hunting and gathering, and in the big flavors
that came as a reward for your efforts. One day I walked down to the
cala alone and lay by a rock pool, watching the tiny shrimps, translu-

cent wisps of nothingness, that paddled placidly at the edge of the sun-warmed pool. I spent the afternoon painstakingly catching them one by one with a butterfly net. When I had a handful and the sun was going down, I walked back up to the house, poured myself a beer, and stir-fried the whiskery, still-twitching shrimps for a second in a spoonful of oil with half a clove of garlic. The shrimps went from glassy to deep orange in an instant, leaching out some of their color into the sizzling olive oil.

Just as well there was no one else around to share that meal, for half of very little is hardly worth bothering with. On the other hand, I curse the fact that no one else was there to feel the mild crunch of their shells giving way to a burst of flavor, rich with minerals. It was one of the most delicious mouthfuls I can ever remember taking.

The Spanish gastronome Julio Camba wrote that just one sardine is the whole ocean. Well, those shrimps were the whole Mediterranean Sea.

2

Valencia

THE SEASON WAS kicking into top gear as I drove north along the highway that hugs the coastline all the way from the deep Spanish south to the French border. Barcelona was 500 kilometers away; Perpignan, 750. On a weekend in late June the big road was a six-lane roller coaster thick with tourist traffic, its broad chicanes swinging between sprawling orange groves and giant estates of back-to-back houses built as second homes for northern Europeans. To the left was a wall of blank, bare mountains; to the right, now and again, a flash of blue sea.

Turning off at the sign for Valencia, I fought my way into the centro histórico, disregarding the signs that advised me not to try, and parked in the cathedral square. The city was flooded with high-summer light. Fountains splashed in the squares; flowers blazed in the balconies. Browsing the tourist shops around the Plaza de la Reina, I bought a few postcards and sat down to write them with a cold horchata, the pale refreshing local drink of earthnut milk, sugar, and water.

At the table next to me a time-honored scene was being played out: the Arrival of the Paella. It steamed in its pan from the oven—or, as was more likely, the microwave oven—while the French couple who had ordered it bubbled over in their excitement.

I leaned as close to their table as I dared, pretending to pick up a fallen paper napkin, and inspected the dish out of the corner of my eye. It had a garish yellow color, more a turmeric or tartrazine yellow than the luscious orange of saffron, and the strips of red and green pepper made an alarming contrast. Lumps of something firm and white, possibly boneless chicken meat, could be seen buried in the rice. The paella gave off a damp, mucky smell, like clothes that have been left too long in a washing machine in hot weather.

Never was a dish so misunderstood, so misrepresented, so abused as paella. The crimes committed in the name of the Spanish national dish—mostly by Spaniards themselves—are horrible to relate. Even the name is a mystery to most of us. One (English) writer traces the etymology of paella to an Arabic word for "leftovers," which could hardly be farther from the truth. In fact it derives from the Latin patella—the English word "pail" has the same root—meaning a cooking utensil made of metal, particularly iron. It follows that, like "casserole," "terrine," and so on, paella refered originally not to the food but to the utensil: a wide, flat, shallow iron pan with handles on the sides.

Of the three picture postcards propped up against the saltcellar on my breakfast table, the first showed a paella de mariscos, the standard beachside paella with fat pink langoustines and prawns and mussels on the half shell artfully arranged across its surface, the pan settled among pine branches surrounded with oranges and lemons. The second was of the original paella valenciana—made with rabbit, chicken, snails and beans, and cooked on a fire of orangewood (you could see twigs poking out from underneath, with a few glossy leaves still attached). And the third captured the making of a particular paella on a gigantic scale. This one was twenty meters or more in diameter, so wide that a special rotating bridge had had to be constructed for the battalion of cooks to reach the center of the pan with their long metal stirrers. This monumental paella, made to feed 100,000 people, was created in 1992, when Valencia's rival city, Barcelona, was celebrating the Olympics and Seville had the Expo. It has gone down in history and the *Guinness Book of World Records* as the grandest paella ever made.

As any Spaniard will tell you, the people of Valencia are lovers of exaggeration, and especially fond of categories such as loudest, brightest, gaudiest, and most spectacular. The baroque, with all its curlicues and furbelows, is undoubtedly the city's favorite architectural style. The famous fiesta, known as Fallas, in which giant painted figures are set afire amid an apotheosis of fireworks and supercharged firecrackers as loud as antitank missiles, is one of the noisiest and most ebullient in a country where noisily ebullient fiestas are the rule rather than the exception.

With regard to the city's central market, said to be the food market with the largest surface area in the whole of Spain—a record it disputes with Barcelona's Boqueria—it is not just size that's important; here are scale and substance, wonderfully combined. Grand and gorgeous, the airy spaces under its domes and halls echoing with the comings and goings of its floating congregation, the Mercat Central is a kind of cathedral.

It had been more than a decade since I'd last set foot in this, one of Spain's temples of good food. Gratifyingly, nothing much seemed to have changed in the interim, except that the building's intricate ironwork and stained glass panels had recently been given a handsome overhaul. Prices had risen hugely, of course, though the change to euros from pesetas made it difficult to tell exactly by how much. Everywhere in the western world, the out-of-town hypermarket poses an ever-present threat to traditional markets such as this. But the Mercat Central showed no sign of buckling under the strain. The market now had a home delivery service: details were available on its website (www.mercadocentralvalencia.com).

Nothing that was good about the old place, however (apart from those low, low prices), had been sacrificed on the altar of modernity. At Caracoles Selectos—Select Snails—I stood for a minute or two to admire the stand with its pots of plastic flowers and fat snails hanging in string bags. Opposite, at the Lettuce Boutique, a greengrocer's stand, painted tiles depicted an idyllic rural scene in the Valencian countryside: a farmer with a square Spanish hoe, up to his ankles in a paddy field, with cabbages in rows stretching behind him. At the herboristería, bunches of dried herbs were tied up with lengths of esparto grass.

The Mercat is an anthology of local ingredients in all their variegated glory. There were four or five varieties of oranges on one stand; six types of green bean on another; eggplants delicately striped in purple and white, taut-skinned and shiny as if polished with furniture wax; cardoons; artichokes at a euro the kilo; and radishes as big as turnips. A box of hard, wrinkly, coffee-brown pellets in a wooden fruit box beside the almonds, hazelnuts, and walnuts turned out to be chufas, or earthnuts, produced in the village of Alboraia and mostly used for horchata. I crunched one; it was mildly bitter and astringent, with a subtle nuttiness reminiscent of almonds. At Vicent Peris, founded in 1870, the variety of cured and salted fish products, a great speciality of Valencia, ran from salt cod and tuna in oil and the classic mojama to rare and exquisite delicacies like sun-dried octopus and bull de tonyina—the salt-cured stomach of the tuna, looking like a relic of a medieval saint.

"Try one of these; they're lovely and sweet," said a voice by my ear as I passed a busy fruit stand. A buxom market woman held out in her hand an orange the size of a grapefruit. I sank my thumbnail into the zest and rubbed the glossy skin on the back of my hand, sniffing the cologne-like fragrance of the citrus oil. I bit into the skin, Spanish style, and ripped off the white pith and peel to get at the cool flesh inside. I gulped down the segments: they were packed with juice and had a freshness that was palpable and tastable. It was a perfect Valencia orange, reminding me forcefully just how much we take this delicious fruit for granted.

AFTER A SWIFT BEER in the market bar, I took the new tramway from the city center to the sea, getting off at Doctor Lluch and walking briskly through some of Valencia's meanest streets. When the old harbor moved away to the grand new container port a mile or two farther down the coast, the Grao neighborhood fell into decrepitude. Indians, Moroccans, and South Americans had made the place their own, living against a tawdry backdrop of convenience stores, video libraries, and neighborhood bars with faded, tattered awnings. Children played in the gutters.

The neighborhoods of Cabanyal, Grao, and Malvarosa were old-fashioned maritime barrios, existing between the poles of harbor and city beach. Cabanyal and Grao were rough harborside places, home to a shifting population of dockworkers, sailors, and fishermen; the Malvarosa was a tatty Brighton on the Med, a seaside pleasure zone where Valencia's poorer citizens once came to spend their Sunday afternoons.

But down at the seaside, change, like the invigorating scent of salt and ozone, was in the air. New buildings were going up as fast as old buildings crumbled. From the top floor of a new block where workers were just putting in the windows, I heard Russian voices, bellowing at each other for more cement. The air was full of dust, the smell of decay and regeneration.

It being almost lunchtime, I directed my steps toward the restaurant that is routinely spoken of as Valencia's best and one of the top ten or twenty in the country. Ca' Sento had always intrigued me as much for its history as for its fundamentalist obsession with the quality of its raw materials.

The Aleixandre family were natives of the Grao, the hard-living fishermen's neighborhood just behind the harbor. In the early 1960s Vicente (Sento) Aleixandre and his wife María Muria emigrated to Switzerland, where they worked for fourteen years; they returned in 1977 to open a bar in the modest Calle Méndez Núñez.

Their place was a sailors' bar with a television blaring in a corner, beer on tap, Coca-Cola, plain table wines, and a bottle of rough brandy kept on hand for the local Gypsy baron when he came in to pay the couple a visit. What kept the business bubbling was the food Sento and María served up at the bar.

"What have you got?" was the customers' cry as they came in the door.

"I've got prawns, langoustine, squid, cuttlefish, crab, red mullet, some nice mussels. . . . I've got grouper, sole, monkfish, hake. . . ." came the reply from behind the bar. In the 1970s Valencia was still an important fishing port, so that this fishy cornucopia was easily available and, what's more, affordable. It was normal, for example, for a workingman to come in at midday and sink a few beers and a plate of gambas.

"How do you want it done? Fried, grilled, a la plancha, with garlic and parsley? . . ."

Over time, the humble harbor bar became a proper restaurant. Sento's natural charm and acumen, María's inborn understanding of the subtle arts of fish and rice cookery, and their shared determination to make something of themselves quickly turned the place into a success. And in the course of things, their son Raúl, born in 1971, became an integral part of what went on in the kitchen. As a child he worked in the bar while his schoolmates played football in the street. Since then, seasons spent in important restaurant kitchens have taught him about the currents of modernity swirling around the world of Spanish food. But in his heart, Raúl is the archetype of the Spanish chef solidly rooted in tradition and family.

Ca' Sento is still to be found in its original location, on the corner of the down-at-heels Calle Méndez Núñez. The place has not grown or expanded, and can serve a maximum of only sixteen customers at one sitting. But the dining room now gleams with marble and the kitchen with stainless steel. The walls are lined with abstract art; several shelves accommodate a magnificent collection of single malts, aged rums, tequilas, Armagnacs, and grappas. On this weekday at lunchtime the majority of the diners were businesspeople and politicians—only they, or their expense accounts, can still afford the prices at Ca' Sento.

Certainly, the cooking here is exquisite. The salad of vieiras (clams) and Dublin bay prawns with baby chard and rocket leaves, turnip tops, and violet flowers with a dressing of orange and lobster coral was memorable as well as beautiful. The rice a la plancha, a dish of Raúl's creation, each spoonful given a golden crust by a few seconds of sizzling on the griddle, came with four enormous, juicy, deep red Palamós prawns. I thought of the workman and his prawns, and wondered what he'd make of the price tag attached to this dish, now that Palamós prawns are a scarce and expensive luxury.

Raúl came out into the dining room and sat at my table to smoke a cigarette. He was a roly-poly, friendly man with a well-suppressed stutter that hinted at shyness.

There are three main types of rice dishes to be found in the region of Valencia, Raúl explained, the classification depending on the amount of liquid left unabsorbed by the rice. Arroz seco is "dry": paella is a dry rice. But then there are meloso and caldoso: "creamy" and "soupy," respectively. The menu at Ca' Sento included all three styles, but tended to concentrate on the lesser-known melosos and caldosos, in part as a reaction against the predominance of paella.

It is the curse of being a Valencian that wherever you go in the world, people want to talk about paella. In the popular imagination the paella has come to symbolize not just Spanish cooking but Spain itself. In its bright colors and hectic but somehow harmonious organization, this dish seems to encapsulate what foreigners believe to be true about Spanish life and culture in a wider sense.

"I always get asked the same question," complained Raúl, tapping his ash on the edge of a saucer. "Where should we go for a good paella? And I have to tell them, the places you can find a good paella could be counted on the fingers of one hand. There is just so much rubbish about. And the worst rubbish is the paella served to tourists, frozen and defrosted in the oven, with a jug of sangría. It's a shame, because that paella is the impression they take away with them. It's also a shame because there are so many good rice dishes they will never try. Rice baked in the oven. Rice with beans and turnips. Rice with pears and raisins—a rice you don't see nowadays, but my grandmother used to make for us. The arroz meloso that my mother still makes in the kitchen back here, with the same pot she's been using for forty years. It's amazing, the variety of the world of rice. It's a universe," he said.

Rice is not just a primary ingredient of the region's favorite dish. The grain *Oryza sativa* has an importance here that is dietary, gastronomic, cultural, and economic. As the mayor of Valencia, a woman of traditional build who obviously enjoys her carbohydrates, is fond of saying, rice has contributed to the promotion and diffusion of the image of Valencia all over the world. One could go further and say, as the Spanish do, that for valencianos rice is nothing less than una manera de entender la vida—"a way of understanding life."

Spain is currently one of Europe's hungrier consumers of rice—indeed, national production cannot keep up with consumption, which runs at an average of six kilos per head per year (much of the shortfall comes from Egypt). But it was not always so. The thirteenth-century *Llibre de Sent Soví,* the earliest surviving cookbook in any Spanish language, includes just one rice recipe, and this is for a sweet pudding with almond milk and cinnamon. For many centuries thereafter rice cultivation was closely associated with disease, since the standing water it required was an ideal breeding ground for the malarial mosquito; and rice as an ingredient, by association, was frowned on.

For most of the history of its cultivation in Valencia, rice was a poor man's food. It took centuries to rise through society; even in the early 1900s, as Lorenzo Millo describes in his monograph *Arroz,* the most typical and popular lunch dish among the Valencian middle and upper classes was not paella, but olla—a stew of pulses, mixed meats, and vegetables, closely related to the cocido of Madrid, the puchero of Andalusia, and the rest of the family of Spanish one-pot stews.

The evolution of rice cookery in the region closely follows its economic development. The earliest paellas were probably made by farming folk in the rural flatlands around the city, cradle of Valencia's important fruit and vegetable production. For the ingredients of these primitive paellas, made over an open fire of orange or lemon wood, cooks would logically have used whatever was closest to hand. Vegetables like Swiss chard, artichokes, and beans, both "broad" (fabes) and "French" (tavella). Depending on the time of year, there might be snails. For protein, a nice fat rabbit might be chopped and added, or perhaps a chicken, since everyone kept a few hens in the backyard. A rice dish was made (and still is) with wild ducks; or with eel and frog, both plentiful; or even, it is whispered, with the fat rats that gorged on the tender rice shoots in early summer. Another of these ur-paellas, dating back at least to the eighteenth century, was arroz con bacalao y col—a potent mixture of rice, salt cod, and cabbage, especially popular during Lent, when meat was off the menu.

From the farmyards of Valencia's rural outskirts the paella gradually took its place in public life. By the mid-nineteenth century it had been adopted as a regional plato típico, with the name paella valenciana. It became a dish for Sundays in the country, the centerpiece of multitudinous fiestas in the open air, and part of the romantic upwelling of nationalist sentiment in the form of folklore and the picturesque. Paella as it is known outside Valencia, a marriage of rice and seafood, came into being in the early twentieth century, in the merenderos (open-air eating places) down by the beach. Compared with the traditional inland paellas, which were relatively dull to look at, the paella de mariscos—the shellfish paella of prawns, crab, and mussels—must have been a revelation, the deep red of the fish standing out against the saffron gold of the rice like the red and gold of the national flag.

VALENCIA SITS ON the edge of what was once a marshy floodplain crisscrossed with rivers and canals. As the city has grown, its consumption of water has grown much more, the water table has plummeted, and as a consequence the plain has largely been drained of surface water.

But the Albufera remains, a freshwater lagoon closed off by a buildup of silt from the Turia and Júcar rivers, and by a slender sandbank on the seaward side. As described by Roman historians in the fourth century after Christ, it covered an area equivalent to 30,000 hectares; it was the Arabs, however, who christened it Al-Buhera—the lake. It was the Arabs, too, during the reign of Abderrahman III in the tenth century, at a time when agriculture in Muslim Spain was making dramatic technical advances, who began growing rice in the rich alluvial plains around the lake.

Driving southward on the A7, I thought the city seemed endless, with a dense tissue of highways gradually strangling the remains of what were once prosperous farms, mills, storehouses, stables. Off the main highway on the old coast road, north of the Albufera, you are in rice country. The rocket-like silos of a factory proclaim their contents as "Arroz SOS": a rice brand as familiar to Spanish consumers as Uncle Ben's is to Americans. During the winter the flat fields are featureless, brown and dry. Then in the early spring, the ground is plowed, the channels (known as acequias or ullals) are opened, the fields are flooded, the rice shoots are planted, and the Valencian countryside begins to resemble the paddy fields of China. Now, at the height of summer, with two months to go before the harvest, the lush greenness of the plantations is startling to the eye.

The restaurant Casa Salvador stood on a modest estuary at the point where the Júcar River meets the sea, on a marshy outcrop, slightly uncanny in its humid silence, poised at the confluence of three waters: brackish, sweet, and salt. The Estany, as it is known, was where Salvador Gascón and his sister Concha came with their parents in 1950 from the inland village of Tavernes de la Valldigna. Despite certain dis-

advantages of the abandoned duck farm in which they installed themselves, such as the lack of electric light or running water, the Gascóns
planned to start a bar serving drinks and snacks to the hunters and
fishermen who visited the Estany on weekends. In the intervening
years (during which the family boasts that it hasn't closed a single day)
the bar has smoothly transmogrified into a fine restaurant, and half a
century later Casa Salvador is famous above all for its rice dishes, over
which it has attained a supreme mastery.

The restaurant is formed of two barracas, the original farm buildings, joined into a wide airy space hung with eel nets, painted ceramics, and other knickknacks typical of the region. The menu at Casa
Salvador reads like a treatise on the rice cookery of the país valenciano,
with curiosities you'd be hard-pressed to find anywhere else, such as a
paella of duck, snails, and eels; another of salt cod and cauliflower; and
a fine-sounding arroz del senyoret—"rich kid's rice," so-called
because the prawns and langoustines and fish chunks come already
peeled, shelled, and boned. I sat at a table on the terrace overlooking
the estuary, where a salty breeze was coming in over the sandbar.
Thirty minutes later, I was happily eating my way through a magnificent arroz caldoso de cigalas, rape, y setas—a soupy rice, cooked not in
the paella but in a high-sided casserole, magisterially combining langoustines, monkfish, and wild mushrooms in a powerfully flavored
saffron-infused broth. I had preceded this with a plate of clams; I followed it with ice cream; and then I sat in a stupor looking at the view
as the afternoon settled into siesta mode. A double café solo would, I
calculated, provide me with just the boost I needed to drive back to
Valencia, find a parking space, and fall through the door of the apartment before collapsing into an armchair.

THERE IS NO gold standard for paella, just as there is no absolutely
archetypal quiche lorraine, no Platonic pizza. But if the tourist industry has messed around with Valencia's most characteristic dish, it
seemed like a good idea to look for paella in its original version, or at
least as close to this ideal as possible. To this end, I would have to travel
a little distance from the coast, for the classic paella valenciana has
been saved from extinction, like some shy wild animal, only by careful
protection away from built-up areas. In the forested uplands behind

the Mediterranean seaboard, rabbits run wild and there is firewood in abundance.

I made a few phone calls and, the next morning, took a train from Valencia's art nouveau jewel of a railway station, the Estación del Norte, to the mountain town of Buñol. The train clattered at a gentle pace through the agricultural zone on which rests Valencia's fame as an important producer of vegetables and citrus fruit. As we climbed uphill, there were groves of oranges and olives, and almond trees, and pomegranates spattered with their scarlet flowers.

These days Buñol is best-known for a mad fiesta called the Tomatina, billed as Spain's greatest food fight, in which thirty tons of tomatoes are hurled in the streets and the world's media turn up to watch. Before the invention of the fiesta in the 1960s, Buñol was an important stop on the seven-day carriage route from Madrid to the coast, and the Venta Pilar was a kind of caravansary where drivers, muleteers, and their charges could stop for the night. The house is a whitewashed, cuboid warren of a place, more than 300 years old; it has a heavy wooden double door where the traffic came in, and sepia photographs hanging in the hall.

"In the old days 100 people might sleep here in a night. It was a tremendous business. But of course, when the mechanical traction engine came in, the carriage business died," mused Enrique Galindo Estévez, who is the elderly owner of the Venta—along with his son, also called Enrique.

Nowadays the place functions mainly as a restaurant, its especialidad de la casa being a paella made in the old-fashioned way, over a wood fire.

"In the old days everyone used wood. Then the gas came in. Now almost nobody does," reflected Enrique. It could be any kind of wood: pine, olive, or almond. But today it was orange, loved by valencianos for the intense, continuous heat it gives out, as well as its fragrance. In a covered section of the backyard was a long stone platform where paellas were cooked on trivets, each on its own fire. The walls and ceiling were coated with a thick layer of shiny tar, the residue of years of paella-making at the Venta.

Hauling a two-handled pan, almost a meter wide, from a blackened stack in the corner, Enrique laid it on the trivet and poured in a generous slug of olive oil. "I do it all by eye," he said.

First he fried chunks of chicken and rabbit, tumbling them in the sizzling oil. The flames licked greedily around the lip of the pan. Then came the beans: a large pale butter bean called the garrofó, found only in the region; and a flat green bean called the tavella. A sloosh of tomato puree (left over from the Tomatina, perhaps, I thought about saying, then thought better of it). Then the rice and chicken stock; the fine threads of saffron, toasted and ground in a mortar; and a generous sprinkling of salt.

And that, said Enrique, was pretty much that. From then on it was a matter of watching the flame, poking in more sticks as the fire burned low. The ideal is a constant level of heat that will cook the rice, not so fiercely as to burn it but just strong enough to leave a crust on the bottom of the pan—this is known as the socarrat, and it's a delicacy that valencianos fight over.

We stood in the courtyard in the spring sunshine admiring the paella as it bubbled appetizingly, waves of aroma billowing out of the pan along with the clouds of steam and smoke. Enrique mopped his brow: it was hot work. After resting for a minute or two he was back on the job, busying himself with a second paella when the first was in the home stretch. It was a Sunday, and the Venta would soon be full of hungry families.

Before long the day's first paella was a great glowing circle of Buddhist orange-yellow. The rice had sucked up all the stock and there were puffs of steam escaping from little blowholes that had formed in its surface. I tried a forkful. The rice was perfectly cooked, and had absorbed all the savoriness of the rabbit, chicken, beans, and saffron. This may not have been the most elaborate paella of all time. It certainly wasn't the cleverest or the most inventive. It was simply authentic. Or authentically simple—which, as with most of Spain's best traditional foods, pretty much comes to the same thing.

3

Costa Brava

THERE HAVE ALWAYS BEEN visitors to Spain, but until the twentieth century they were just a few intrepid souls who were able to overlook the discomforts of travel in one of Europe's most backward countries for the sake of its magnificent artistic heritage. Spain never really featured on the grand tour: it was far too difficult a destination for those young aristocrats of the nineteenth century who flitted lightly from Switzerland and Tuscany to the English lakes, sketchbook in hand.

Tourism had its official birth 100 years ago, with the creation of the National Tourism Commission by the count of Romanones in 1905, but scarcely took off in a commercial sense until mid-century, by which time the stage was set for the extraordinary tourist boom of the 1960s.

In 1950 there were 290,000 foreign visitors. In 1959 the Francoist policy of autarchy or closed economy was officially discarded. After that, foreigners, and foreign investment, flooded into the country. From 1960 to 1973 Spain had the second highest growth rate in the world, after Japan. In 1981 the number of visitors reached 40 million; three years later it had soared to 54 million tourists in 1984. According to the World Tourism Organization, based in Madrid, the Spanish tourist market will grow 5 percent a year over the next ten years, reaching 75 million foreign tourists in the year 2020. But by then the industry itself might be unsustainable, as a report by the United Nations on the future of the Mediterranean recently predicted, with another 4,000 kilometers of hitherto virgin coastline destined to vanish under the concrete tide, and the region as a whole nearing total environmental collapse.

Indirectly, the impact of tourism on the nation's food habits has been hugely beneficial, since the income it generates has allowed more people to eat more and better. There is no doubt that tourism has provided an audience for the new Spanish cuisine of the 1990s, an audience it might have lacked if local tastes alone were available to appreciate it and local pockets to pay for it. With regard to the package tour, however, poor cooking in hotels—the greasy paellas and insipid gazpachos (paella and gazpacho were found to be perfect hotel dishes, since both could be made in enormous quantities)—perpetuated the bad reputation of Spanish food in general.

In his novel *Un Artículo de Encargo,* Miguel Sen has his principal character, chef Eudaldo Manera, describe the unsavory culinary practices of the 1960s in the hotels of the Costa Brava—from where, says Manera, comes the Spanish saying "Among the bad builders are the good cooks," since the kitchen staff in tourist hotels often found work on building sites when the season was over. The picture of package tourists drinking themselves into oblivion in "hotels that were built in four days and are now falling apart," is convincing, if depressing. The hotels had fixed times for lunch and dinner, and anyone who was late had to pay a supplement. So the hotel managers got together and arranged for their guests to go on long boat rides around the bay of Lloret de Mar, ensuring that their charges arrived late for lunch. Waiting for them in the dining room, says Sen's character, might be a slab of breaded meat which he swears was mortadela, dipped in egg and bread crumbs and fried, "for all I know, in engine oil."

From Valencia I set a course for the far northeast corner of the peninsula, where the Pyrenees meet the Mediterranean Sea and Spain meets France. I was heading for Roses, a small coastal town at the northern end of the Costa Brava about which I knew nothing, except that it possessed what was routinely described in restaurant guides and magazine articles as the most innovative and exciting restaurant in Spain. That Saturday the national press was full of excited reports that the *New York Times* had proclaimed it the most important restaurant in the world and had printed a full-face portrait of the chef on the cover of its weekly magazine. I was due to have dinner at El Bulli on Sunday night. But I had a night and a day to go till my reservation, and until then, foodwise, I was on my own.

Roses: The name of the town made it sound fragrant and floral and postcard-pretty. But on a hot night in July, Roses smelled of sunflower oil and canned tomatoes. I watched the tourists come and go through streets lined with gift shops and boutiques. They dined in waves: first the Brits, with their stodgy-looking suppers of spag bol and pizza; then the Germans and Scandinavians (grilled meats and french fries); and finally the French (paella, fish, and plates of *fruits de mer*).

It was my strong suspicion that finding anything really good to eat in this heaving holiday town would be a challenge worthy of Hercule Poirot. Sitting down at a table on the seafront, I asked for a plate of ham, a bowl of gazpacho, and a side order of pa amb tomàquet, the Catalan national snack: bread rubbed with tomato, anointed with olive oil, and sprinkled with salt. The tomato was out of a jar, the olive oil nearly rancid, the sliced serrano ham as sweaty and pink-tinged as the tourists filing past on the promenade. The gazpacho had a dull, lifeless taste, like something insufficiently seasoned that had been sitting around for too long in a crowded fridge.

This might have been the sad end of my night out in Roses, were it not for Carmen Casas, doyenne of Catalan restaurant reviewers, whose bible-like guide to the restaurants of Catalonia recommended Can Campaner, a little restaurant in a back street, off the beaten track, family-run, which, according to Carmen, served nothing except local seafood simply but perfectly cooked. I practically ran the few hundred yards uphill, to a bright dining room with white paper tablecloths and wall tiles painted with romantic scenes of the Costa Brava, the fishing boats plying the coast, the unquiet sea, the wild cliffs and sinewy pines. Around the walls were team photographs of the Barcelona soccer team. Late on a Saturday night the restaurant was humming with locals, and the rubbery tones of Catalan voices bounced off the walls. Every so often the decibel level rose another notch, when a blast of sizzling came from the kitchen at the back.

Senyor Magesté reeled off the menu for tonight, and immediately brought me a plate of rock mussels, their shells stippled pale green with lichen, their pale little bodies vibrant with intense sea flavor. My spirits were lifted in an instant. Thereafter a series of dishes arrived, each more sensational than the last. The prawns, locally caught, were plump, russet-red, incomparably fresh. The razor shells were chewily delicious strips of golden meat; the soles, the size of my outstretched hand, came with a greenish, gleaming lump of perfect allioli, the Catalan emulsion sauce of garlic and olive oil, as piquant as mustard. There were monkfish chunks and baby octopus and langoustines, all caught the night before in the deep sandbanks along the coast of Roses, L'Escala, and Palamós, and tumbled briefly on the sizzling plancha. And there was a bottle of fizzy white Blanc Pescador, the so-called "needle wine" (vi d'agulla) whose acid bite and freshness are a perfect foil for the richness of Mediterranean seafood. It was all so good and so genuine that it almost restored my faith in Spanish seaside eating.

THE ROAD TO Cala Montjoi begins unprepossessingly among the suburbs of Roses; winding up into the rocks and stones of Cape Creus; becoming a dusty, roller-coaster track of hairpin bends and wide-screen vistas; and finally depositing you, breathless and wild-haired, in the harbor town of Cadaqués. At the height of the high season there is a permanent stream of cars on the narrow road, as visitors head for these barely accessible rocky coves in a vain attempt to leave the Costa Brava crowds behind. Cala Montjoi's claim to fame, unlikely though it may look to the casual observer, is that it has probably the world's most famous, not to say notorious, modern restaurant. If "paella" and "gazpacho" are the first two terms of the international lexicon of Spanish food, then "El Bulli" is probably the fourth or fifth.

Getting a table at El Bulli is, in the world of international haute cuisine, something like winning the lottery. The restaurant is open from April 1 to October 1 but serves only dinner, and the dining room has a capacity of just forty customers on any given night. Except in high summer, it closes on Mondays and Tuesdays. The number of diners El Bulli can serve in any given year is therefore around 8,000.

So much for supply. To say that demand outstrips the supply is putting it mildly. For those 8,000 dinners the restaurant receives no fewer than 400,000 requests every year. The faxes, the e-mails, the anxiously handwritten letters begin to arrive not long after October 1, when the restaurant closes and chef Ferran Adrià and his acolytes decamp to their workshop-laboratory in Barcelona to dream up new wizardries for the following season. Surprisingly for a restaurant of such stratospheric world renown, there are no quotas at El Bulli, no PR invitations, no freebies, no tables kept vacant in case Antonio Banderas should turn up one night with Melanie. Not even chef Adrià's closest friends and associates are guaranteed a table. Legend has it that when chef Juan Mari Arzak, the grandmaster of modern Spanish cuisine, who is held in deep respect by Adrià, was in the vicinity of Roses and inquired after a table, he was turned away.

On the evening of the appointed day, a Sunday, after a long siesta and a long hot shower, I drove out once again from Roses. At this hour the tourists had all gone back to their hotels, and the sinuous road was empty. Down below the sea was laid out flat, colored a silvery gray in the evening cool.

El Bulli has a curious history going back to the earliest days of tourism on the Costa Brava, when a German couple, Hans and Marketta Schilling, set up a bar in their new house, catering for the divers who were drawn to the crystal-clear waters of Cala Montjoi. (The name of the place derives from the couple's bulldog, Bulli.) The house stands at the entrance to the cala, still undeveloped so far, apart from a few vacation chalets built in the free-for-all days before 1969, when a law put a stop to any and all building within fifty meters of the water. The low white house stands between road and beach, but almost nothing could be seen through the protective curtain of cypresses and Mediterranean shrubbery. The name was stenciled on a rusted iron plaque.

Finding a back gate open, I walked down toward the kitchen. A group of young guys in black shirts and trousers were lounging by the kitchen door, sitting on upturned fruit boxes, smoking cigarettes. A pile of empty wooden crates bore witness to the fact that the restaurant gets its melons from Valencia, its asparagus from Navarre, its lettuces from Barcelona. The building looked rather plain, a whitewashed Spanish seaside house with terra-cotta roof tiles and a terrace out front looking down to the beach through white arches. Closer to the sea, a wall of plate glass gleamed like a mirror. Beyond the glass was the sanctum sanctorum, the kitchen of El Bulli, a place of alchemical mystery and magic where even now my dinner was being conjured up.

I found the man himself sitting by himself at a table on the terrace, the arch behind him framing a view of the cala's modest arc of sand and water, an image of calm after the frenzy of a summer day at the seaside. He was scribbling something in a small notebook.

Not since the days of Escoffier and Carême has a chef scaled such heights of fame and admiration. Yet the details of Ferran Adrià Acosta's early life hold few clues to his eventual gastronomical stardom. He was born into a working-class family in Hospitalet de Llobregat, a dreary suburb of Barcelona, in 1962. Thus he represents a generation whose knowledge of life under the dictatorship is almost entirely second-hand: in the year of Franco's death he was just thirteen. His generation is that of the Transition; it bridges the gap between black-and-white television and the iPod, between one-pot chickpea stews and molecular cuisine.

Adrià has a well-fed, lived-in sort of face, and shortish brown hair mussed up so that you can't tell at a glance whether it is naturally curly or straight. He is neither thin nor fat, tall nor short, good-looking nor ugly. As he sits in front of me in his whites, he looks entirely neutral: neutral and normal.

"Mine was just a normal family," he said mildly. I had asked him to tell me about his roots. "What did we eat? Normal things; the same kind of normal things that millions of people normally eat. My mother cooked. But the fact that I ended up devoting my life to haute cuisine had nothing to do with the way things were at home. Normal families have twenty or twenty-five regular dishes: ours were rice, a baked fish, tripe. My mother wasn't big on casseroles; our thing was more vegetables, fish a la plancha, fried fish. My family is mainly Catalan, but with ancestors that came from Andalusia and Murcia. So we had gazpacho, which is not from Catalonia. Except that nowadays, you find it everywhere.

"I remember, from my childhood, four or five things. One was something they used to shut me in the toilet for not eating. Whenever we had lentils, I would refuse them point-blank. I was quite a fussy child when it came to food. If there was one taste I hated more than anything in the world, it was Dalky brand strawberry ice cream." He made a pouting face, a child's expression of disgust. "To me it's antiflavor, like antimatter. I've never got over my hatred of that taste. The other thing was green peppers, and I still can't bear them even now."

A kitchen worker came striding across the terrace to show him something. I caught a flash of it, a dark little pillow of something on a plate.

"Yes, fine. But don't let it dry out too much. Let's present it with a little of the stock. OK?"

His parents, I asked him gently. What did they think of it all, his worldwide fame, the restaurant and its extraordinary food, the cold soup of lychees and fennel granizado, the avocado sorbet with sunflower seeds, the electric milk?

He shrugged. "Like any parent who sees his son succeed, that's all. They don't understand what you might call the international dimension. They know that something's going on, but they're not quite sure what. Maybe it's better that way." He shifted in his seat. "They are postwar people. They tell me that after the war, they didn't exactly go hungry, but almost. The fact of having a tomato or an aubergine was something you valued. So."

Adrià's relationship with his background, his cultural surroundings, is interesting and puzzling. He is undeniably Catalan and Spanish, and identifies with both nationalities. On the other hand he strongly resists the pull of place; he is a postmodern creator, picking up diverse influences from cultures all across the globe. This tension remains a vital element in his work; there's a sense of being rooted and yet somehow rootless—psychologically anchored, yet free.

"My surroundings are these," he says quietly. Behind him on the water a small boat pulls up to the gray sand. A first cool breath of wind comes up from the bay. "But I don't believe in *terroir*, not in that French sense of earth and roots. *Terroir* is feeling; the earth is nothing without people. Don't look around here too much, for as much as you look you'll see nothing."

I tell him about my curate's-egg experiences in the restaurants of Roses, and he gives another small shrug as if to say, Well, what on earth did you expect? "Listen, I've been in Roses for twenty-one years, and I've never had a good tapa, a decent paella. . . . People accuse me of lowering standards: 'It's your fault there are so many young kids trying to do modern food, and doing it badly.' Maybe, but isn't it much worse that there are millions of tortillas and paellas all over the country that are cooked so badly? Ordinary food in Spain is in a much worse state than haute cuisine, and that's a fact."

Adrià started in ordinary food and crept higher and higher, to the very summit of haute.

His professional journey has been a long haul. He has been at El Bulli since 1984: more than half his life. When he arrived at Cala Montjoi the sum total of his work experience was a summer washing plates in Ibiza, a year in the kitchen of the military barracks at Cartagena, and another few months at the restaurant Finisterre in Barcelona.

"I got here in April, and in October they made me *chef de cuisine*," he said wryly.

The restaurant had already been functioning for twenty years, first under the Schillings, who upgraded the original bar into a grillroom with miniature golf; and then with chef Jean Louis Neichel, who now has his own Michelin-starred place in Barcelona. Adrià cheerfully admits that at first, his dishes were far from the works of art we have come to expect from him. One of his earliest creations was a salad of charcoal-grilled vegetables, clearly derived from the Catalan escalivada, which was common enough in simple restaurants but a radical novelty in haute kitchens where vegetables were served in the French style, boiled or steamed.

His "road to Damascus" moment came during a chefs' conference in Nice in 1984, when Jacques Maximin defined creativity in cooking as *ne pas copier,* and the young Adrià sat up and took notice. The first fruits of that revelation were the early "adaptation" dishes giving a twist to classic Spanish dishes and techniques, such as the lobster gazpacho and ajoblanco of langoustines. The early 1990s saw the first of the apparently crazy combinations—bone marrow with caviar, rabbit with octopus, chicken wings with lobster. And in 1994 Adrià brought in the big guns: the famous foams, a genial invention that involves impregnating a liquid with air for an ethereally delicate futuristic version of mousse. The foams (he calls them clouds) were born in a juice bar in Barcelona, when Adrià noticed the fruit-flavored foam that remained in the bottom of his glass and wondered if the effect could be reproduced. The notion of "deconstructive" cuisine—separating the constituent parts of a given dish, modifying them in various ways, and then putting them back together so that the result preserves the genome of the original dish—was another of Adrià's immortal contributions to modern cuisine. Initially applied to the Spanish white-trash dish known as arroz a la cubana, white rice with banana and tomato sauce, the technique was subsequently applied to tortilla de patatas, gazpacho, vegetable menestra, and whatever other classic preparations seemed to lend themselves to Adrià's dazzling intelligence and wit. Thereafter we had spherification, freeze-drying, and cooking on a cold plancha fired with liquid nitrogen; we had the new ravioli using milk skin or translucent-thin slices of prawn in place of pasta; the new aspic, using agar-agar instead of the traditional gelatin; the sponges, "airs," and "clouds." Quite apart from the techniques, to date Adrià has created more than 1,500 individual dishes, fulfilling Maximin's maxim to the letter.

Success, when it happened, astonished even him. In 1993 the otherwise strictly French guide Gault-Millau made El Bulli the first and only foreign restaurant to be included (giving it nineteen points out of twenty). In 1997 Adrià won his third Michelin star. When Joël Robuchon, reigning genius of French cuisine, proclaimed Adrià his successor, he only confirmed what many foodies already suspected: that El Bulli was the most important restaurant in the world. While Adrià has been happy to act as its public face and cover star, there are at least two other geniuses among his fellow workers: Albert Adrià, patissier and brother of Ferran; and Juli Soler, business partner, restaurant manager, éminence grise. Soler was the brain behind the amazing new kitchen at El Bulli, 325 square meters of high-tech wonderment carved out of the rock, with one whole wall of glass which floods the interior with Mediterranean light.

"Do you want to see my kitchen? Come." Adrià gets up, suddenly brisk and businesslike, and I follow him inside, my nerves of this afternoon now replaced by bristling excitement.

First things first. At some restaurants, if you're lucky, you are invited into the kitchen at the end of the meal, when the service is over and startled sous-chefs look up from their cleaning at the tipsy stranger who has wandered into their realm. At El Bulli the invitation comes before the meal, when the kitchen is firing on all cylinders— but firing with a sort of gentle, streamlined power, like the engine of a fabulous Italian sports car. It is not your standard restaurant kitchen— all harsh white light, noise, and heat—but an elegant space of generous dimensions with an atmosphere halfway between laboratory and monastery. And indeed, the almost medieval aspect of the functioning of El Bulli, its blend of scientific rigor and alchemical fantasy, high seriousness and holy fooling, has made it into a place of pilgrimage for idealistic young food folk the world over.

From the kitchen, Adrià leads me to my table. The dining room is white-walled, warmly furnished in orange, purple, red. The other tables seem distant in space-time; similar things are happening there, but in another dimension. I can hear Italian, German, French voices. There is a hush, but it's not the solemn hush of chintz and velvet. There are smiles and giggles; I feel mischief in the air.

There are things that matter in El Bulli's universe, and things that are passed over lightly. The menu is nothing much to look at, for instance. Nothing could be simpler, almost disingenuously so, than this folded sheet of paper, only a little larger than a postcard, with retro publicity for El Bulli on one side (dating, I see in the small-print copy- right, from 1964), and the menu for tonight on the other. There is a striking difference between this sober, cheaply produced document and the extravagantly decorated folders you find in most other high- end restaurants, menus that invite you to hold them aloft in both hands like a choirboy and study them as if you were about to read from Saint Paul's Epistle to the Corinthians.

Tonight's dinner would consist of thirty-two dishes, listed in small dark type with no capitals, like a piece of concrete poetry. Adrià was the originator of what came to be known as the "long, thin" menu, a series of tapa-size dishes over which the diner has no choice. Some of these dishes, such as the homemade mozzarella or the sea snails with crab, sounded like more or less conventional cooking. Others sounded like nothing on earth. I could only speculate on the nature of "spherical melon caviar," "Tennessee infusion," "popcorn cloud," or "thaw 2005." I knew that Adrià was given to tricks and humor in his work, and that he loved to bewitch his guests with theatrical flourishes like the flowers handed around to be sniffed between mouthfuls, the natural essences sprayed into the air above the table. I reminded myself to be ready for anything. Three black-shirted waiters appeared beside me, smiling beatifically, like the Three Boys in *The Magic Flute*. I took a deep breath.

And the show began. A little green ball of tarragon paste, presented on a flat silver spoon on a delicate web of some other precious metal poised above a black plate. The tarragon ball was to be placed in the mouth and allowed to dissolve, flooding the palate with a powerful rush of herbal flavor: aniseed, spearmint, licorice . . . Meanwhile another waiter was busy concocting a caipirinha with fresh lime juice, sugar, and Brazilian cachaça, using a bowl of liquid nitrogen at minus forty degrees Celsius. Clouds of dry ice billowed out of the bowl as he stirred the cocktail, serving it up in a glass the size of an eggcup. After the cleansing flush of the tarragon, the cocktail's acid sweetness was an exhilarating assault on the taste buds, leaving the palate gaping. As an opener to the menu it was a coup de théâtre, a spectacular curtain-raiser.

The meal's first act is a succession of "snacks," recalling an innocent era of childhood pleasures. These "tapitas," as Adrià calls them, give free rein to the playful side of his genius. A springlike shape, made of spun sugar and olive oil, to be placed on the finger and eaten in a single mouthful. A pistachio caught in a shell of crystallized yogurt. A cookie made of black olives and cream, an exact visual replica of an Oreo cookie. I laughed out loud. A kind of communion wafer, made of air-dried mango, that vanished on the tongue with an intense burst of tropical fruit. Sensations, surprises. Chunks of air-dried and fresh melon, in jewellike colors of orange and green, served on ice in a silver flowerpot, with cool white fresh almonds. . . . A white shivering cloud, which the waiter instructed me to convey to my mouth in my fingertips. The cloud seemed too big for a single mouthful; I crammed it in, laughing at the indignity, but it then seemed to melt away to nothingness and a distant, ethereal memory of cinema popcorn.

And it goes on. None of the dishes on this menú degustación is bigger than a few mouthfuls, and some are virtually virtual, a single brushstroke or scribble of flavor. These little dishes are brilliant statements, essays, experiments, provocations.

The dishes gain in intellectual weight, if not in actual size. A tempura of samphire, perfumed with saffron, and a spoonful of oyster sauce: quintessence of oyster. Walnuts with walnut sauce: quintessence of walnuts. Tiny quantities; vast, echoing flavors. Miniature rock mussels like the ones I had last night at Can Campaner, here served with a multicolored mini-salad of various types of seaweed. Strips of monkfish liver the size of your fingernail, cooked at the table in a little pot of hot stock and then swiped across a spoonful of sesame sauce: delicious beyond imagining. There was almost no meat: with a few exceptions, it was all fish and shellfish, vegetables, fruit, and herbs. One exception was crunchy rabbit ear. Adrià blanches the ear, skins it, and fries it. This seems an outrageous idea. But why not? If there is one body part that identifies the rabbit more than anything, it's the ears. And the ear was a fantastic, savory and crisp and somehow a throwaway gesture, like the best pork crackling in the world.

The morphings are to the end of the menu what the tapitas are to the beginning. (More things . . . The excruciating English pun is purest Adrià.) They were sweet fun things, done on a kind of plancha filled with liquid nitrogen, so that the marshmallowy exterior actually "cooked" on the ice-cold surface, and the steam rose into the air in big white cold sticky clouds. A draft came in from an open window, pushing across the dining room—which, I realized, was now entirely empty apart from myself and the waiter with his Frankenstein dry-ice machine.

I turned on my mobile phone to look at the time: it was two in the morning. I had been the first to arrive, and now, five hours later, I was the last to leave. Feeling a little unsteady on my feet, I shuffled out to the terrace and sat down again at the table by the arch, the one with the neatly framed view of beach and sea. The warmth had gone out of the air; I wished I'd brought my thin summer sweater.

Adrià came out to sit with me, now that his night's work was over. He asked me what I thought of the dinner; I said I thought it was OK. He seemed tickled by this lukewarm response, and smiled indulgently. I told him I had spent much of the meal feeling I needed to laugh, or actually laughing out loud, at the sheer zaniness of the food on my plate and the sensations it was producing in my brain.

He nodded. This is an important part of what he wants his customers to feel. The most wonderful of all the wonderful things about El Bulli, it might be said, is the exquisite balance it maintains between pleasure and science, between lighthearted enjoyment and an intensely serious approach to gastronomic experiment.

"Good; that's good. I do believe in a sense of humor in the kitchen. Food can be a way of having fun."

Like a latter-day Marco Polo, he scours the world for strange and delightful novelties. On a recent trip to Japan, he had found a source of transparent rice paper, which he had been rolling and folding into an empanadilla, stuffing it with berries flavored with eucalyptus. The bone marrow from the spine of the tuna. Fresh pine nuts, gathered in May before the nut is fully formed. From the Amazon basin, a series of strange fruits and stranger herbs, like the bizarre vegetable jambu, which briefly sends the mouth to sleep. Adrià's inspiration is childlike. It is based on a permanent delighted curiosity about the world around him.

Curiosity, however, often depends on a deep-seated sense of security. A taste for the exotic springs from a profound knowledge of the familiar. And this is the central antithesis: the world, for Ferran Adrià, is at the same time both familiar and exotic, local and global, provincial and international.

He has had offers from all over, and millions of dollars, to set up shop abroad, in Las Vegas, Tokyo, Paris. Yet seeing him here with the sea behind him, sitting out under the stars, drinking a well-earned glass of white wine, the warm silence surrounding us both, insects clicking and whirring in the darkness, the smells of pine sap and rosemary and seaweed drifting across the terrace, I realize that he might not have achieved what he has in any other situation, any other context, any other landscape. Roots and family mean everything and nothing. Like the big black sea down there in the bay, you can't always see them, but you know they're always there.

4

Cádiz-Málaga

ZAHARA DE LOS ATUNES sat squatly behind a wild stretch of sandy beach at the southernmost tip of Europe, where the continents seem almost to touch, but then to change their minds. It was a rough-and-tumble, knocked-together sort of town, more of a village, that now lived off tourism in a small way, but had not altogether shaken off the salty, stinky charm of a place whose life, if not livelihood, still revolved around the culture of fish and fishing.

After the gastronomic mountaineering of El Bulli, I figured, it would be good to breathe some less rarefied air. Back home, I had asked about somewhere on the coast of Spain that had not been irredeemably spoiled, where the cooking would be simple, savory, and unadorned. All my informants had mentioned Cádiz, because the strategic importance of the coastline had kept much of the Costa de la Luz in military hands, thus saving it from destruction, and the popular fish cookery of Andalusia was still practiced on a day-to-day basis. So it was that on a Sunday afternoon in the dregs of late August, when the country has been in vacation mode for so long it is secretly rather bored with the lounging, languid life of summer, I was lying beside the pool of a three-star hotel on the outskirts of Zahara de los Atunes, where the probing tendrils of new development pushed ever farther along the coast.

Zahara has always depended economically, and continues to depend in other ways, on the tunafish that swim past the town in giant schools on their way through the Strait of Gibraltar, to spawn in the warm waters of the Mediterranean.

There was not very much to do in Zahara except sleep, walk along the windswept beach, and sit down to fine meals of fish prepared in the various forms of the local cocina marinera. The menu at the town's restaurants was a litany of Andalusian coastal cooking. There were tortillitas de camarón, one of my absolute favorite things in all of Spanish food, essentially a batter with tiny shrimps and chopped parsley, fried on the plancha in a splotch until it turns into a crisp little pancake. There was cazón en adobo, chunks of shark marinated in vinegar and herbs, then fried. There were baby squid and sole and cuttlefish and anchovies, and a legion of little fish with names that sound familiar in Spanish and wildly exotic in English. All, or nearly all, were prepared in the same manner: which is to say, dredged in a mixture of chickpea and wheat flour (the speciality flour used in Andalusia for frying and nearly impossible to find outside the region), before being briefly plunged into boiling olive oil.

An often repeated adage holds that "The south fries, the center roasts, and the north boils." It's a wild generalization, but with a generous helping of truth. The cooking of Andalusia, if the truth be told, makes the apparently simple act of frying into a pillar of its culinary practice.

Pescaíto frito, or mixed fried fish, in any case, has always been a major element of life on the Costa de la Luz. In 1929 the gastronome Dionisio Pérez, in his witty and still relevant *Guide to Good Spanish Eating,* described the city of Cádiz and the villages along its coastline as "the headquarters, the Olympus of pescaíto frito." It was true then, and it's true now. In Cádiz, and in the nearby Puerto de Santa María, the custom is to buy a big paper wrap, or cone, heaped with freshly fried pescaíto. This wrap known as el papelón ("the big paper"), is taken away for eating in the ozone-fresh air of the sea wall, or conveyed to a bar or bodega where the fish is eaten with the fingers and washed down with beer, wine, or fino sherry.

In Zahara there was no traditional papelón, but there were plenty of simple eating houses with upturned sherry barrels for tables and thin paper napkins scrunched in drifts on the floor, and menus that majored in all forms of fried fish. After an exhaustive investigation, I found that the Bar Paquiqui was the one I liked best. It was hidden away in a flower-filled corner of the oldest part of the village, in a pitched-roofed fisherman's house with Arab roof tiles. Inside, the atmosphere was that of a proper village bar, with the World Cup roaring away on television and a tremendous noise of frying from a tiny kitchen at the back. I found a table outside and sat drinking tinto de verano ("summer red"), the iced refresher of red wine and sweet fizzy soda.

From inside the kitchen came a frenzied sizzle and clatter. A round pink face in a white kitchen cap poked around the hatch in a cloud of fishy smoke. A cry was heard: "Table two, prawns, cazón, tortillitas, on their way!" Antonia, owner of the face, stood in charge of the fryer, and she was truly a master of her craft. She called me in from outside to show me how she turned the pieces of shark in the flour, shaking them from side to side on a special rack to remove the excess, and then deep-fried them just long enough to form a crisp golden shell that sealed in all the tenderness of the fish.

She had learned the art of frying from her father, Francisco, who had retreated from the front line of the kitchen and was now responsible for the backstage business of dealing with suppliers, preparing the marinade for the cazón en adobo, and cooking up in his own home the menu's few long-simmered dishes like atún encebollado, a delicious stew of tuna and masses of onions flavored with oregano, sweet pimentón, bay leaf, and wine vinegar.

Francisco Martínez, known to the world at large as Paquiqui, had presided over the Bar Paquiqui in Zahara since the late 1980s, when he had finally given up the ways of the sea for the stability of a life on land. I found him sitting in his special chair at the back, making sure everything ran smoothly on this late-summer night when Spain was playing France and the atmosphere at the bar came perilously close to rowdiness.

He came out to sit with me, sipping a glass of wine while he watched me eat. For many years Paquiqui had been a professional ship's cook, so there was not much he didn't know about catering for hungry and demanding customers.

"I worked on fishing boats, deepwater, for thirty-five years," he told me. He was a serious yet amiable elderly gentleman, with heavy gray brows and a gaze that became solemn when he needed to concentrate on a recipe, statistics, or a particularly intractable memory.

"The boats always left from Barbate, heading for the Canaries, Casablanca, or farther south, the coast of Africa. . . . We might be at sea for eleven days, twelve days, or if we were going south, twenty-five days, or more. My salary was 1,000 pesetas a month. This in 1950. Life on board ship was hard. The boats had no bathrooms; there was very little water. . . . You shaved once every ten days, when the boat got back to port."

At least the food was good—or at least Paquiqui made it sound good. I had heard about cocina a bordo, or "onboard cooking," the particular genre of Spanish fish cookery in which many classic dishes of cocina marinera have their origins. It is a genre that is fast disappearing, since big fishing boats these days have freezers and microwaves, and fishermen probably live off pizza and pasta like the rest of humanity, but Paquiqui was a living testament to its richness and variety.

"Fishermen, when they're working out at sea, want big meals at midday and in the evening," he said. The repertoire ranged from soup-stews based on beans and vegetables, or chickpeas with baby cuttlefish, to rice dishes with cardoons (arroz cardúo), with hake tails, or with canned tuna and red peppers. Paquiqui's speciality was a soupy rice based on monkfish with a sofrito of dried ñora peppers, tomato, and garlic; he used the liver of the fish and a piece of fried bread, mashed together in the pestle and mortar, to thicken the stock toward the end of the cooking. It sounded wonderful, and I told Paquiqui so, and he launched into a step-by-step description of the recipe, which I scribbled down on a napkin and still have somewhere, among my disorganized piles of Spanish kitchen notes.

Surprisingly, fish wasn't the only thing eaten on board. There was also meat, since the province of Cádiz is an important producer of beef cattle. "We ate the beef until it ran out; then we started on the fish." There might be estofado en amarillo, a beef stew with red pepper, garlic, bay leaf, and pimentón, which he still cooked up for the workers at the Bar Paquiqui though it never appeared on the menu. The name means "yellow stew," though from the red pepper and pimentón, you'd think it would be closer to a rich dark red.

As for Zahara and the sea, they were like a divorced couple still living in the same house. Only a few old men still fished from the beach, more out of habit than necessity, bringing their boats in at midday to make a few euros by selling their meager catch to friends and neighbors. In the last fifteen years the town had thrown in its lot with the money-spinning businesses that had brought fame and fortune to the rest of the Spanish coast: tourism and construction.

"Since I retired, I haven't been back to the sea. I was that fed up with it," Paquiqui said. "There is more work about. Life is better than before. There's no need for the young people to go to sea, and it's just as well. The sea is very bad."

STEAMING IN THE midday heat, Zahara had the feeling of a faded beachside outpost somewhere in Latin America: Cuba, perhaps, or the coast of Venezuela. It had flat-roofed houses with peeling whitewashed walls, and a sixteenth-century fortress that had once served as a storehouse and factory for Zahara's tuna industry, but whose limestone walls were crumbling into the dust.

The market at Zahara was a humble affair except when it came to fish, in which it would have surpassed many a market in a town ten or twenty times larger. I picked one of the three stands at random and stopped to talk to the attendant, a short, loud woman with short hair and thick black glasses. The range of fish, laid out in front of her in a kaleidoscopic arrangement of pink, orange, scarlet, and coral red, testified to the considerable biodiversity of the oceans off the Costa de la Luz. The quality was peerless, as it would be, when the fish had come in only a few minutes ago from the fishing port at Barbate, a few miles up the coast.

The fish woman pointed out the ugly urta, which is much prized around the coast of Cádiz, where it is cooked a la roteña (in the style of Rota, a town famous for this dish and for its American naval base) with a sauce of tomato and peppers. I looked with covetous eyes at some red mullet, a fish I have always loved for its subtly flavored, meaty flesh, so good when stuffed with fresh herbs (it goes particularly well with fennel) and slapped on the barbecue.

On the coast of Cádiz neither of these species, however, could ever be the main attraction. At the top of the stand, crowning the display, was a hunk of fresh tuna that had come in from the harbor not half an hour ago. It was a large piece weighing at least five kilos, as rosy as a cut of prime beef, and so fresh that it proudly kept its shape when the fishmonger gave it a hefty slap. At twenty-two euros a kilo it was a good deal more expensive than the priciest rare-breed beef sirloin. You might imagine that in one of the least prosperous parts of Spain, this fish would have few takers. You would be wrong: after me in the line came three local women in blue-and-white aprons, the traditional uniform of the working-class housewife, and each took away a couple of juicy slabs, for cooking vuelta y vuelta in the frying pan, just a moment or two on each side.

"Around here, what we know about is tuna, tuna, tuna," said the woman who ran the stand. She then sketched for my benefit the basics of the local tuna industry: the four remaining almadrabas, the tuna-fishing installations founded by the Phoenicians and still operating in much the same way, though with catches that plummet every year to new and ever more alarming lows; and the habits of the species *Thunnus thynnus thynnus* (repetitiously so-called to distinguish it from the inferior Pacific subspecies *Thunnus thynnus orientalis,* as well as from tuna knockoffs like the albacore and yellowfin tuna, both of which have the same family name but cannot hold a candle to it in quality).

The atún rojo is a noble fish that reaches giant size. It spends most of the year in the cold but rich waters of the Atlantic, until early summer when it heads south, like much of the population of northern Europe, in order to spawn in the bath-like waters of the Mediterranean. In order to reach their goal these enormous fish must make their way through the Strait of Gibraltar—where the almadrabas are waiting for them.

The etymology of this word is plainly Arabic—it is supposed to derive from *daraba,* to smite or hit, the almadraba being a place of smiting or hitting. The craft of tuna fishing by this method was invented by the Phoenicians and perfected by the Romans, before receiving its modern name from the Moors. The glory days of this traditional craft were the 600 years the almadrabas of the Andalusian coast were controlled by the duchy of Medina Sidonia, from the thirteenth century until the nineteenth. There were formerly almadrabas all along the Spanish Mediterranean coast, but now only four remain, and all are on the Atlantic side of the Strait of Gibraltar: one each in Barbate and Tarifa, and two in Zahara de los Atunes.

It is hard to imagine what an almadraba actually looks like without seeing a plan of its complex underwater structure of deep nets through which the tuna are led as through a maze, and finally corralled in a central net from which there is no escape. This net is then raised through the water—the so-called levantá—and the enormous fish, which can weigh 300 kilos or more, are left high and dry. The spectacle of the levantá is powerfully impressive. The few outsiders who have witnessed it describe the scene as one of tremendous violence and danger, as the giant fish thrash about in their death throes, the fishermen jump into the fray to stab them with giant hooks for loading on board, and the water seethes with blood and foam.

The fish woman pointed out a picture on the white-tiled wall of her stand, showing a levantá in full swing: a square of boats around the silvery mass of flailing fish; the fishermen in their uniform of bright orange and midnight blue.

"I've seen it once," she said grimly. "And that's it. I won't see it ever again."

The tuna boats leave the harbor for the almadrabas at dawn, returning halfway through the morning. Sometimes there is nothing in the nets, and they come back empty. It is hardly a surprise to learn that the catch has dramatically declined over the last few years, to the point where it seems likely that the whole tradition of almadraba fishing, with its 3,000 years of history, will have disappeared before the decade is out.

I got to the docks at Barbate just as the boats were arriving. Today they had been lucky, and there was jubilation in the air. No fewer than fifty-four tuna had blundered into the nets. This was regarded as a fine catch, though by the standards of an earlier time, when the norm was 300 or 400 fish per day, it would have been a meager haul.

I stood on the harborside and watched the proceedings, the gray-painted boats as they moored one by one, each with its cargo of corpses covered in gray winding sheets. A small crowd had gathered to see the tuna winched up from the floor of the boat, to be received at the door of the warehouse where they would be weighed and checked. Their giant bodies swung above the crowd like modern sculptures; they were sleek and hard and gleaming, as shiny and cold as if made of solid steel, and their mouths gaped open in a tragic mask of horror.

Out here on the dock, the heat was rising. There were shouts from the joshing fishermen, excited noises from the crowd, and a mingled harbor smell of diesel fumes and fish remains. Inside the warehouse, the scene was very different. Computers clicked and beeped. Outside, the tuna had been a lump of meat, a dead animal. In here, it was science and big business. A slender, neatly dressed man with Asian features was working away with some kind of clinical probe, designed to measure the body temperature of the fish and thereby determine its exact time of death. To the Japanese, who are the major buyers of atún rojo de almadraba, the freshness of the product is of paramount importance. In the sophisticated universe of Japanese fish culture, there is no more exquisite delicacy than this. The Japanese word for the belly meat of this tuna is *toro*—which is also, by coincidence, the Spanish word for "bull." And this is not the only lexicological link between tuna and beef. Among the words for cuts of tuna, we have solomillo (sirloin), lomo (loin), and espinazo (spinal column).

It's in the form of salted and cured tuna, en salazón, that atún rojo reaches the summit of excellence and value. Of the two remaining salazón houses in Barbate, most people you ask around the town will tell you the better is Herpac (the other is Salpesca). From the harbor I walked to Herpac's shop and factory on the outskirts of town, where at the back door of the building the beep-beep-beep of a reversing truck announced the arrival of three tuna from this morning's levantá. Inside the shop a girl in a white coat explained the process behind mojama, the star product of Barbate's tuna industry and one of the finest of all Spanish foods. The tuna loins are salted and hung up to dry on the roof of the shop for a month, two months, or three months, depending on the weather and "what the tuna tells you," until they shrink and harden to the texture of a fine serrano ham. The firm's other top products were hueva—tuna roe cured in the same way, perfect for grating over pasta as the Sardinians do with their *bottarga*—and atún de ijar, the belly meat preserved in fillets under olive oil. The price of these goodies seemed agonizingly high, but I fought off the pain to buy one small piece of hueva and one of mojama. As I left the shop, I was already thinking how I would slice it thinly, dress it with a little olive oil, and invite a select group of friends to a luxury aperitivo with fried almonds and a bottle of cold manzanilla from one of the sherry houses of Sanlúcar de Barrameda a few miles up the coast.

By now it was lunchtime; and in Barbate at lunchtime, if you want to eat tuna and are willing to pay for it, there is one restaurant above all that fills the bill. The parents of José Melero once had a bar in nearby Vejer de la Frontera where locals went for wine and tapas and to play cards in the evening. In 1978 the family moved down to Barbate and opened a small restaurant called El Campero, which is still going strong, though it has mutated into rather a smart little joint with a striped blue-and-white awning and scary air-conditioning, where the rich landowners and sherry barons of the province go to talk business over fino sherry and heavenly cocina marinera.

I sat at a corner table and chatted with José, who was a short stocky man with a neat mustache and wearing a short-sleeved shirt, the garment worn by three-quarters of all adult males on a summer day on the Costa de la Luz. José was amiable and quietly spoken, but his voice registered an extra point or two on the emotional Richter scale whenever he got onto the subject of tuna. The tuna was the great marvel of our culture, the culture of Cádiz, of Andalusia, and of Spain. It was la joya del estrecho: "the jewel of the Strait."

José was an expert on the traditional cooking of Barbate, which made cunning use of the less prestigious cuts of atún rojo in such homey dishes as tuna entrails with chickpeas, cuts of mojama with tomato, tuna "ears" with sauce, and casserole of tuna skin. There was also facera—the head meat and cheeks of the fish, cooked with potatoes in a classic of the local fishermen's cuisine—and parpatana, just behind the head, which was oven-roasted. Of all the various local tuna recipes, the most elaborate and the most often prepared (since many of the others were falling rapidly into disuse) was atún encebollado.

But the menu at El Campero didn't stop there. It was an exhaustive adventure in tuna cookery, running from the humblest tapa of tuna heart, served cold with a vinegary dressing, through tuna sashimi and tuna tartare, to tuna in a bitter orange sauce (the analogy between the oily-rich meats of tuna and duck does have a certain logic), and a slice of morrillo a la plancha with anchovy mayonnaise. The morrillo is a long tube of muscle held together with delicate fat, not unlike the finest sirloin of ibérico pork. Traditionally this was a humbler cut, classified as vísceras (entrails). So was galete, a small piece of gelatinous meat located deep inside the head which lends itself to long, slow cooking. José brought out a plate of galete to round off the proceedings: it was dark and meltingly tender in its rich concentrated sauce, more like rabo de toro than anything else in the world of seafood.

What tricks history plays on us, and how dumbly we fall into the traps it sets! What are now luxuries were once common or garden-variety staples. When things are abundant, they are scarcely valued, or are even looked on with contempt. (Oysters, a poor man's food in nineteenth-century London, are an obvious example.) It is only when they become scarce and expensive that they are finally given the appreciation they deserve, by the minority who can afford them. But by then, sadly, it is too late for the rest of us.

MARJORIE GRICE-HUTCHINSON is principally remembered today for her work in economics as a disciple of Hayek. Her study of 1952, *The School of Salamanca: Readings in Spanish Monetary Theory, 1544–1605,* is a key text in Spanish economic history. But she also wrote two books in a genre that might be known nowadays as "the good life abroad." In *Málaga Farm* (1956), now out of print, she paints a brightly colored picture of life on the Costa del Sol in the last few years before tourism was to transform it out of all recognition, documenting local life with a curiosity occasionally tempered by a quiver of puzzlement.

She had arrived on the Costa in 1924, when her father, George William Grice-Hutchinson, bought the Finca San Julián, a farmstead just outside Málaga on the fertile coastal plain known as la vega (hence las vegas, the plains). In the years before the civil war he and his daughter were well known in the area for their philanthropic work, in particular the school and medical dispensary they founded in the village of Churriana.

For a person who had lived so long among the Spanish, Marjorie Grice-Hutchinson is revealed in *Málaga Farm* as oddly squeamish about some of their habits. Describing a busy market, housed in an old Moorish harbor building known as the Atarazanas, she mentions the Arabic inscription over the entrance, "There is no conqueror but Allah," and goes on to comment, "The motto has not entirely lost its old force: for who shall arbitrate in the severe though bloodless struggles that are waged in the market?" Bloodless, or bloody: she found "disagreeable" the sight of live hens and turkeys tied together by the legs, and wrote, "I still feel revolted when I see a woman choose one of these unfortunate birds, look on unmoved while its throat is cut, and watch its death-struggles with detached interest."

With her professional eye for the details of social reality, Grice-Hutchinson saw clearly that in the era before tourism, the lives of the working classes on the Costa del Sol came perilously close to poverty. Housing for ordinary people was generally bad, and conditions were often insalubrious. The diet of the malagueño farmhand, however, she thought "fairly good." The typical breakfast of such a person would have been bread, leftover fish, and "a beverage made from roasted barley and slightly resembling coffee." Lunch might be soup, followed by a "substantial stew" of rice, potatoes, and vegetables. And supper was fried fish, potatoes, and something called gazpacho, which she describes—it is clear that the dish would have been unfamiliar to British readers in 1956—as "a refreshing concoction made of garlic, cucumber, and tomatoes floating in a bowl of oil, vinegar, and water."

Later on in the book, in the section "Food and Drink," the author informs her readers that gazpacho is "served as the first course of fashionable luncheons and dinners, and for the poor often constitutes an entire meal." The recipe she gives for the dish hardly conforms to her image of vegetables bobbing in a bowl, and I have never heard elsewhere of apples being added to the mixture. But the idea of the vegetables and bread being "pounded" sounds authentic, at a time before handheld mixers and food processors, since anything that had to be mashed, crushed, or liquefied would have been worked at laboriously by hand in a mortar and pestle.

Few dishes anywhere in the world are more rigorously seasonal than gazpacho. This is a dish which for most of the year is all but inconceivable, not just because the ingredients are out of season, but because the dish derives its meaning and raison d'être from a particular time of year. You would no more eat an ice-cold gazpacho in the frosty month of January than you would eat a mighty cocido madrileño with all the trimmings in the middle of August. During winter gazpacho retreats into hibernation, not to emerge until one of those days in June when an early blast of summer heat takes the country by surprise; you realize that everything you need for the dish is out there in the garden, minus one or two things which can be bought at the corner store; and suddenly gazpacho is back on the agenda, where it stays, an irreplaceable staple of summer eating, until the first chilly days of autumn once more consign it, like Persephone, to another eight months of oblivion.

There are gazpachos that stick in the mind, along with places, people, and moments. The first "milestone gazpacho" of my life was one I made myself. As a child I liked to cook, but more than cooking itself, what excited me was the business of planning the menu, setting the table, and creating the atmosphere. I devised a series of dinners based on national themes, at which the guests were the members of my family. The Spanish dinner consisted of gazpacho and paella—naturally enough—and sliced oranges for dessert; the menu cards were typed up individually and adorned around the edges with Spanish flags, bulls' heads, and castanets. I remember nothing about the paella, though it was probably a travesty. But that gazpacho has stayed with me. I must have whizzed it up in my mum's old Kenwood mixer, which was the sort that required you to hold down the lid with its rubber seal—or else whatever you were whizzing would end up decorating the walls. Gazpacho struck me then not only as amazingly easy to make, for such a classic dish of world cuisine, but improbably delicious. Which of course it is.

No one is quite sure about the origins of gazpacho, though the idea of a watery salad goes back a long way, perhaps predating the Romans. The word, however, has been traced to the Latin *caspa,* implying small pieces or flakes. (The modern Spanish word for dandruff [caspa] off-puttingly has the same root.)

Until the tomato and the pepper arrived in Europe, gazpacho would have been made without either. Before the twentieth century this was not a well-known dish, and rarely figured in cookbooks. Angel Muro's encyclopedic *Practicón* of 1894 makes no mention of it. Perhaps Muro thought it too embarrassingly primitive a concoction to be worthy of inclusion. Yet, oddly, not a single one of the Andalusian repertoire of sopas frías makes it into his culinary Parnassus: the only cold soup to be found in the pages of the *Practicón* is an iced consommé, hardly representative in any sense of Spanish regional cooking.

As the influence of France faded from the Spanish culinary scene, which it had dominated for the whole of the nineteenth century, the excellences of traditional cooking began to be seen for what they were. For the great doctor and humanist Gregorio Marañón (1887–1960), gazpacho was an inspired piece of popular gastronomy anticipating some modern ideas about healthy eating. He wrote, "The learned folk of a few decades ago marveled at the fact that with such a light dish, harvesters were able to toil for so many hours in the heat of the midday sun: they were unaware that the common instinct was many centuries in advance of the professors of nutrition, and that this emulsion of oil in cold water, with the addition of vinegar, salt, pimentón, crushed tomato, bread, and other ingredients, contains everything necessary to sustain workers engaged in the most tedious of labors."

There are gazpachos of all colors, textures, and aromas—some of which do not even bear the name. And the king of them all, in my book, is not a gazpacho at all in any real sense. Ajoblanco (literally, "white garlic") is a soup of raw almonds with a little garlic, salt, olive oil, and water. It is one of those dishes that, primitive though they sound in theory, become in practice a great deal more than the sum of their parts. Ajoblanco is often eaten with the inspired accompaniment of sweet muscat grapes or chunks of ripe melon. It is a thoroughly traditional dish, yet it could have been invented last week. Cool and ivory white, with a creaminess that leads many people to the mistaken assumption that it contains a dairy product, ajoblanco has a minimalist modernity that belies its age-old popularity in the city of its birth.

THE CULINARY SCENE in the city of Málaga is not what you might call buzzing, but there is one place at least that is often cited as a point of reference: the Café de Paris. The name is terrible, but after twenty-five years of existence and a shining reputation in the city, there must seem little point in changing it. When José Carlos García's father ran the kitchen in the Café de Paris it was famous for French-style cooking, which ran to such things as beef Wellington and soufflé Grand Marnier. But when José Carlos took over—fresh from La Cónsula cookery school outside Málaga—the menu underwent a radical change.

I first went to the Café de Paris in the mid-1990s, when José Carlos had just taken the helm. By then his ajoblanco malagueño with a red wine and cinnamon granizado was already a firm fixture on the menu. As a dish it made a great deal of sense, not only because the silk and ice of soup and sorbet made for a fabulous combination, the deep red on ivory white a dazzling visual contrast, but also because it tapped into the traditions of the city, breathing new life into a recipe as old as the hills.

Now I was on my way back along the coast toward Málaga, sitting in sluggish, angry traffic on the highway linking Cádiz and Algeciras with the Costa del Sol. I was already late for my two o'clock reservation, and I was also running out of gas. I could feel my anxiety level rising with the temperature inside the car. As I crawled past endless shopping centers and car dealers I noticed a turnoff for San Julián, the finca where Marjorie Grice-Hutchinson had lived and written until her death in 2003.

Few times in my life have I more urgently needed a cold gazpacho—or an ajoblanco, for that matter—with or without the red wine granizado. I conjured up the thought of something cold, and refreshing, and relaxing, as I limped the last few miles into town, found a space in the ferocious sun beside the bullring, and dashed for the door of the restaurant.

In a matter of minutes my wish was granted. The dining room was silent, cool, and calming. The waitress brought me a gazpacho of red fruits, with marinated sardines in tight curls, and a plate of José Carlos's famous ajoblanco. Then there was red mullet in fillets, arranged on a risotto of beets and chives. The bold use of color, contrast, and intensity reminded me that the city of Málaga was the birthplace of Pablo Picasso.

Ajoblanco ran, so to speak, in the García family. José Carlos's grandfather, who came originally from Rincón de la Victoria, a little way down the coast, where the family originally ran a churrería for the fishermen of the village, had loved the dish almost to distraction. "He ate it with grapes and a little fresh cheese," said the chef as we chatted in the kitchen after lunch. "It was his dinner, almost all year round."

José Carlos's parents had told him about the original, rustic gazpacho, which sounds more like Marjorie Grice-Hutchinson's description of roughly crushed vegetables swimming in oil, vinegar, and water than the smoothly liquefied soup of modern times.

"My dad tells me that farming people used to eat it in the countryside as a working lunch," José Carlos said. "The women would bring it out to them in a clay bowl covered with a cloth. It must have looked quite unattractive—everything just mashed up with a fork."

The cold soups of Andalusia have turned out to be a rich resource for the new Spanish cooking, giving rise to modern classics such as those created by the malagueño chef Dani García: gazpacho of cherries (with goat cheese "snow" and salted anchovies), gazpacho of green tomato (with sliced sea snail), and pine-nut ajoblanco. Among Ferran Adrià's earliest inventions were a luxurious gazpacho with chunks of lobster and a salmorejo of lobster and rabbit. Nowadays it is no surprise to find a designer restaurant in Madrid offering tataki of salmon on a pool of porra antequerana. The fashion has even spread to Paris, where Joël Robuchon serves a tomato-based gazpacho with fresh almonds and basil oil at his chic new restaurant L'Atelier. Sopas frías are everywhere.

As for José Carlos, he has taken this central plank of his culinary heritage and fashioned it into dozens of curious and interesting forms.

"Gazpachos? I've made them out of everything!" he laughed when I asked him the obvious question. One of his first variations on the traditional theme was gazpacho de fresa, in which he replaced half the weight of tomato with the same weight of strawberries. Raspberry also works, as do cherry and beet. I myself make a gazpacho with watermelon that is hauntingly sweet and subtly perfumed. José Carlos's experiments have led him to try gazpacho of avocado, a thick greenish cream; and gazpacho with a garnish of roast scallops, fried eggplant, or marinated tuna from the almadrabas of Cádiz. His most radical creation was gazpacho transparente, a normal gazpacho decanted and filtered again and again until nothing remained but the watery essence of the tomato and cucumber and green pepper. It was a long way from the English gazpacho of my childhood, farther still from the dull tourist gazpachos of the Costa Brava—and a million miles from the harvesters with their scythes, amid the dust and prickles of a cornfield in high summer, gratefully tucking into their midday meal of raw vegetables mashed in a clay bowl with vinegar, oil, salt, and water from the spring.

5

Galicia

MEDITERRANEAN AND ATLANTIC. Two seas, but also two cultures, two communities, two ways of looking at the same set of circumstances.

The peoples of the Spanish Mediterranean have turned their back on the special relationship they once had with the sea. Tourism and the construction industry have long since overtaken fishing as the principal occupations of Mediterranean society. Pockets of the old maritime culture still survive, it's true; I had found a few of them over the course of a summer's travels along the coast. To find this way of life in robust health, however, you need to look toward the northwest, and the great stretch of coastline abutting what the Spanish call the Cantabrian Sea, from Galicia in the west to Asturias and Cantabria and the Basque country in the east.

Looked at on a map, the coast of Galicia is a crazed doodle, an intricate tracery of estuaries, peninsulas, and islands. The region has a higher ratio of coastline to total surface area than any of Spain's other coastal communities.

Of all the autonomous communities in the new Spain, none but Galicia has such a close and fruitful relationship with the sea. More than half of the Spanish fishing industry is concentrated here, and Galicia is unique in that fish still forms a pillar of its economy, despite pollution, European quotas, and falling catches. The community also has a greater consumption of fish and seafood than anywhere else in the country.

I stood on the sand in the weak September sun. On a calm afternoon in the Rías Baixas, the five sea estuaries that push inland along the northwest coast of Spain, it is easy to kid yourself that you are still in the south. Lemon trees, figs, orange trees, and vines thrive surprisingly in the mild microclimate of the rías. The sand on the beach where I stood, on a peninsula jutting into the Ría de Arosa, was made up of crushed shells of cockles, winkles, and clams. The whiteness of this sand under the shallow sea, flat calm in the sunlight, gave the water a turquoise-pinkish hue that, if you half-closed your eyes and painted in a few waving palms, dared you to believe you had beamed down on some gorgeous atoll in the Pacific.

THE POUSA FAMILY were natives of this coast, gallegos to the core, attached to their origins like limpets to a rock. Even when they lived in Madrid, on the fifth floor of an apartment house, they spent their August vacations here almost as a religious observance, the whole troop of eight children, parents, and grandparents decamping every summer to O Grove, a little town on a peninsula of the Ría de Arosa, taking fourteen hours by car along roads that, even in the 1960s, were little more than winding asphalt-coated tracks.

Cold salt water ran in their veins. Even the eldest Pousa brother, CEO of a blue-chip company in Madrid, still came back for an occasional weekend to dress up in old clothes and potter around with fishing rods and baits and floats, feeling his stress drift out with the tide.

Julo was a sailmaker in Villagarcía, on the other side of the ría. He showed me to my quarters, one of the original fishermen's houses in the tiny harbor at Rons, and then took me out again to the beach, where a soft drizzle had begun to fall. There, pulled up on the sand, was the family's pride and joy: a wooden fishing boat, one of three or four of the same curious, lean shape, with a high curling prow. The dorna, as it's known, is a relic of Viking and Norman incursions along the Galician coast in the early Middle Ages, and related to the Viking drakkar. Proof of its origins, apart from that evocatively curling prow, can be found in the construction of the boat, which uses the Viking technique of overlapping panels—known in the Galician language as tingladiña.

The little dorna, the *Nuka*, had been in the family for decades. Julo ran his hands over its red-painted hull, showing me its primitive mast and sail, its special rudder (timón orza), and the fish-scale construction of its hull. He remembered how as a child he used to fish for octopus, attaching a stick and a hook to a live crab, tossing it over the side of the boat attached to a line and buoy, and coming back next morning to haul up the flailing beast.

We repaired to a bar behind the beach, owned and ruled by a fierce-looking but sweet-natured woman named Joaquina. She poured us glasses of Ribeiro, the gallego table wine whose clean green fruit and thirst-quenching acidity are like stuffing your mouth full of ripe white grapes, and a couple of her homemade empanadillas: little turnovers stuffed with mussels in the mild pickle known as escabeche.

The conversation turned around the Festa do Marisco do Grove, a ten-day fiesta that was reaching its apogee this weekend, in a series of giant tents specially erected along the harbor. This seafood fiesta had been celebrated in O Grove annually for the last forty-two years and was one of the great exaltaciones—the orgiastic homages to various foodstuffs, from potatoes, to leek, to octopus, that have become a characteristic element of the Galician festive calendar. According to the *Faro de Vigo*, the local newspaper, which was lying on the bar, the Festa do Marisco had made O Grove nothing less than the "world capital of seafood." The full-page article was a potpourri of statistics: 250,000 visitors; 125,448 servings of seafood; more than 500,000 euros in takings.

The recent history of the town was closely caught up with the story of the fiesta. When the civil war ended, O Grove was a small seaside town that subsisted, barely, on what it could catch in the sea, dig up in the ría, and grow in its orchards and vegetable patches. The humblest townsfolk, when they had nothing else, survived by eating clams and cockles scratched out of the mud at low tide. In Galicia, as recently as the 1970s, it was an indicator of a person's truly desperate financial state that he was reduced to eating marisco.

There was nothing desperate about the scene that met my eyes in the port of O Grove, when I arrived there with Julo and his little son later that evening. Marquees had been put up around the town's fish market, trestle tables stood in serried ranks, and stands around the edges of the tents offered a compendium of all that is best in Galician seafood: shrimp, Dublin Bay prawns, razor clams, crabs, and mussels in vinaigrette; octopus in the Galician style, dressed with olive oil, salt, and pimentón; and a rice dish with local shellfish which, with admirable restraint, the organizers had refrained from describing as paella. There was plenty of good gallego bread, chewy and crusty in a way that no other Spanish bread quite achieves; and there was a mighty quantity of Ribeiro, fresh and bracing as the breeze off the sea. Between the tables, the various stands, and the computerized cash registers, milled a huge crowd, filling the space with the noise of their happiness and appetite. At the back of the tent was a stage on which Galician musicians and dancers were currently performing, and the fast and furious music of bagpipes and tambourines, like a cross between Scotland and Andalusia, together with the intoxicating wine and the exhilarating seafood, was whipping up the atmosphere as the wind whips up the sea.

At the octopus stand three big women in white coats were working with a slickness born of repetition; while one fished a pink, dripping octopus out of a bubbling cauldron, another snipped the legs into slices onto a thick wooden plate like a medieval trencher, and a third busied herself with the dressing: a slosh of olive oil, a hail of rock salt, and a dusting of sweet pimentón. Pulpeiras are specialist octopus cooks who go from fiesta to fiesta the length and breadth of Galicia, taking with them their great copper cauldrons, their octopus scissors, their cans of pimentón, and their years of experience in the art of making pulpo a feira: octopus "in the style of the fair," the style in which Galicia as a whole most enjoys its octopus. (The wooden plate adds nothing to the taste, though it certainly looks nice and does facilitate spearing the octopus slices with the toothpicks usually provided. I am told that the wooden plates date from the days when the pulpeiras traveled by horse and cart on some of the bumpiest roads in Christendom, making the transport of hundreds of china plates severely impractical.)

Beside us at the trestle table an elderly man in a black beret had laid out in front of him a bottle of Ribeiro, a large hunk of bread, and a pile of paper napkins. He was either awaiting the arrival of a person bearing plates of marisco, or preparing to tuck in by himself to what would be, given the circumstances, a very frugal Sunday supper. Images caught in my retina as I stood at the table: a small child with a big drum; a cohort of housewives on a night out, with near-identical perms and cardigans; a svelte young dancer in a long black satin gallego skirt, worn specially for the whirling, bagpipe-accompanied dance called the muiñeira, hurrying past with a heaped plate of steaming mussels, the shells of the shellfish the same glossy jet-black as the skirt.

The rain now thundered on the roof, dripping off the edges of the tents into the plates of food being ferried to and fro, mussing up the hairdos of the señoras in their Sunday best, reducing the floor to a mess of soggy napkins and mussel shells. Rainfall in Galicia being a fact of almost daily life, however, there was no way the seafood-scoffers at the festa were going to have their party spoiled. If anything it made the whole thing even more fun, since now, with this driving rain, you were pretty much here for the duration, and what with the noise on the roof and the shrill music of bagpipes and drums you had to shout even louder to be heard above the din. As long as the Ribeiro lasted, in any case, there seemed little point in being anywhere else. And the seafood kept on coming—plates and plates of it, juicy clams a la marinera, and huge lanky langoustines with crackable claws containing nuggets of dense white meat as big as your thumb, fat lobsters split down the middle and flash-grilled a la plancha with olive oil and garlic, and octopus a feira, and more mussels a la vinagreta, and yet more octopus. Julo and his son tried a few steps of the muiñeira, while I fell into a state of mild hypnosis that I remembered from another great seafood feast, in the port of Santander, years ago. The wine, the squalling bagpipes, and the noise of the people all seemed to coalesce into a single, collective sensory experience, a feeling that was pleasure and well-being and forgetfulness all rolled up into one.

In the slow morning of the following day, I looked out of my window toward the quiet water of the ría, only to find that it had disappeared. The low tide, never an important feature of Mediterranean life, had left a landscape as messy as the floor at the festa: brownish mud and rocks plastered with seaweed and the gurgling water of the outgoing tide. On the horizon was the island of Arosa, shrouded in mist; and beyond it on the opposite of the ría was the town of Cambados, cradle of the Albariño vine and its gorgeously perfumed white wine.

Examining the scene more closely, I saw figures in this landscape: there were human beings down there in the mud, doubled over, shuffling slowly in rubber boots, some wearing head scarves and aprons, each with a bucket in one hand and some kind of tool—a small rake or pick—in the other.

I squelched out over the mud to speak to the nearest of them, Maruxa, a small woman with deep furrows in her face and a permanent stoop, a slight curvature of the spine, that seemed to suggest a lifetime of hard work, much of it bending down. In fact, Maruxa told me, she had been a sequeira—someone who operates during the seca, the "dry" low tide—all her life, just as her mother had been before her. The craft, or profession, of gathering shellfish often passes from woman to woman down the generations, sometimes along with the right to work a particular stretch of beach.

It had always been women's work; the men went out in boats.

"Sí, señor, I used to go out with my mother and grandmother when I was just a little girl. I used to come back with a few clams, even when I was tiny. There were more of them then. And there were more of us out here. They were what you lived on," she said matter-of-factly.

She showed me the contents of her bucket, half full of big clams still begrimed with the smelly estuary mud. Even in the 1960s, since shellfish had practically no commercial value, there was no control over who fished the stuff and how much anyone fished, and people could take home whatever they could carry. Those days were over, said Maruxa. You needed a permit, and there were no more permits being given out. Marisqueo, the business of shellfish, was strictly monitored. You were allowed a maximum of three kilos per day, no more. The sequeiras were now so jealous of their harvest, Maruxa told me, that they even took turns as security guards on the best shellfish beaches, watching out for poachers.

THE HISTORY OF TOURISM in Galicia—not counting the pilgrimage of Saint James, which is one of the world's oldest forms of mass tourism but was confined to the interior—begins on the island of La Toja, just across the water from O Grove. Since the late nineteenth century there has been a spa on the island, with a grand hotel catering to its well-to-do clients. When the first bridge to the mainland was built, in 1908, some of these wealthy folk began to venture daringly into the village, and their first stopping point was the small stone house just beyond the bridge, where Pepe "O Coxo" (so called because he was lame in one foot) and his wife Doña Carmen "A Andaluza" (so called because of her glossy black hair and dark features, unusual for a gallega) ran a grocery store that doubled as a bar. Neighbors and friends could drop in there for a glass of wine and a bite to eat. The tourists from La Toja were fascinated by this rustic setup, and Carmen was happy to serve them a plateful of whatever she happened to be cooking up at midday, which might have been a succulent rib of local beef braised with onion, carrot, and white wine; a piece of hake a la romana (fried in batter); or a fresh crab from the ría. Before long Casa Pepe was a fully functioning restaurant, the first in O Grove and the seed from which a dynasty of restaurants, run by Pepe's children and grandchildren, would subsequently spring.

There was a lot going on at Casa Pepe. Apart from the bar and shop, Pepe O Coxo's main businesses were wine, which he bought in barrels locally and sold to the taverns of O Grove, and octopus. The family business had eight legs. Pepe went every morning to the fish market and bought up the best locally caught octopus. At the back of the shop, on a gentle slope leading down to the ría, there was a yard for drying octopus. Here the octopuses were beaten on rocks to tenderize their flesh—traditionally, three blows for every leg—then turned inside out and strung out on lengths of barbed wire like so much laundry. While the octopuses were drying the whole family kept an anxious eye on the sky, and at the first sign of rain they would be whipped off the line and taken into a stone storeroom used for wine, until the sun came out again. When they were dry and rubbery, but not hard, they would be packed in sacking and sent off to O Carballiño, an inland town famous for its traditional mastery of pulpo a feira.

In the front room of her restaurant, Pepe's daughter Marisol brought out a framed photograph of herself as a young girl in a red-and-white head scarf, grinning at a thickset man with a jowly, imposing face, wearing a white shirt and a black tie that came halfway down his chest. The man was laughing at something, while the two of them leaned on the marble bar at Casa Pepe. He was her daddy, the paterfamilias, patriarch of the clan. She hugged the frame, caressed it with her hands, posed with it for my camera. She told me: "He was the motor that drove our family. He was a kind man, a good man. Dear Daddy."

His three children all went into the restaurant business in their various ways. When the patriarch died the business was split up between his offspring; his son Pepe took over Casa Pepe, and Luis married a woman called Lourdes, who opened an octopus bar (naturally) in O Grove. Like her elder sister Digna, who started her own place down by the harbor, Marisol decided to go it alone, and opened Restaurante Dorna, just over the way from Casa Pepe, in 1959. She married a man from the next village, a seaman called Baldomero, and they set up home above the restaurant. But it was always really Marisol's show. She carried the torch.

She was a bright, breezy, good-looking woman with the easy charm that comes from years of attending to the public, and she was nicely turned out in a lime-green and white striped shirt and matching necktie, with her auburn hair cut short and neat. She wore two pairs of glasses: one perched on her nose, the other hanging around her neck. She radiated perceptiveness, generosity, and restless energy.

While she busied herself with lunch, her daughter María, my hostess in the house at Rons, gave me a tour of the family home above the restaurant, which rambled up into the living quarters and beyond, into a twilight zone of storerooms and attics. We poked around in a darkened shed, finding boxes of the old china bowls that wine was once served in, and piles of discarded clamshells which Baldomero had been hoarding for years. At the top of the house was a fine surprise—a proper backyard, following the slope of the hill beyond, where giant pumpkins stood in rows and washing was hung out to dry; and above that a vegetable garden with cabbages on high stalks, overarching vines, and a lemon tree at the back.

Down in the restaurant a big table was laid by the open window, with the ría at low tide just across the street, and the island of La Toja just across the water. This was a quiet day in the restaurant, and we were to be the only table. It was a big family lunch with mum: there was also Rocío, another of Marisol's daughters, who had just opened a restaurant in her grandfather's old storeroom at which, happily and not entirely coincidentally, charcoal-grilled octopus was the house speciality; and there was María and Josee, and two other sons, Victor and Baldomero. First Marisol brought us a delicious empanada, the Galician flat pie, filled atypically with salt cod; a plateful of bright red shrimp; and a big dish of mussels from the ría with a proper Spanish vinagreta (a cold sauce of chopped onion, oil, vinegar, and chopped hard-boiled egg). Then came the grand second course: a real octopus encebollado, the excellent plato típico of O Grove and its environs.

"Now, this is el plato rey de la casa—the king of the dishes in our house," said Marisol with a touch of solemnity, explaining how she first simmered the octopus and then the potatoes in the same water, before dressing both with a mixture of onions fried in plenty of olive oil, with pimentón, salt, and a final topping of bread crumbs. It was incredibly good: the potato meltingly savory, the octopus sweet and tender, the pimentón giving a hint of spice to the oily, oniony sauce.

While her guests devoured the octopus Marisol jumped up again and moved behind the bar to roll up a platter of filloas—the Galician version of crêpes, filled with a sweet pastry cream. I asked her about the earliest days of the restaurant, the turbulent years when half of Galicia emigrated to Argentina, London, or Madrid. The 1960s and 1970s were years of massive emigration, in Spain as a whole but especially in Galicia, where conditions were harder than anywhere else.

"Yes, people did leave the town," said Marisol. "But it wasn't because we were poor; we weren't really. People just didn't realize the possibilities we had, the richness of the ría, the money to be made. At my wedding banquet, as part of the aperitivo, my father served oysters, shrimp, crab, spider crab, and mussels with vinagreta. And people were surprised: in 1967, it wasn't something you expected to be offered, at a wedding of a certain—how shall I put it?—social standing."

She showed me a book documenting the growth of the festa from a modest exhibition of shellfish down by the harbor, displaying monster specimens of lobster and crab, to the multitudinous exaltación it is today.

The background of the festa is the policy of desarrollismo—of stimulating the national economy at all costs. In 1957 Franco's recently appointed cabinet agreed on a Plan de Estabilización which would bring much-needed capital into the economy from three major sources: foreign investment; money sent home by the 1 million Spanish migrant workers; and, crucially, tourism. Tourism, of course, was to prove a money-maker beyond anyone's wildest dreams. The lion's share of the tourist's deutsche marks, pounds, or francs, would go to the various costas—Blanca, Brava, and del Sol—while the Atlantic coast received almost nothing. Even so, on October 5, 1963, on the occasion of the first Festa do Marisco, the *Faro de Vigo* touchingly described O Grove as "the land of aristocrats of the sea" and predicted that its principal product, shellfish, would become the "artifice of a new era, the era of the tourist, the dollar, and progress."

NORTH OF THE Rías Baixas, the microclimate changes. Just over the upper lip of the Ría de Muros, the landscape becomes rugged and barren; and the sea, so benign in the rías, becomes obstreperous and unpredictable. The Costa da Morte, as this stretch of coast is officially known, is a wild, windy corner of the peninsula, beautiful in a stark and sometimes forbidding way, and mercifully free (for the time being) of hotels and second homes.

I drove up there at five o'clock one morning, skirting the complex coastline of the northern rías, and arrived in the harbor of Lira in a sepulchral predawn darkness. Figures in woolly hats skulked around the still closed harbor bar—all of us dreaming of café con leche.

From the point of view of marketing, the Costa da Morte is at a severe disadvantage relative to the other Spanish coasts. Imagine the scene in the hairdresser's salon: "Going anywhere special this year?" "Yes, we've got a week's package on the Coast of Death." It is so called because the ocean there is so treacherous: the water can rise up into a fury without warning, and deepsea currents pull ships toward fearsome cliffs and barely concealed jet-black rocks. More boats have gone down on this coastline than on any other in Europe, and mariners still live in dread of it. The area hit the headlines internationally on the morning of November 19, 2002, when the oil tanker *Prestige* sank 250 kilometers out to sea, discharging 80 percent of its 77,000-ton load of crude oil, which eventually found its way onto the rocks and beaches of Galicia, Asturias, and Cantabria.

The port of Lira has a fleet of twenty boats, ranging in size from the tiniest dorna upward, but most are after the same catch: *Octopus vulgaris,* pulpo in Spanish, polbo in the Galician tongue. After the *Prestige* sank, when their livelihood was threatened, the fishermen of Lira got together to form a cooperative with some decidedly modern ideas. One was an online fish market: anyone can order fish over the Internet and have it delivered by courier. Another was the notion of "fishing tourism," similar to agrotourism, a brave attempt to make the fisherman's craft more widely known and earn a few extra euros in the process.

The *Nuevo Perla* ("new pearl") was a pioneer of this brand-new form of tourism. It was a traditional wooden fishing boat, looking as one would, ideally, like all fishing boats to look: with a squarish cabin in the middle and a rounded prow, painted in classic fishing-boat colors—bright blue, green, and red. The three-man crew had all been born and bred within a few miles of Lira: Jesús, known as Chuchu, the captain and owner of the ship; silent Cristino; and José, a sly-faced brash young man, nicknamed Rápido for his quick efficient work. These three follow a well-worn routine. Leaving harbor in the early morning, they take up the octopus traps left on the seabed the day before, remove any occupants that have just moved in, and put back the traps with new bait. They are back in the harbor in time for lunch.

At six-thirty in the morning we chugged out of Lira toward the first of the catch sites, just a few hundred meters from the shoreline. A force-eight gale had battered the coastline the day before, and the *Nuevo Perla* had stayed in port. Today it seemed the storm had passed, though the sea was still unruly and threw the boat rudely to and fro. The stars shone in a cloudless, moonless sky.

As the sun rose the coast came slowly into view: sandy beaches backed with dunes and rising to sculptured moss-green hills; a wide bay stretching away to the hulking, shadowy cliffs of Finisterre to the north; and the straggling villages of Carnota and Corcubión, their plain, low, gray-painted houses seeming to huddle against the wind and sea spray.

The smell on board the *Nuevo Perla* was the usual maritime cocktail: engine exhaust, which came at my face in belching clouds as I stood at the stern; and the reek of three big boxes of mackerel a little less than gleamingly fresh, just now being sliced for bait with a heavy, sharpened, wooden-handled fisherman's knife. The deck was slithery with fish remains; seagulls swooped and gaped, their squalling barely audible over the rattle of the engine. The wind came in chilly and damp. I was grateful for the green plastic wet-weather sea suit the crew had lent me.

I sat on a coil of a thick rope, watching the three of them go about their work. They had been on the same boat for seven years, day in, day out, excluding weekends. "If we hadn't worked together for so long, we wouldn't be so well coordinated," reasoned Chuchu—and it was true. They were a well-oiled machine. When we reached the catch site, marked by a pink buoy, a primitive motor was set in motion, winding the rope that pulled up the traps from the ocean bed. The traps, called nasas, were drum-shaped iron structures lined with netting, with a hole for the octopus to enter, attracted by the bait hanging in a bag, and a drawstring at one end for its easy removal.

I looked over the side as the traps floated up through the dark water. The crew of the *Nuevo Perla* dealt with them as slickly as a factory production line, pushing the cages along a metal rim installed on the side of the boat. They were quiet as they worked, cigarettes clamped in their lips.

The traps came up full of writhing life. There were black conger eels as thick as your arm—half a meter of twisting muscle—and big orange starfish, huge sea snails, and twitching prawns. The octopuses were harder to see, splayed like weeds against the side of the traps in their doomed attempts to escape.

After years of close contact with the octopus, Rápido knew a thing or two about the creature and its ways. Pulling one out through the drawstring hole at one end of the trap, he held it by the head in his rubber-clad hand, and the beast did its best to break free, plastering a mass of tentacles over his forearm.

"See the suckers here, all up the legs? See that some are bigger than others? That means it's a female," he said, as, taking a penknife, he made a deep cut at the base of the head. Out poured a gush of black ink. The eight legs went limp; the suckers seemed to lose their suck. Also—and this was the oddest thing—the octopus changed color in an instant, its tortoiseshell brown and black fading immediately to a dull gray.

"We have to kill them, or they climb all over the boat," said Rápido cheerily. "They're not as stupid as they look, you know. I saw a documentary. There was a crab in a bottle, and the octopus had to get it out. They timed it. And each time it was quicker. Clever bastard." And he tossed the dead octopus into a fruit box along with the rest of them.

A cold sun sparkled on the pewter sea. During the course of the morning we had moved three times along the coast, edging ever farther toward Finisterre, and in each of our three catch sites the procedure had been the same: an exhausting process of pulling up, emptying, and replacing a total of almost 800 octopus traps. The results of such backbreaking labor would pay for the ship's gasoline, three big boxes of mackerel bait, and a living wage for each of the crew.

A few hours later the four of us were sitting in the harbor bar, eating two wooden platefuls of pulpo a feira and drinking several beers. Rápido was laying into the pulpo with a wooden toothpick, stabbing at the octopus chunks as if each one were a whole octopus it was necessary to kill before it slithered off the side of the plate. Plainly, he at least hadn't lost his liking for the Galician national dish, although familiarity is supposed to breed contempt.

"It's good food, octopus. Sí, señor," he said through a full mouth, taking a large swig of beer to wash it all down.

By THE NEXT DAY the cold front had come and gone. It was a serenely lovely morning in Rons, and the shallow water beside the sands of my private beach was misleadingly turquoise. It was to be my last day in Galicia, and I still hadn't seen at close quarters what has become one of the region's principal sources of wealth: the platforms called bateas, on which millions of mussels are cultivated on ropes hanging down in the plankton-rich waters of the ría.

Down by the diminutive harbor, Alberto had just come back from a day's fishing and was cleaning up his boat before heading home. His boxlike traps were smaller and lighter than the ones used for octopus, though, as he said with a grin, the odd octopus might easily find its way in along with the crab and shrimp he was supposed to be catching.

Alberto—Berto for short—was a young man who had spent all his life in O Grove, and when he tried to speak Castilian, the roly-poly vowels of gallego came tumbling out. If he would take me out to the nearest batea, I cautiously proposed, I would invite him for a beer at Joaquina's bar. He looked at his watch, decided there was time, and said sure, come aboard; and I jumped into the floor of his flat-bottomed launch, the *No Hay Otra* ("there's no other"). We sped away into the choppy water of the ría, the boat crashing among the waves.

Seen from the shore, the bateas are dark shapes crowding the surface of the ría, and have a faintly sinister aspect, like a top-secret military installation whose purpose can only be conjectured. The first bateas appeared in the early 1950s; now there are some 5,000 of them in this ría alone. Each has a name, a number, and an official sign, staking the claim of its owner to a piece of this peculiar undersea goldfield. We pulled up alongside the first batea we came to, and I climbed onto the edge of the raftlike platform, made from tree trunks bolted together with oil-barrel floats, the whole thing secured to the seabed with giant concrete weights.

A fishing boat fitted with a crane had pulled up at the platform. Three men stood on deck in orange plastic dungarees, sorting the mussels by pushing them through a rattling grille. The crane pulled up one of the ropes on which the mussels grow, depositing the clump on the deck with the loud smash of 1,000 shells scraping against each other. They formed a black mountain of shells as high as your waist, stinking of undersea mud and rotting seaweed.

On the far side of the boat stood a row of net bags the size of small sacks. One of the three mussel men strode over and swung one of the bags over his shoulder, holding it out over the side of the boat for me to grab.

It was a present, a reward for coming to see them on their factory ship out here in the ría. I could barely lift the sack, and as I stretched out to grab it, ten kilos of mussels almost returned to their tranquil home on the bottom of the ría. It wasn't the kind of souvenir that could be placed on your mantelpiece and forgotten about. I wondered how long so many fresh mussels might last in a warm car before turning into a weapon of mass destruction. Twelve hours? Twenty-four? Thirty-six?

There was only one thing for it: I would invite my new friends María and José, daughter and son-in-law of the matriarch Marisol, to a mussel feast this evening. If there were three of us and we were hungry enough, we could easily dispatch a kilo each, or possibly two, given that most of the weight of a mussel is made up by the shell.

From the window of José and María's small apartment I could see where I had just been with Berto. According to the theory of "food miles," the ideal foodstuffs are those that have traveled the shortest possible distance from their place of production. Tonight at least, by this reckoning, I was doing well. The ría was like a vegetable garden where you might nip out for a lettuce and a bag of tomatoes in the afternoon and eat them as a salad in the evening.

The French may do their mussels with parsley, wine, and shallots; and if it were me, I might have tossed in a little chopped onion, a glug of wine, salt and pepper. But María, bless her, had simply cleaned up the mussels, torn off their beards, and heated them in a big enamel cauldron until they opened. She then somehow staggered to the table with the cauldron and left it in the middle, with a few chunks of lemon from a neighbor's tree to squeeze over the mussels if we felt like it. The true simplicity of Spanish food is a kind of daring, a challenge to the diner that seems to say: "Let's see if you can take this just the way it comes."

On the face of it, there wasn't much to suggest that this very late lunch for three would be anything out of the ordinary. But with two bottles of Ribeiro; a big round loaf of the best Galician rye bread, nutty, chewy, and yeasty; and this big tub of juicy, just-cooked mussels—fat pillows of a pale salmon-pink—it felt as if we'd organized an impromptu seafood fiesta of our own.

Afterward I sat with my hosts in their glassed-in balcony and looked out at the sea. The tide was up and lapping at the beach below us. José was in an expansive mood.

"What do I need satellite for, when I have a view like this? This is my television screen," he said, framing the vista with his outstretched arms. "I see the boats come in, and I see the boats go out, I see the storm clouds on the horizon, and there's never a moment to get bored. See that guy in the orange suit? He's a friend of mine, goes out to fish for crabs. Works at night, sleeps during the day, and takes his catch to market in the afternoon. It's not a bad life. Though I think mine's better, sitting up here watching him work."

The man in question was puttering about in a little boat under the single flickering lamp of the harbor wall, loading a heap of crab traps from the harbor to the deck. His fluorescent seaman's jacket shone out weirdly in the lamplight. As dark and rain began to fall, we sat in silence with our glasses of Ribeiro, watching him chug out of the little harbor and phut-phut out into the glassy waters of the ría, his orange suit becoming a bright spot in the dark distance.

Land

W HAT MUST IT BE LIKE to live in a rural society? I mean a really and truly rural society, one that lives off and understands the land. What must it be like not to think the countryside merely pretty or romantic? To look at a plowed field, an olive grove, a vineyard, and see a piece of land either shamefully abandoned, poorly maintained, or correctly tended, its trees well pruned, its plantings neat, healthy, and productive? These are questions that have traveled with me for years, and I find that I am only now a little closer to giving them some kind of answer.

I finally left Ibiza in the year 2000, in search of a place to live that would be quieter, cheaper, and farther from the suffocating presence of the sea. After a series of serendipities, flukes, and unforeseen circumstances, I eventually found myself living in a small rural community in the deep interior of the country, as far from the coast as it was possible to go. On the far western edge of Spain where it bumps up against Portugal, Nacho and I bought a small farm with olive trees and a vineyard and set about restoring its long-abandoned water tanks and dry stone walls. We bought a cow, pigs, chickens. Before long we were growing our own vegetables and fruit, as we had been doing for years but on a bigger scale and with ever greater success. We were doing things we had never done before, like making wine and olive oil. And for me it was both a great adventure and a real education. I have learned more in the five years we have lived here about the way food is produced in the traditional societies of old Europe than I would ever have thought possible when I first arrived in this country in my brown Mini all those years ago.

Modern western societies have created a yawning chasm between the realities of country and city, to the point that a recent television program in Britain revealed that children in an inner-city school in London were incapable of recognizing an onion. In the Spain of the early twentieth century the gap between one world and another was created not so much by ignorance as by an abysmal disparity in the quality of life.

Spanish cities were beginning, by the 1920s, to enjoy the benefits of modern conveniences such as electric light, telephone, running water, and a functioning sewer system. Out in the villages, however, communications were still miserable, and rural society was permanently haunted by disease and starvation.

I have seen photographs of Spanish rural communities in the early years of the twentieth century, and the best of them are documents of a reality that, in the context of European history, lasted practically until the day before yesterday. The faces of the people—shy, suspicious, defiant, haunted—sometimes remind me of the faces of those vanished or vanishing tribes you see in *National Geographic*: faces of the third world, cruelly exposed to the curious, judgmental, or pitying gaze of the first.

In many respects the rural Spain of a hundred years ago was more third world than first. There were few houses even in the cities with running water or toilets; in the countryside such luxuries were unthinkable. Doctors were a rarity, and even when they were available, had to be paid for. Those without resources relied on folk medicine, herbal remedies, and traditional figures such as the curandero (quack doctor) and comadre (midwife). Education in the villages was scant, mostly insufficient, and teachers were paid so little, often relying on donations of food from parents to survive, that a popular saying grew up: "Hungrier than a schoolteacher." Children were put to work at an early age, often in simple tasks like bringing in the sheep, picking fruit, or watching over a grazing pig. The routines of the campo took precedence over everything, including school.

During the first half of the twentieth century Spanish agriculture was one of the most backward in Europe. Few of the innovations that had progressively transformed agriculture in, say, Great Britain had reached the farmers of the Iberian peninsula. Timid advances in agrarian reform were made during the Second Republic of 1933, but the outbreak of civil war in 1936 prevented any further development, and agriculture during the 1940s more or less returned to the conditions prevailing in the nineteenth century: minimal use of machinery, a labor force consisting mainly of landless campesinos hired daily, with no contracts and no legal protection. In the southern half of the country the land was still largely tied up in latifundios, in which laborers and their families lived under the control of the amo or señorito, often in precarious conditions. Those who had access to their own land, the subsistence farmers, were scarcely better off: while a good harvest lowered prices and reduced their income, a bad one might mean they were forced to buy food at market, incurring a debt that they could barely pay off—or worse, the family went hungry.

In June 1922 the celebrated doctor Gregorio Marañón accompanied King Alfonso XIII on a safari to what was thought to be the most backward and isolated place in Spain: the region of Las Hurdes, in northern Extremadura. Marañón later wrote in his memoirs that rickets, paludismo, and other diseases associated with malnutrition were rife. Some of the peasants of Las Hurdes, he recalled, came to him clutching their stomachs in pain. The gesture was not a symptom of dysentery, thought the doctor, but of "Las Hurdes disease," otherwise known as "acute hunger."

During the 1920s a Madrid newspaper published a series of "Letters from the Cortijo," purporting to show readers the reality of life and work on a large privately owned estate near Jerez de la Frontera. The agricultural year traditionally began on Saint Michael's day, September 29, when the fallow fields were prepared for sowing. Workers were paid 21 cuartos (a cuarto was a copper coin worth three cents) and a ration of food consisting of three pounds of bread and a cupful of olive oil to be shared between ten men, plus salt and vinegar. "With these three pounds of bread and the accompaniments they make three gazpachos; two hot ones for the morning and night and the other, cold, at midday."

The working day started early, especially during the plowing season. "Before dawn the foreman says: 'Praised be Christ' and everybody stands up straight, and the laboring men go out and take hold of their plowshares, and never let go of them till the sun sets, except for two breaks for lunch and a few moments to smoke a cigarette . . ."

During the winter work at the cortijo was scarce and many of the laborers were sent back to their villages in Grazalema, Benaocaz, or Arcos de la Frontera. The picture the "Letters" paint of these men's lives at home is pathetic. "At this time of year the thistles and sprue asparagus are just appearing, and many of the men are busy collecting them with their families for sale in the village, so as to earn a few cuartos which aren't enough for bread, and they eat these thistles cooked in water and almost always without oil; never, for them, the convict's tasty and enviable ration of chickpeas and tocino."

In the year 1900 around 70 percent of Spaniards lived in the country. A century later the figure had fallen to below 10 percent. So that within 100 years Spain has developed from a predominantly rural society to an urban society living from industry and services. In time, the new metropolitan Spain will triumph over the old, the gap between country and city will become an abyss of ignorance, as in the rest of the West, and the rural environment will be entirely given over to agro-business and agro-tourism, a suburban zone that is neither urban nor properly rural but something in between.

But the Spanish character was forged by its deep historical connection with the land, and for the moment, the values of the old rural society are proving surprisingly resistant. Many city dwellers feel a powerful emotional connection to the land. Most can trace their roots a generation or two back to some pueblo in the provinces, and they will say proudly when you ask them where they're from, "I'm from Brime de Urz, province of Zamora," when their only real connection to that minuscule village (population: 143) might be the occasional visit on summer vacations, or a phone call twice a year from their last surviving elderly relative, who lives alone in a stone house without central heating, urgently in need of repair.

SPAIN IS NOT a single entity but a patchwork of identities cobbled together into a state. Each of the regions of Spain has its own distinct culinary tradition, and for this reason there is no such thing as a unified, definable national cuisine. Even so, the conditions of rural life unite more than they divide, and the lifestyle and food of a village in the province of Navarre clearly resemble those of an equivalent village in, say, the province of Córdoba.

More than anything, the cooking of rural Spain is a collective response to the realities of climate, weather, organized religion and its strictures and structures, and, above all, the need to provide the body with the calories necessary for hard physical work. Manuel Vázquez Montalbán neatly defines the relation between environment and food as "eating the landscape," implying a close connection with the natural world, which, as (sub)urban habits invade the rural space, is fast coming undone.

The basis of the rural diet was always bread. Bread was a basic ingredient in such standard Spanish dishes as migas and gazpacho. (In fact the Spanish word for bread, pan, is practically synonymous with food in general.) Protein came overridingly from pulses: chickpeas, lentils, and dried beans (alubias). Such meat as there was would have been predominantly pork, since many families kept a pig and fattened it for the annual slaughter. The coastal zones might have had access to fish and shellfish, but little of this catch ever reached the villages of the interior, unless it came in the form of salt-cured bacalao. There might be a rabbit or partridge or pigeon from time to time, if there was a hunter in the family. Vegetables were and are highly prized, and Spanish regional cooking is rich in dishes that give star status to humble ingredients like potatoes, broad beans, artichokes, Swiss chard, cardoons, spinach, peppers, tomatoes, and eggplants. Another crucial chapter of the rural Spanish diet is made up of wild foods. Without snails, asparagus, wild garlic and greens, and mushrooms, the traditional gastronomy of Europe would be much the poorer, and the rural Spanish poor would have been less well nourished.

If there is one word that captures rural Spanish food habits more precisely than any other, it is "resourceful." The make-do-and-mend habits of a people that never had a great deal of anything to spare have become part of the DNA of Spanish food culture. The ingenious use of leftovers is certainly a dying art, but it lingers on in the kitchens of the pueblos, where no one would ever consider throwing anything edible into the trash.

Economy comes naturally to the Spanish country cook. Nothing is wasted; as much as possible is recycled. Oil for frying is strained and reused time and time again, and finally turned into soap. From the leftovers of the Sunday cocido or puchero, for example, proceeds the pringá of Andalusia, the shredded meats and sausages transformed into a kind of pâté; ropa vieja, "old clothes," in which the chickpeas and vegetables make their reappearance fried up with olive oil and garlic; best of all, the croquetas of leftover meat, creamy on the inside, crisp and golden on the outside, which the best Spanish home cooks still make from time to time. In traditional food cultures all over the world, it's often the case that creativity and parsimony go hand in hand.

AS SUMMER STAGGERED to a close and the afternoons turned the hillsides a mournful shade of sepia, I got out the road map again. In my travels along the Spanish coastal zone, I had tried to understand the pressures that had come to bear on its way of life and food: most obviously, a benign climate, access to the bounty of the sea, and the transforming presence of tourism. Now I planned a series of different journeys: inland, toward the rural heart of the country, as far away as possible from the *dolce vita* of the coast. I looked for destinations where the industry of mass tourism might not yet have distorted the economy or blighted the landscape, and the roots of traditional cooking might lie more deeply in the ground.

I would be traveling in autumn and winter: low season on the coast but the culinary high season of the interior. When temperatures fall and the days shrink and sputter like cheap candles, the true character of rural Spanish eating comes into its own. There would be rib-sticking stews of pulses and meats, fat-rich products of the matanza, bread-based soups, and slabs of charcoal-grilled meat. After the bright summery flavors of the coast, my taste buds would need to be retuned for bigger, stronger, heartier flavors, and my digestive system primed for generous servings of carb-heavy, protein-rich food.

I would start with a place I knew from hearsay as a land of good trenchermen, the northern kingdom of Asturias, and then make my way down into the flatlands of La Mancha, source of some venerable culinary, as well as literary, relics. I would need to think deeply about products, especially the two great contributions to Spanish inland gastronomy, namely olives and olive oil and the complex culture of the pig. From La Mancha I might slip sideways to Jaén, world capital of olive oil production, then veer left toward the pork-obsessed lands of western Spain, close to my own home. My eyes would be open for history and the way it leaves visible traces in the food customs of a people. For insight into the Arabic influence on Spanish eating, I might revisit Granada. For a sense of the way medieval practices lived on in one of Europe's richest historical cuisines, I would have to make time for Catalonia. And with that, I imagined, I ought to have my hands full—not to mention my stomach—until the spring.

6

Asturias

WHILE I HAD BEEN racing up and down the coast, Nacho had spent the summer working on the land, processing carloads of produce into every possible jam, sauce, pickle, and preserve for which recipes could be downloaded from the Net. Now he was due to leave for Jerusalem, where he would be working with the Palestinians to boost their nearly nonexistent production of fruits and vegetables. When he departed at the end of September, I stayed on for a week to sort things out on the farm, then set off on the mission I had set myself: to track down the culinary roots of the Spanish interior.

I left home on a late-summer afternoon when a pall of accumulated heat hung heavily in the air. The farther north I drove the farther the temperature dropped, until I reached León, when I finally turned off the air-conditioning and opened the window. I pulled through the Pajares mountain pass with a palpable sense of relief: suddenly, and at long last, it seemed, the summer was over.

To someone coming from the south of Spain, the Mediterranean coast of Spain, or anywhere else in Spain for that matter, Asturias genuinely seems like another world. When the rest of the country is a scorched symphony in beige and brown, here the landscape is decked out in a dozen shades of green. When there is not one drop of fresh water to be had from the riverbeds of Andalusia, here the streams rush heedlessly, one might almost say wastefully, down the mountainsides, bringing freshness and greenness to everything they touch.

To a Spaniard, the word "Asturias" suggests one overriding image: rolling fields of green grass, dotted with Holstein cows. As children, Spaniards sit at the breakfast table sleepily examining the milk carton with its Asturian brand name and its symbolic imagery of cows in a pastoral setting, until a subliminal association is eventually made: Asturias = pasture = milk.

Asturias is dairy land. Some of the most familiar names in the Spanish fridge are those of Asturian origin, even if most of them are now part of massive food conglomerates. The trucks of Arias, Pascual, and Central Lechera Asturiana thunder by on the region's modest roads, rushing milk to the central depots. In a country that has not traditionally been fond of dairy products, with the notable exception of cheese, this is one region that not only loves them unashamedly but has almost single-handedly managed to export dairy culture to the rest of Spain. Until the advent of modern distribution, packaging, and fridges, most Spaniards never ate or cooked with butter. Yogurt, fat-free with fiber added and vitaminized and flavored in any number of ways, fills whole aisles in the modern supermarket. Yet it was virtually unknown until the 1980s. And all of it is traceable, by some means or other, to the pastures of the principality.

I had no particular agenda beyond finding out just what Asturians ate. Not being quite sure where to head for, I turned off the highway at random and ended up at the town of Ribadesella, where the salmon-rich Sella River meets the sea. As the evening darkened a gentle drizzle began to fall, sending locals hurrying home and emptying the streets like a bad DJ empties a dancefloor. I rolled down the sleeves of my thin cotton shirt. Five hours of driving had left me with hunger pangs, and my clothes were now clammy from the rain. It all seemed to point to an early dinner at some simple little place where I could dry off and eat something restorative, típico, and tasty.

As well as being the headquarters of the national dairy industry, Asturias is known as the cradle of Spanish cider culture. A region of the north coast around Villaviciosa is actually known as la comarca de la sidra ("cider county")—such is its commitment to the production of fermented apple juice. (When Asturians have anything to celebrate, they crack open a bottle of fizz, just like anyone else. In their ease, though, it is not fizzy wine but a carbonated cider presented in a thick-mouthed bottle to reinforce the association with real champagne made from grapes.)

I headed straight for the harbor front and pushed through the door of the Sidrería Tinín, one of several simple cider houses in this part of town. It had wood paneling and squat wooden tables, and old photos of the town in earlier days, and two large oil paintings illustrating the art of pouring the cider. In the paintings, two men wearing track suits and serious expressions showed exactly how it's done, with the bottle held at arm's length in one hand and a thin stream of cider splashing a long way down into a flat-bottomed glass in the other hand.

The cider house rules are simple enough. Either you can pour the cider yourself, or you can ask your waiter to do it for you. You must serve yourself only a small amount, pouring from as great a height as possible, as in the picture on the wall; be sure to drink it quickly; and always leave in the bottom of the glass a little cider, which you may dispose of either onto the floor or in a special receptacle provided for the purpose. At the Sidrería Tinín a stainless steel channel ran around the bottom of the bar, and in the corner, a sawed-off barrel held a white plastic container underneath. The spillage of cider is a natural part of Asturian life and gives rise to one of the characteristically Asturian smells—a sweetish, slightly fermented moist sort of odor, mingling with the natural humidity of the air.

I sat down and ordered a bottle of cider, and the waiter brought me a thick green glass bottle of an old-fashioned shape, with round shoulders and a generous lip, the kind of bottle you might send messages in.

At a nearby table a bearded old gent had finished his bottle and was murmuring quietly, lost in a reverie. The waiter glanced at me as he opened my cider.

"'Tá cantarina," he said with a smile of complicity—meaning, in the Asturian dialect, that this was the kind of cider that, if you drank enough of it, would make you sing.

I let my man pour the first glass, the second, and the third. His technique was unerring, and impressive to watch: the cider fell a good meter in a steady stream, landing plumb in the middle of the thin, flat-bottomed cider glass, splashing a little and turning the cider cloudy with the oxygen acquired on the way down. (The process is known as escanciar.) On each occasion he presented the glass to me with a flourish and I swigged the cider down, remembering to leave the statutory mouthful as a polite symbol of my lack of greed, my willingness to share. The cider was a dusty gold color, and so palate-scouringly dry it made me shiver. It tasted like the smell of apple trees in autumn—woody, spicy, and fruity. When the time came for the fourth glass the waiter was nowhere to be seen, and, emboldened by watching the first three poured, I thought I would try my hand at the business of escanciar. It was not quite as easy as it looked. You needed a certain chutzpah to try it at all, being surrounded by locals who were used to seeing it properly done and would surely be scornful of your risible attempts. The stream of liquid tended to land on the floor or on your hand—anywhere but inside the glass—and this was not only embarrassing but also highly wasteful. I cast a shy glance around the bar. If the others disapproved of my efforts, they were too polite to let it show.

Tipsy from the journey and the cider, I now had a raging appetite. Outside it was dark, and raining heavily. The food arrived on tin plates: crisp fried morcilla, the Spanish blood sausage, dark and delicious; and a bowl of fat clams swimming in a sauce that was nothing more or less than the juices released from their shells as they expired in the heat of the pan. Then came a plate of juicy sliced lacón, the salt-cured pork of northwestern Spain; and, best of all, a platter of five Asturian cheeses cut in generous slices, each more rustic, farmyardy and fabulous than the last. Each was a distinct creation, but they all had the taste and fragrance of milk, the aroma of pasture, flowers, and (there's no other way to put this) warm cow. I thought of the sheep I had seen on the journey north, nibbling the dry herbs and stalks of the high Castilian plains. Here all was lushness and abundance, and you could taste it in these cheeses. There were a soft, yielding, fresh taramundi; a creamy, piquant afuega'l pitu (the name means something like "fires in the throat"); a powerful, fruity blue cabrales; and an ahumado de pría with a haunting taste of smoke. Cheese number five was the rare gamonedo, which is produced in tiny quantities and rarely found outside the region. It was presented as a much smaller piece, and slightly set apart from the other four, as if to emphasize its rarity. Gamonedo is a cow's milk cheese and, like cabrales, is veined with a delicate greeny-blue tracery, but there all similarities end, because the gamonedo has a dry, crumbly texture that looks rather alarmingly as though it'll gum up the palate, but actually melts in the mouth into a salty, creamy, almost Parmesan-like richness.

Asturias is a happy hunting ground for cheese lovers. Some forty different cheeses are produced within its borders, three of which have denominación de origen status; few places in the world—even in France—can boast of such variety over such a modest area.

By morning the weather had cleared, the air was sparkling, and the colors of the countryside were turned up bright. Thinking I would look for the sources of some of this cheesy excellence, I turned onto the old highway leading up the Sella River, then turned east into the sunlight, Ray-Bans on and windows down, feeling like the king of the road. There was almost no traffic. Farther inland, gentle hills rose to a wall of glittering, sugar-iced mountains: the Picos de Europa, "peaks of Europe," so called because their snowy caps were what mariners saw on returning from long expeditions in distant seas.

In the village of Poo de Cabrales I screeched to a halt to take a photograph of its road sign—superbly appropriate, given the powerful odor of the cheese in question.

A few villages farther on, where rushing streams arrived breathless from the mountain range above, filling the air with therapeutic negative ions, I stopped at a small bar beside the Grena River. This establishment doubled as post office, tobacconist, grocery, and general supply store, and also sold raciones of cheese. It was gloomy inside, and the ceiling was hung with cowbells, harnesses, baskets, drinking horns, and hams. Sacks of dry goods stood open-mouthed on the flagstone floor: I saw walnuts, hazelnuts, and fabes—the big white beans for fabada, the Asturian regional dish número uno. Behind the bar were highlights of the range of articles that locals might require in their work or leisure, from pocketknives and wooden clogs (still worn by Asturian country folk, for going about in the mud) to lottery tickets, fat cigars, and pairs of thick woolly socks.

At the Formica bar I asked for a beer and a serving of cabrales. When in Rome, it makes sense to try the Roman speciality—after all, this is the region's most famous cheese, one of its most famous foods, and a source of justifiable Asturian pride. It is puzzling to me that cheeses like Stilton and Roquefort, though both wonderful in their own way, should enjoy worldwide fame while cabrales, which is more than a match for either, should be so little known outside its homeland. The woman tending the bar cut me a slab from a whole cheese she kept behind the counter, a big roundel covered in a green-and-red wrapping. At the center of the label was a kind of heraldic shield showing two goats and a bear on their hind legs, taking fruit from a tree. In the old days cabrales used to be wrapped in leaves of the plágamo tree, which grows beside streams in these parts. But the health police of the European Union were suspicious of the leaves, and banned them.

The cheese came on a square of greaseproof paper on a Pyrex plate. It was quite a cheese. Pungent to an incredible degree, with a blue-green veining that had nearly edged out the creamy whiteness. You needed a beer, or perhaps a glass or two of cider, to get it down without scorching the walls of the esophagus. There was a spicy kick to it, with a touch of citrus fruit, and a potent aftertaste that stayed on your palate for ages and clung to your fingers for hours however vigorously you washed them.

Cabrales shares its homeland with gamonedo, the other great Asturian cheese, which is even less well known and considerably harder to find. On the map, I noticed the name Gamonedo at the end of a meandering lane that seemed to head upward, toward the peaks, the mountain lakes, and the famous monastery of Covadonga, birthplace and symbol of Christian resistance to Moorish domination in the darkest days of the eighth century. I needed no encouragement to turn the car around and follow this lane, which ran along a valley dense with chestnut forests. From here the hillsides plunged away steeply, losing themselves in dark ravines clogged with woodlands with grand stone ruins of farmhouses or churches hidden in their depths.

Gamonedo turned out to be a pretty, if basic, mountain village of stone houses and square wooden granaries. The granaries had rough slate roofs, poised on four flat mushroom-shaped stones at the corners to keep out the rats. Up here in the crisp mountain air, these granaries had a Tibetan look, like Buddhist pagodas. It was a quiet morning. Cockerels strutted in the street. I stood at the edge of the village looking out toward the crystal spires of the Picos de Europa. Brown cows, their bells tolling in the distance, grazed on steep slopes of thick green pasture sprinkled with wildflowers. It is always reassuring to find the source of a product, there in front of you, before you buy it. And the source of this product did look particularly happy and fulfilled, working its way methodically through some of the tastiest pasture on the peninsula.

A woman in a black head scarf and clogs came shuffling past, and we spent a few minutes passing the time of day. Yes indeed, it was very quiet up here in the pueblo. All the young people had left, though there were new people coming in, buying up the houses for vacation homes. They were outsiders, not people from here—a family of madrileños, a couple from Bilbao . . . She could hardly imagine what they saw in a village like this, so far from the city, with nothing, not even a school. She shook her head.

I was looking for cheese? In that case, I should come with her immediately to the house of a friend. We walked slowly through alleys spattered with cow dung, past the village washing fountain, now unused, half full of stagnant water.

"That's where I washed my clothes, for years. Now I have a washing machine. My son bought it for me," explained the woman cheerily.

Her friend Belarmina González lived in a large house in the lower part of the hamlet. Outside Belarmina's front door, beside a flowerbed flaming with pink hydrangeas, stood a pair of clogs like the ones worn by my guide, and next to them their practical modern equivalent: plastic overshoes like sawed-off Wellington boots. Just across the way was a lovely old granary, one of the finest I had ever seen, with strange primitive designs, naive symbols etched in whitewash on the weather-beaten wooden panels. Behind these panels, up near the roof, corncobs hung in pale yellow bunches. I was reminded of the importance of this crop in the rural life of Spain's northern communities, from Galicia to the Basque country. Corn, or maize, was food for chickens, pigs, cows, and people. A dense maize bread was even made from it, and, though the taste for this broa has largely died out in Asturias, it continues in Galicia.

Belarmina González got up from her chair in the morning sun and ushered me inside, while the other woman clacked away down the street. The first room in the house was a sitting-dining room with a solid wooden table and, along the rear wall, a glass-fronted cabinet loaded with fancy silver cups in a variety of designs. But Belarmina did not run a soccer team: these were prizes for the Gamonedo cheese she makes with her husband and son.

To the right was a simple kitchen, its walls lined with bathroom tiles.

"We used to make the cheese in there," said Belarmina, gesturing over her shoulder to the kitchen as she pottered about the dining room. "But then they stopped us."

She took me outside the front door again and pointed across the valley, high up toward the celestial landscape of the Picos, where a series of glacial lakes lie in mirrorlike stillness beside the monastery of Covadonga. That was were the flocks were, with her son and husband watching over them. "Up at the lakes," she said.

There were few makers of gamoneu, as the cheese is known in Asturian dialect, still in operation, she continued. This was hardly a surprise in itself, since all over Europe many traditional food products are threatened with extinction. But the reason for gamoneu's decline is unusual, to say the least. It is due to the increasing number of wolves, which are attacking flocks in the area and making life impossible for shepherds. The Iberian wolf, *Canis lupus signatus,* is now a protected species in the Picos de Europa National Park and its numbers have grown, forcing farmers into a vicious circle: the more farmers sell their flocks and give up the business, the more the wolves' food supply diminishes and the farther down the mountain the wolves will venture in search of fresh meat.

Gamoneu is a seasonal cheese, made mainly in spring and summer when the flocks are up at their mountain pastures. It is made from a mixture of milk from Casina and Carreña cows—both traditional Asturian breeds, long-horned and big-eared—with goat and sheep milk. Morning and evening milk are combined, lowering the pH, as milk acidifies over time. This cheese owes its character to the social history of the shepherding population. The shepherds of Asturias spent summers in the high mountain, living in wooden shacks where, during the chilly nights of May and June, they might need to light a small fire to keep warm. Most mountain refuges in the north of Spain lacked a chimney, so the smoke simply lingered in the atmosphere, eventually finding its way out through the roof. This meant, in turn, that the chorizos and hams hanging from the ceiling, and the cheeses left out to cure, would naturally receive a dose of smoke, preserving and subtly flavoring them.

Belarmina brought out a whole cheese, weighing almost two kilos, from a cupboard in the kitchen. It was three months old but seemed much older; it was dry and hard to the touch, with an interesting nubbly rind colored with an impressionist wash of rust-red, gray, and pale green molds. She wrapped it in a page from the local newspaper, *La Nueva España,* with stories about farm subsidies and local saint's-day fiestas.

"Now, when you get home, you must take a cloth and wet it a little under the tap, and you must wrap the cheese in it. That way it won't dry out," she advised me.

And she took my pocketful of euros, placed them carefully in a drawer in the cabinet groaning with all those silver cups, and went back to her place in the sun.

ASTURIAS WAS NEVER COLONIZED by the Moors, and the Asturians are basically a Celtic people, light-skinned and fair-haired. The climate is mild in summer, but harsh in winter, with cold fronts that sweep in from the Atlantic. Crops that are common, not to say ubiquitous, in the rest of Spain won't grow here: it is strange to see no olive trees, no vines, hardly any citrus fruit. The result is that traditional Asturian cooking is based on a different premise from most Spanish food: the natural frying medium, for example, would be butter or pork fat, rather than olive oil. There is virtually no wine—Asturias is, together with Cantabria, Spain's only non-wine-producing region.

The winter matanza or pig-butchering is, or was, of vital importance in the nutritional and culinary life of this community. Armando Palacio Valdés, in his novel *Sinfonía Pastoral* (1931), gives the basic ingredients of the Asturian rural diet (he doesn't specify whether in order of quantity or of nutritional importance) as maize, chestnuts, eggs, hazelnuts, walnuts, milk, lard, cider, spelt-wheat bread, cecina (dried beef), pumpkin, cabbage, onions, potatoes, beans, pulses, and the products of the matanza: lacón, chorizo, morcilla, and tocino.

Traditional Asturian cooking is solid, dependable, high in calories, and fiercely loyal to its origins. There is variety here: each of the region's seventy-eight concejos, or councils, has some sort of edible speciality. But the local cuisine hinges on one great dish, which for Spaniards as well as Asturianos neatly sums up the region in one monumental edible symbol: the fabada.

The Castilian word "haba" tends to refer to the broad bean, which is generally eaten fresh. What "faba" refers to is what most Spaniards would understand as alubia: a bean that is grown specially for drying. There might be several dozen different types of faba grown locally: a whole hill of beans. We know from the diaries of Jovellanos, a central figure of Asturian literature, that even in the eighteenth century the faba was cultivated all over the principality, in dozens of varieties. The roxa or colorá, deep vermilion red, is like our kidney bean. The pale green verdina, highly fashionable, goes nicely with rabbit, hare, or partridge. The pinto bean comes in extraordinary colors and designs, jewellike, spotted and striped, so pretty they could be threaded on string for a necklace. But the king of them all is a big, flattish, longish, straight-sided bean, roughly the size and shape of the final joint of your little finger. The fame of the faba de la Granja, or del Cura, as it is also known, is based on its smooth, melting, buttery texture when cooked, its fine skin, and its considerable capacity for absorbing liquid.

This is the best faba, and the favorite faba for making fabada. It grows best in a warm, damp climate in which the temperature doesn't drop much below eighteen degrees Celsius or exceed twenty-four degrees—and exactly these conditions prevail in Asturias from May to September, the bean's productive cycle. Fabes de la Granja were traditionally planted as a mixed crop with maize, so that the bean had the maize stalk for support. Nowadays more than 2,500 hectares of agricultural land are given over to fabes, and the average yield ranges from 800 to 1,000 kilos per hectare. So that's . . . work it out: Between 2,000 and 2,500 tons at every harvest. It's a lot of fabes. But then Asturias eats a lot of fabada.

Lentils, chickpeas, or beans, simmered for hours with a ham bone, a hunk of tocino, a chorizo, and a morcilla or two, and perhaps a vegetable, potatoes, turnips, or cabbage. . . . Every region of Spain has its own variant of the ur-dish of pulses and pork, or pork and beans, from cocido madrileño to the puchero of Andalusia, the olla podrida of Burgos and the Catalan escudella i carn d'olla. Their common ancestor was possibly the adafina, a chickpea stew made popular by Sephardic Jews, who made it on Fridays to be eaten on the Sabbath. The meat in adafina was originally mutton or beef, until Ferdinand and Isabella made the enthusiastic consumption of pork an article of faith. The fabada is Asturias's own version of the basic recipe. Its other main ingredients, apart from the fabes, are called the compangu, the accompanying stuff: salted tocino, lacón, chorizo, and morcilla. The beans and meats are soaked in cold water overnight and then are bubbled together for several hours with no extraneous element other than a few threads of saffron and a sprinkling of salt. It is not by any means a complex dish, but everything must be just right: the beans soft and creamy; the sauce not too watery, not too thick; the meats tender enough to cut with a spoon; the sausages just maintaining their shape in the simmering pot.

On a chilly day when I had spent the morning thinking about fabada, it seemed only logical that I should find one to eat for lunch. I drove westward and southward, through landscapes that varied between stark, bare moorland and leafy valleys of chestnut and oak woods. And at two-thirty that afternoon, zero hour for the Spanish midday meal, I found myself in the village of Pola de Allande, seventy-five kilometers or more off the beaten track, in a part of inland Spain as little-known and unreconstructedly rural as any.

There was only one proper eating place in town, a hostel and restaurant that had been there nearly forever, but was nevertheless known as La Nueva Allandesa. The dining room was a big echoing hall, with the television news rattling away in one corner, and a large number of tables with white paper cloths. It was a comedor like hundreds of others all over the country, a place serving big lunches for small money, unpretentious, brisk, and noisy.

As three o'clock rolled round the customers were arriving in a continuous single file. I congratulated myself: this would surely be a good place. I ordered a bottle of cider and poured myself a glass, spilling only a little on the floor. The menu was fabada or pote asturiano, a variant of fabada which also includes cabbage, vegetables, pig's ear, and the smoked and cured Asturian sausage called chosco. Unthinkingly I ordered fabada, and it was brought to me on two steel platters—the beans on one, the meats on the other—in a serving of terrifying quantity, enough to feed four effete city dwellers or one large Asturian countryman who's been out with the cows since dawn. The tocino had taken on a translucent, glassy quality, like a slice of caramelized melon; the chorizos were smokily sweet; the morcillas were succulent and spicy. Best of all were the fabes, big fat white beans, so tender and fine-skinned they melted in the mouth, with a flavor so meaty it was hard to stop eating them until you were so full you wondered how your digestive system was ever going to cope. A politician in Asturias once invited Julio Camba, the famous journalist and gastronome, to a fabada. Six months later the politician happened to run into Camba again in Madrid, and asked him: did he remember that fabada? To which Camba replied dolefully, holding his hand to his belly, "It's still here, my friend, it's still here."

When I went to visit Nacho Manzano the next day, we talked about the vexed question of digestibility, and he nodded sagely. One had to be careful with fabada. When it was good, it was a marvel, a masterpiece, and like all the greatest dishes of the Spanish rural repertoire, an example of what elegance there can be in simplicity. It was not, however, a dish to be taken lightly, or partaken of heavily.

Señor Manzano—"Mr. Appletree"—runs one of the most fascinating restaurants in Asturias. He represents a particularly southern European paradigm: the chef (usually a man) of a successful modern restaurant which was once run as a bar, or as a simple eating place, by his parents.

Casa Marcial, Nacho's restaurant, is a little place in a hamlet outside the village of La Vita, which in turn lies four kilometers outside the town of Arriondas. I first read about the restaurant in a review by a Spanish journalist of a more delicate constitution than most, who loved Nacho's food but was primly disgusted by the bucolic details of the surroundings, particularly the cow pies in the driveway and a "slobbering" dog that approached him in the parking lot. It was precisely this sort of detail that made me want to visit. Casa Marcial sounded like an honest sort of place that wasn't so dazzled by its Michelin star that it failed to keep in touch with the reality of its rural context.

And so it proved to be. The restaurant was a gray stone building among a group of cottages and hórreos, with a view of rolling green hills wreathed in downy mist. Chickens pecked around the hedgerows. Every house in the hamlet had its own vegetable patch: I could see potatoes; peas; jade-green onions with thick juicy stalks; and the year's last beans, climbing in thick green garlands on strings hung from an A-frame of chestnut poles.

Nacho came out to meet me in his chef's whites. He was a quick-bodied young man in his early thirties, small of stature, drily humorous, with dark hair, dark eyebrows, and a pale kitchen face, who spoke rapid-fire Spanish with such a strong local accent I had to retune my ears. It was well before lunchtime on a weekday, and Nacho was in no particular rush to get back to the kitchen, so we wandered around the property chatting about food, his family history, and the importance of staying true to your roots.

"I grew up here, in this house, in this environment," he said, matter-of-factly.

The house had belonged first to his great-grandmother, who had passed it on to his grandmother, who had sold it to her nephew, who was Marcial, Nacho's father. For a century or more the house was a vital resource for the people of the neighborhood: it was a bar and a store that sold everything from shoes and socks to canned sardines, and it even had a dance hall on the upper floor. Mothers on outlying farms would send their children down to pick up the bread every morning, and come down later themselves to do the daily shopping. In what is now the restaurant's beam-ceilinged dining room there was once a cider press, where every autumn the family produced its annual supply. This was a typical arrangement in the villages of northern Spain, where mountain landscape and bad weather threw rural communities in on themselves. There were no cars, so the bar and store played a vital role in the commerce and society of the neighborhood.

Nacho left me in the dining room and retreated to the kitchen to prepare for me a nine-course menu that brought nicely into focus the contemporary sensibility that he applies to his culinary roots. As I sat quietly eating, tractors rumbled back and forth outside the window, carrying bales of hay.

The meal began with a cream of gamonedo cheese, lightly flavored with sage and garnished with confit of tomato and fresh apple. I remembered the cheese I'd bought from Belarmina and its crumbly richness, laced with piquant blue, and the faint reminiscence of woodsmoke which also came through in this delicate cream. Nacho thinks gamonedo the principality's greatest cheese, and the best for cooking, thanks to its dryish texture and salty piquancy.

Then he brought me his best-known dish, one of the flag-waving inventions of the new Asturian cooking: maize torta with poached onion and scrambled egg. Thereby hangs a tale. Maize flour was the subsistence food of the rural poor. Tortas were thick cakes of maize flour cooked on a piece of sheet metal over a coal fire: highly indigestible, but with the advantage that they filled you up nicely. At the very least, you could serve the torta with a fried egg, and this was a popular combination. In the hard years following the civil war, when half of Spain teetered on the edge of starvation, there was often little else in the cupboards of rural Asturias.

Pondering the solid virtues of the torta but trying hard to make it easier on modern stomachs, Nacho came up with his own version. His torta is still made of maize flour, from the maize that grows outside the window; but the doorstop of dough that took a day to digest has been replaced with a thin pancake that when fried in smoking-hot oil puffs up into something miraculously light and airy. The onions Nacho uses are grown in the neighborhood. Thanks to all the rain, Asturian onions are sweet and mild, and they caramelize beautifully into a melting puree. The eggs are from the farm next door. "The dish is no big deal, I suppose," he shrugs, "but it's harmonious, pleasant, easy to eat. Everyone likes it, even the highbrow critic I read the other day, who called it 'delicate, feather-light, wholesome, and humble.'"

The third dish was a more recent creation, also a product of the Asturian *terroir*: a crisp slice of salty panceta, sitting on a few finely sliced almost raw vegetables, with a light vinaigrette based on the perfumed juice of the fabada. A couple of tender fabes served almost as a point of reference, a way of saying, "This is where it all comes from."

This made me curious to taste Nacho's fabada in its complete form, in which, he said, he uses morcilla and chorizo from the Arriondas area, and which he himself loves cooking almost as much as eating. But this would have to wait for another day. I also would have to forgo Nacho's famous pitu de caleya, the cockerels he buys from a neighbor at a year or so of age. As their babble name implies (caleya means country lane or track), these cockerels live in semi-wild conditions and are fed on barley, maize, and wheat, as well as whatever they can find for themselves in the fields and hedgerows. Nacho cooks them in a casserole until their dark, close-textured, flavorsome meat has released all its goodness, and he serves the pitu with rice made with the stock.

But I was now only halfway through: still to come were zucchini flowers stuffed with crabmeat, with peeled green peas; fillet of grouper roasted for a few seconds, with peeled broad beans; *parmentier* of squid; and a stunning dish of simply roasted wild salmon from the Sella River. The salmon was the best I can remember tasting in a long time—the flesh a delicate pink, flaky, and almost completely lean, nothing like the greasy orange slithery farmed salmon.

Looking back over the menu after a refreshing dessert—a jellylike tocinillo of muscovado sugar with green apple juice and rocket leaves—was like looking back over a long walk in the country. There was nothing attention-seeking about this man's cooking: it was modest. Though contemporary in every way, with light sauces that gently underpinned the generous flavors of the main ingredients, it seemed to draw its strength from deep below the surface: in memory, personal and collective; in the sureties of home and family; and in the timeless world of country people, country cooking, country life.

7

La Mancha

L OOKED AT ON one of those oddly fascinating relief maps, which invite you to run your fingers over their rumpled surface, La Mancha appears as a vast, flat tableland, stretching uninterrupted across the center of Spain roughly from Madrid southward to the Sierra Morena. There are no summits, no hills to speak of, yet this plateau has an average height of 600 meters.

Nowhere else in Spain has these wide horizons, these endless vistas, this unremitting flatness. The extremes of climate are brutal. Winter is cold and stark; summer is four months of blow-to-the-head heat. Rainfall is hardly a major feature of the local weather forecasts. There are few trees on this high plateau, apart from the plantations of olives and grapevines. No wonder the Arabs called it Al-Manchara: "hard and dry."

I traveled in an afternoon all the way from the humid forests of Asturias to the imperial city of Toledo—capital of the autonomous region of Castile–La Mancha and, until 1560, of the whole of Spain. My hotel room that night had views over palaces and convents whose towers and steeples were inhabited by dozens of nesting storks.

A paperback copy of *Don Quijote* lay on my bedside table; a gift from the management. This being the four-hundredth anniversary of the first publication of Miguel de Cervantes's novel, in 1605, the whole of Spain was in the grip of Quijote fever. New editions—illustrated, abridged, annotated, for children—were coming out every few weeks. The tourist board of Castilla–La Mancha had gone into overdrive, putting up special green "Quijote Route" signs on the outskirts of every village, whether or not it could boast any real connection with the events of the novel. The Don himself, always envisioned as a scrawny figure with a thin face and pointy beard, was everywhere: modeled in porcelain in a ceramics store, in pewter in a jeweler's, and in sugar icing in the window of a pastry shop.

What *Don Quijote,* the novel, has to say about Spanish food is revealing. Lorenzo Díaz, author of *La Cocina del Quijote,* a disquisition on the role of food in the novel and manchego food in general, argues that no other cuisine in the world has been promoted so nobly in literature. It is true, and famously so, that the very first paragraph of the novel presents a broad-brush portrait of its principal character in terms of the dishes he habitually partakes of: "a stew with rather more cow in it than lamb, salpicón on the other nights, duelos y quebrantos on Saturdays, lentils on Fridays, and the odd pigeon on Sundays." (Salpicón was a kind of salad of leftover meats dressed with vinegar and spices. As for duelos y quebrantos—the term means something like "harm and suffering"—we have no very clear idea about what they might have been. Suggestions range from a stew made of the poorer cuts of a cow that had died of natural causes, to a scrambled omelette of lambs' brains and fatty bacon.)

Food certainly plays an important role in the novel; in a sense, however, the more powerful force in its depiction of seventeenth-century Spanish society is not eating but hunger. The perpetual search for food, and the ingenuity this presupposes, is certainly an underlying theme of many Spanish novels of the time, especially those of the picaresque genre, including Quevedo's *Buscón* and the anonymous *Lazarillo de Tormes,* with their characters whose overriding obsession is to get themselves a decent meal. This was an era in which Spain, as a superpower, was forced to spend enormous sums in order to maintain its explorations, its warring armies, and its established colonies. Meanwhile the homeland went to rack and ruin: crops were abandoned, villages were deserted, and the streets of the cities were invaded by legions of beggars. The blind man in *Lazarillo de Tormes* keeps his food in a knapsack, which he closes with a padlock; but his cunning guide, the book's narrator, manages to unpick the fabric and extract choice morsels of bread and fatty bacon. On one occasion he even swipes a sausage the old man has cooked over a fire, leaving a turnip in its place.

I flicked through *Don Quijote* to the part where Quijote and Sancho attend the wedding of the rich hidalgo Camacho. On the morning of the wedding Sancho, forever dreaming of food, awakes to an aroma that promises well for the Pantagruelian banquet to come.

"From the direction of this leafy arbor, if I'm not mistaken, comes a vapor and smell a good deal more of roasting bacon than of rushes and thyme; wedding celebrations that begin with such smells, by my life, must surely be abundant and generous," he declares.

Indeed, the banquet proves to be magnificent. Sancho's eyes are on stalks, his mouth watering uncontrollably, as he beholds a whole steer roasting over the embers of a whole elm tree. Two piglets had been sewn into the stomach of the roasting steer, a technique which, Cervantes comments en passant, "served to give it flavor and keep it tender." Six bubbling cauldrons, each big enough for "a marketful of meat," held chickens, hares, birds of various kinds, and whole lambs. There were two giant pots of oil for frying sweetmeats, previously drenched in honey; cheeses galore; and masses of the whitest bread imaginable.

Though the feast has yet to begin, Sancho cannot resist begging the cooks to allow him to skim off the foam from one of the cauldrons and eat it with a piece of bread.

Tragically, this is all that Sancho will eat today. Don Quijote is in a hurry to meet his next villain, and his trusty sword bearer is destined to go hungry once again. Sancho's disappointment at having to leave without partaking of the banquet is poignantly described as a "darkness" falling on his soul.

FOR SUCH A HARSH and barren landscape, La Mancha produces a prodigious range of edibles. The cereal crops grown on a large scale throughout the region mean that manchego bread is far superior to the (admittedly lamentable) Spanish average. The huge flocks of sheep that roam the plains are responsible for Spain's most famous and most marketable cheese. The region makes a splendid olive oil, especially in the gentle uplands of the Montes de Toledo. The town of Las Pedroñeras, near Cuenca in the southeast, more or less keeps the world in garlic. Not least, the region as a whole is the world's single greatest producer of wine—"great" in the sense of quantity, not quality, though the situation is improving.

There is plenty of bulk production, then, but there are also exquisite things from particular places. Consuegra, Madridejos, Villafranca de los Caballeros, and a few other manchego towns provide the saffron that perfumes the rice dishes of Valencia and Alicante, and, despite strong competition from large-scale producers in Iran and China, can plausibly claim that theirs is the finest in the world. The pickled eggplant of Almagro, pungent with cumin and vinegar, is a delicacy that, once tasted, is never forgotten. The list of dulces, the regional sweets, is endless, every town having its own speciality—which, it has to be said, often closely resembles that of the town next door.

As for the cuisine, we need to distinguish between the two parts of this "autonomous community." On the Castilian side, game and roast meats are the order of the day. Partridge a la toledana is the main dish of Toledo, and the northern part of the region is obsessed with game birds. In La Mancha proper, the cooking has its roots in the hardship rations of shepherds and country people. The feast-day dish here is gazpacho manchego—nothing to do with the gazpachos of Andalusia, but a stew of mixed game with a crisp flatbread (the dough for which was traditionally kneaded on a dry goatskin) crumbled into it. The region's everyday dishes—migas and gachas—are simple preparations that can be thrown together using ingredients carried easily in a knapsack without spoiling, such as dry bread, flour, oil, garlic, cured or dried meat, and olive oil. Migas ("crumbs") is a true subsistence dish, based on dry bread rehydrated a little with water and fried to a crisp with garlic (chopped chorizo, tocino, and even red pepper are added in better-off households). Gachas is even more basic. This is a kind of savory puree, rich in protein yet horribly indigestible, made with the flour of the almorta, a relative of the lupine, and a good deal of pork fat and garlic. It belongs to the family of thick cereal sludges, like porridge and polenta, which are principally designed to fill the stomach and stave off winter's biting cold. I once ate gachas on a hot summer day, and paid for my mistake with sweat from head to toe, a thirst barely quenched by a liter bottle of Vichy Catalan, and a comatose state from which I would emerge, dazed and dripping, after three hours of deep siesta.

Toledo was a handsome city, full of poignant reminders of tolerance and cultural exchange among the three great faiths—Catholicism, Judaism, and Islam—probably never to be repeated. But the few inhabitants of its museumlike centro histórico seemed a little too serious-faced and sober for my liking. I busied myself with the task of visiting as many of the city's legion of pastry shops as possible in a single morning, and came to the conclusion that the apparently upstanding folk of Toledo were secretly in thrall to sugar. If they scuttled by me like ghosts in the street, it was only in their haste to get home, stretch out on a sofa, and gorge on their city's enormous range of sugary goodies: deep-fried honey-drenched flores manchegas; pumpkin-stuffed empanadillas; marzipans, mantecados, and milhojas.

Above the door of Saint Ursula's convent in Calle Santa Ursula, I noticed a sign in Japanese, English, and Spanish advertising the sweets made by the nuns. I ducked inside and there, in the gloom of the hallway, was a small window behind which were displayed the various specialities of the house, including pastas de almendra (almond biscuits), yemas de Santa Rita (egg yolk and sugar in a little cake), and the strange "Anguila Número Uno"—literally "eel number one," a snakelike form in yellow marzipan decorated with whorls of sugar icing.

There were footsteps in an adjoining room. Saint Ursula's being a cloistered convent of Augustinian nuns, all transactions with the outside world take place by the torno, a wooden cylinder similar in concept to a revolving door. Clank, clank, as a nun unchained the torno. I caught a glimpse of black sleeves and the lily-white hands of an elderly woman, her skin as delicate as crepe paper.

She coughed, once. "Ave Maria purísima," she said in a toneless voice.

I'd been briefed, and I knew that when buying at a convent, just as when buying online, you need to log on with the correct password.

"Sin pecado concebida." Conceived without sin. Well, it goes without saying.

A box of marzipan and an eel, please. The torno clattered around, first to deliver the goods and then to convey the money; then it made another half turn to return the change. Finally there was a moment of idle chatter. The recipes? "Oh, we've been making these things forever. World without end, amen." And I wouldn't have mentioned the plainly Arabic origins of something like marzipan, if the nun hadn't done so herself. "They do say it goes back to the Moors," she muttered, with distaste audible in her voice.

She gave another little cough and busied herself with the cash box, padlocking the torno again.

"It's a shame we have to lock it. If we don't, they'll steal whatever they can lay their hands on."

ALL THAT MARZIPAN has to come from somewhere. South of Toledo, among the furniture warehouses and car dealers, I see the first almond groves. Then a couple of partridge farms, to satisfy the local hunger for perdiz a la toledana. The city straggles out into expanses of olive grove. The earth here is rust-red, and the contrast with the gray-green leaves appeals to eyes tired of dust and flatness. Then the vines begin, hectare after hectare of low corridors, like a simple maze in which, nightmarishly, you could lose yourself forever. Concrete vats stand like obelisks in the fields, discarded and forgotten since the wineries installed stainless steel en masse in the 1980s, begging to be considered for some alternative use—perhaps as a shower room for that urban pied-à-terre.

The roads were straight, flat, and long, furrowing the sea of vines. Hulking shapes in the fields moved slowly between the ripples of this yellow-green ocean: an army of grape pickers, some with the head scarves and dark faces of immigrants from Africa or South America. It was only mid-October, but there had been almost no rain this autumn, so the countryside looked blasted, the tomato plants in the gardens browning, feeble, faded. What must La Mancha look like in August? What must the heat be like? No wonder the towns seem turned in on themselves, as if hunkering down until the first winter rains. Only the vine and olive stay green, giving a false impression of lushness when everything else has long since shriveled away.

Lulled and slightly mesmerized by the manchego roads, I wound up in Consuegra. The unusual name means your child's mother in law. Visible from miles away, a line of whitewashed windmills crowns the crest of hills above the town, and these windmills, with their quixotic connotations, provide Consuegra with its major tourist draw. Food lovers, however, have a more important reason to visit. This corner of La Mancha is the source of the world's most costly foodstuff, by weight, worth more, notoriously, than gold. During October and November the dun livery of the manchego countryside is suddenly scattered with patches of exotic color, as the violet flowers of the saffron bulb, *Crocus sativus,* emerge from their crown of fine emerald-green leaves.

Beside a house on the edge of the village I spied two women, down on their knees in the reddish earth of their saffron plot. They wore the bata de casa, a thin blue-and-white apron tied around the neck and waist. I stopped the car and chatted with them as they worked, watching them pluck the flowers whole into baskets, nimbly and at great speed. Their names were Dionisia and María.

There had been a heavy dew, and a thick crowd of new flowers had come up during the night. It was what is known in La Mancha as un día de manto, when an extra-large quantity of saffron flowers are there for the picking and a mauve-colored carpet or blanket (manto in fact means "cloak") seems to hover just above the ground.

"We always start early, with the dew still on the flowers. When they dry out it's much harder, you know, to pick them whole."

Dionisia had a husband and three grown-up children but still tended her patch of saffron, which she shared with María, her friend. The family economy had always depended on her husband's work as a farmer—he grew barley and wheat—but the saffron brought in a nice little extra income, which would be saved up. In the old days saffron was kept in a safe place along with the family's other precious things, the bits of jewelry and cutlery, and in the event of an unexpected expense, such as a wedding, a funeral, or a purchase of land, would be cashed in for the best price.

Few things in the world are more valuable than the blood-orange pistils of the saffron crocus, and few crops are more torturously labor-intensive. A single celemín of 235 square meters (the standard size of a plot) produces just one pound of saffron, and every pound requires no fewer than 80,000 flowers. They must be picked by hand, since no machine has yet been invented to match the delicacy of the human thumb and forefinger. The process of removing the pistils from their flowers, known here as la monda, is also done by hand.

"We sit around the kitchen table of an evening, with a pile of roses—we call the flowers roses. And we work away. And we chat as we work, and sometimes the neighbors come around to lend a hand. At the beginning it's not easy," said Dionisia.

"But over the years you do get used to it," put in María.

I leaned down to watch the two of them closely. Their fingers seemed to flutter over the ground, and the "roses" piled up in their baskets.

"You have to be careful. The saffron, it's very light, it weighs nothing. When we're working in the kitchen, we keep all the doors shut. The worst thing that can happen is a breath of wind coming in and blowing it all away. It happened to my cousin one year. She was down on her knees for hours, on that kitchen floor."

Despite being one of Spain's most famous products and a spice whose rich, exotic perfume has few rivals, saffron has very little presence in the national cuisine. Apart from paella, I can think of only two traditional Spanish dishes in which it features at all: fabada asturiana; and gallina en pepitoria, a classic casserole of hen or chicken thickened with ground almonds, pine nuts, and pounded hard-boiled eggs. Now I understood why. In a rural society with limited resources, to use up the family capital in cooking would have seemed a deeply reckless act.

We were a few days away from the town's big fiesta, which falls in October. The fiesta includes a saffron-plucking competition, in which local roseros compete to see who can remove the most pistils.

"I won it once, a long time ago," said María with a chuckle. "I'm not so quick anymore. The arthritis has got to my fingers, see."

The sun was coming out, and the women would soon be setting off home for another morning's monda. The look of the two of them, hunched over the ground like that, bent like windblown tree trunks, made me wonder it wasn't back problems María suffered from, rather than arthritis.

LATE ON A Monday morning in Almagro, I sat in the Plaza Mayor and ate a fine Spanish brunch of migas with fresh grapes and a big glass of café con leche. Almagro was a collection of whitewashed streets around a perfect plaza that was not so much a square as an avenue of balconied, columned arcades, the rooftops above them irregular with history. Blank facades opened up to reveal a palace, a convent, a patio.

Thanks in part to a sixteenth-century theater that has miraculously survived—for centuries it was just a residential courtyard where plays were performed—Almagro has become a magnet for Spanish playgoers, who converge once a year for a festival of classical theater. In terms of food, the town's major point of interest is its unique recipe for pickled eggplant, which is eaten cold as a refreshing appetizer and is one of the most addictive of all Spanish delicacies.

Traces of the Moorish legacy are visible everywhere in Spain, if you keep your eyes peeled and your mind open. Berenjena—eggplant—is Arabic in more than one sense. The vegetable was introduced by the Arab and Berber colonists of Al-Andalus and the etymology of the word is also Arabic, and before that Persian: *bedinyena.* The Catalan alberginia and the French aubergine have the same etymology.

Wherever the eggplant comes from and whatever it's called, there is not much you can tell a person from Almagro about it. To someone such as María del Carmen Sánchez Serrano, for example, it is an indissoluble part of life, work, and family history. There is a word used in Almagro to describe Mari Carmen and women like her: berenjenera, "one who occupies herself with eggplants." Here, it's a normal trade, like being a butcher, a baker, pharmacist, or farmer.

I went to see Mari Carmen at the factory, a small warehouse on the outskirts of town with a sign outside reading Berenjenas La Jaula, which was the name of the firm. It was late afternoon by the time I got there, and Mari Carmen had just come back with her sister from a street market, where the company sells eggplants, olives, and other cured goods by the kilo. I waited by the door for them to finish unpacking. As I breathed in the characteristic and quite unmistakable aroma of vinegar, cumin, and pimentón, my mind was transported to a Mediterranean beach and a picnic on a warm spring day a decade or more ago, when the crunch and sourness of these pickled eggplants, bought in a can from a local supermarket, came as a new and surprising experience. A puddle of bright orange—seepings from the pickling liquid—crept across the factory floor toward the drain.

No doubt about it, berenjenas are part of the identity of this town. The inhabitants of Almagro have always sold their pickled eggplants at fairs and fiestas all over the region. Their arrival was greeted, as one manchego writer remembers it, como agua de mayo ("like May rain")—that is, with delight, for on a torrid August night there was no more refreshing and restorative food than the vinegary crunch and spice of berenjenas de Almagro.

Mari Carmen had her hair tied back and wore gray sweatpants tucked into Wellington boots. We sat in a small, dark office with peeling walls and old-fashioned gray office furniture. The way she sank into her chair made it look as if this was the first time she'd sat down all day; and maybe it was.

"I started work when I was eight, and I've never stopped," she began, impressively. "I know eggplants like I know my own family. When I was born, at the exact moment, my mother had a pot of eggplants on the boil. Funny, after forty years I ought to loathe the things. But the fact is I don't. I still love them." She smiled wearily. Her face wore a colorless, early-to-rise look.

"Where is the recipe from? Oh, it goes back centuries, to the Moors. That's what I've been told. We've been doing it forever. Nothing's changed; it's all still done by hand, mostly. All natural, nothing artificial."

The fame of the berenjena belongs to Almagro, but the special little eggplants, no bigger than a child's fist, are grown in the hamlet of Aldea del Rey, where the soil is better. The aldeanos plant the seeds in May and harvest from July onward, picking the eggplants when they are still green and the rounded fruit has barely emerged from its spiny base. (The green parts are edible and pickling makes them tender. In Almagro even the stalk is peeled and eaten, though most Spaniards would leave it on the plate.)

The crucial part of the process is not the pickling but the boiling. "It's years of experience, years and years, that tell you how long to cook them for," said Mari Carmen.

We walked out into the factory to see the steel cauldrons where the eggplants are boiled until they take on their golden color—a moment too long and they simply go black—and the vat where they are plunged into cold water. In the old days they were laid out on cloths in the patios of the houses and sprinkled with well water.

Then comes the aliño—an important concept in Spanish culinary practice, associated mainly with salads (aliño means dressing or seasoning) but also commonly applied to sausages like chorizo and salchichón, olives, and any other food that is flavored after curing or cooking. The eggplants are opened, stuffed with a slice of red pepper, and closed with a fennel stalk cut from the wild plants that grow along the hedgerows and on fallow ground. Then they are tipped into terracotta jars with a mixture of water, wine vinegar, cumin seed, salt, and sweet pimentón. After eight or nine days they are cured and ready to be sold.

Mari Carmen slipped off the plastic covering of one of the jars and fished out an eggplant for me to taste. Anything you try in its place of production is always better than when you buy it in a shop, and this was a superb example of its type: fresh and crunchy, neither excessively vinegary nor aggressively spiced. I peeled the stalk and ate that too, finding that it wasn't at all woody and fibrous, but perfectly toothsome.

It was delicious, but then Mari Carmen and her family had had forty-five years to perfect the recipe. We stood in the storeroom filled with that special aroma and I wiped my hands with a paper towel (eggplant is messy to eat) and we got to talking, and little by little, detail by detail, a family saga unfolded. Mari Carmen was one of eight children, and their mother worked her fingers to the bone to keep them fed. Their education was not all that it might have been. Mari Carmen's eldest sister was taken out of school at an early age because the mother couldn't cope on her own. The school principal tried to remonstrate—it was a shame; the girl had brains and might go far; if it was a question of money she would see what could be done. But the mother insisted: the girl was needed at home.

Mari Carmen shook her head, leaning her shoulder against the whitewashed wall. "We never knew hunger in our family, but there was hardship. I remember the neighbors' children, sitting on the steps with a bag of candy. And us—well, we knew there was no way we'd be getting that candy."

Her father had grown up among seven siblings and no parents, his own father having been killed in the civil war.

Mari Carmen's father was a fighter, a survivor. First he worked in a flour mill. Then he kept pigs on a borrowed patch of land, curing the hams at home and selling them. When this failed to support the family, he turned his hand to eggplants. He tried boiling them in a zinc cauldron his wife used for washing clothes, and curing them in a terra-cotta jar that had been her entire dowry. He had no very clear idea of the recipe, and the first three attempts were disasters.

"They went black on him!" laughed Mari Carmen, her face coloring a little. "He got the timing wrong! They came right only on the fourth time, and he was furious—imagine it, all those eggplants gone to waste." Her eyes glistened at the memory.

And so La Jaula was born. The name means "cage," in reference to a proverb that was popular in the family: "Nice cage, shame about the birds." And from then on it was hard work and more hard work. She and her sisters were out on the road in the van with the eggplants, going from village to village, setting up in the early morning, packing up in the raging heat or aching cold of the afternoon, then going back home to wash up the basins. . . .

I said good-bye, and she stomped off to load up the van. Tomorrow she had a delivery. We shook hands. Her arms were stained orange with pimentón—the permanent tan of the eggplant maker.

"Berenjeneros, berenjeneros, that's what we are. And it's too late to be anything else," she said with a smile of resignation and tiredness and satisfaction.

MANUEL DE LA OSA has a restaurant in a village near Cuenca that has discreetly, almost reluctantly, become known as one of the best in Spain. Señor de la Osa's surname sounds very like the Spanish word for bear, oso, and thus one tends to think of him as bearlike, physically: burly, not to say hugely proportioned; bearded, with his charcoal-dark hair in a messy mane; and with fingers like thick game sausages and arms like serrano hams. But his glance and smile are timid; skeptical; and, despite his fame, free of ego.

Manolo (everyone who knows him even slightly uses the familiar form of his Christian name) is not one of those chefs who spend most of their time away at conferences, workshops, and guest appearances in other people's kitchens. He dislikes airplanes and finds travel generally tedious.

"If people want to meet me, let them come and see me," he says firmly.

Las Pedroñeras is a scratchy brick-built plains town that has very little to recommend it to the tourist, with the obvious exception of his restaurant, Las Rejas.

A big sign as you enter Las Pedroñeras reads "Capital of Garlic," in three words encapsulating what the town does best and what its economy almost entirely depends on. Warehouses on the outskirts are given over to thousands of tons of garlic, which lies in pale lumpy piles and hangs in curtains from the roofs. In fact a faint whiff of garlic hangs over the whole town, drifting into shops and offices, stealing into people's bedrooms and disturbing their dreams. The reputation of Las Pedroñeras hangs on ajo morado, streaked with pinkish purple, which is said to have a greater fragrance and subtlety of flavor, as well as fatter, juicier cloves, than the run-of-the-mill white garlic now flooding into the European market, mainly from China.

It is hard to convey just how extraordinary it is to find a restaurant like Las Rejas in a place like this. On a concrete wall, half obscured by the dust from the trucks that thunder past on the N301, a notice in big black letters reads: Restaurante Típico, Cocina Manchega. This makes it sound like one among hundreds of roadside joints, where rows of trucks parked outside are no guarantee of a decent meal, that flash past at regular intervals as you drive through southern Spain.

At midday the kitchen at Las Rejas was simmering with activity, a backstage area alive with the sounds of chopping and scorching, the whiz of the blender, the bubble of the stockpot. Through the back door came a constant stream of people carrying boxes and briefcases, offering samples, wielding forms to be signed, or simply dropping by to say hello. While Manolo gave a young junior chef a crash course in how to work a new ice cream maker just delivered from Madrid, I stood by the bar in the back room and drank coffee with some of the suppliers who happened to be on their rounds that morning. There was a man who grew peas, a man who grew garlic, and a cheese maker who had brought cheese handmade from the milk of his own manchego sheep.

It was just before one o'clock. Plenty of time until lunch, then, for a brief incursion into a region that is to garlic what Bordeaux is to wine: the heartland, the cradle. My guide, Francisco, the town's only producer of organic garlic, leaped into his Land Rover and roared off in a cloud of dust down a dirt track that wound away through an undulating landscape of vines, olives, and bare earth the color of rust, under the sunroof of a cold blue sky. In the background the town sprawled away, looking not unattractive from this distance, and the squat square tower of the church with its pyramid-shaped roof gave the view a civilized, French look.

We walked out along the rows into the middle of the field and got down on our haunches to examine the crop. The water sprayers had been on all night, giving moisture to a crop that, in the month or so since planting, had seen no more than a day or two of rain.

Francisco pulled a full-grown bulb from his jacket pocket, passing it to me for inspection. I pierced the purple skin with my fingernail and punctured the juicy clove beyond: it smelled, not sharp or acrid, but mild and sweet.

Garlic and Spanish cooking would seem to be inextricably connected. The Spanish are supposed to love garlic, and to hurl it with abandon into every one of their dishes. It's a historical prejudice, the notion of the garlic-stinking Spaniard, reaching back at least to the time of Richard Ford, author of the great *Handbook,* who in typically caustic fashion declares: "It is curious to see to what an awful extent the Spanish peasant on the eastern coast will consume garlic: we caution our traveller against the captivating name of Valencian butter, *manteca valenciana.* It is composed (for the cow has nothing to do with it) of equal portions of garlic and hogs' lard, pounded together in a mortar, and then spread on bread, just as we do arsenic to destroy vermin." To give him his due, Ford also says of garlic that "the evil consists in the abuse, not the use," and in this of course he is absolutely right. In fact the Spanish do not use garlic in everything, and Spanish cooks are generally respectful of its power, especially when it is used raw. An intelligent discussion of garlic and its correct use in cooking comes from the pen of the Catalan Josep Pla, who hated the way that, to paraphrase his words, any food cooked with garlic tastes only of garlic. Pla makes the important distinction between the fresh garlic of the new season, sweet and innocuous, and the thing it becomes after a few month's storage, which has "such an expansive force, such a decisive presence, that it destroys all the flavors and all the delicate gradations of taste" in the food to which it's added. Interestingly, Pla suggests that garlic may owe its traditional popularity in Spain to hunger, since its powerful aroma created "an illusion of nourishment" in people whose diet was scanty and monotonous.

Traces of garlic juice were still on my fingers as I sat down at a table near the kitchen where Manolo could keep an eye on me. At the next table a dressed-up couple were each talking animatedly into their separate mobile phones, while plates of food came and went beneath their noses. Opposite me stood an antique bottle rack in rough-hewn wood, with a row of terra-cotta jars standing sentinel as they had doubtless done for generations.

For Manuel de la Osa, like other Spanish chefs working close to the roots of their particular regional traditions, taste and memory are intimately connected. Flavors and textures refer both backward, to tradition and childhood; and forward and outward to the new worlds of multicultural and high-tech cuisine.

"As I see it, the kitchen isn't a laboratory full of test tubes, siphons, and other devices. . . . A place for experimenting with flavors, sure; but for that the best tools are the tongue and the palate," he said as he stood at my table, looming over me like Mount Rushmore, holding in his hand a plate of lychee sorbet with caviar and olive oil—the first of three stunning little aperitivos preceding the menu proper.

It was certainly a most un-manchego start to the meal, but the aromatic, refreshing lychee, the salty-rich caviar, and the piquant grassy olive oil were a brilliant fanfare. What came next was a little more "rootsy": a rock mussel with saffron foam and fried cheese with quince and black olive. Still more earthbound was a cold garlic soup, one of de la Osa's most enduring inventions, presented in a cocktail glass with crisp wafers of ham poised above egg yolk, parsley, and fried cubes of bread. Like the dish in its original form, this deconstructed version was satisfying and simple in equal measure. The garlic was absolutely discreet: subtle and sweet.

Now came the fireworks. A dish of roast squid with pisto manchego and a raviolo formed of a transparent slice of tocino filled with peeled baby broad beans. The sweet surprise of the bright green baby beans in their parcel of salty tocino was amazingly good. So was a potato cream whipped up with sheep's milk, along with a pair of lamb sweetbreads and another pair of asparagus tips. Such wild and earthy flavors . . . By the time I reached the roasted John Dory sirloin with rosemary, parsley oil, and crushed potato, it was becoming obvious that the creator of these dishes was a man with perfect taste. I hardly knew what to do with the menu's final savory dish, a suckling pig confit with apple and quince sauce perfumed with vanilla and truffle, except to wolf down every last forkful of it and clean the plate with a hunk of bread.

The clock ticked around to five; the well-to-do lunchers paid their bills, couple by couple, and left, toting their Prada bags as they prepared to cross the threshold into the prosaic, cash-strapped outside world; and still Manolo kept bringing me more and more dishes, pouring me glasses of curious and innovative manchego wines, and generally treating me with the kind of amiable generosity one doesn't expect, somehow, of a famous chef with much more important fish to fry.

His multiple desserts were a gorgeous blur, a farrago of ice creams and granizados of yogurt with spices, hazelnuts, white chocolate, fennel, coffee, saffron, orange, and blackberry. A rich sponge cake soaked in red wine reduction, respectfully nodding to the importance of wine in the culture of the region, signaled the end of my capacity to eat, drink, or think, for the time being. At this postprandial point, as the afternoon turned snoozy, Manolo appeared at my table once more and sat down to tell me something about his philosophy of life and food.

He called for two big tumblers of ice and a bottle of J&B.

"The story is as follows. Whisky?" Glug, glug, clink, clink. "This is a farming town. Ninety-nine percent of us are farmers. What kind of gastronomic activity is there going on in a town like this? Very little. Even so, my grandparents were already doing this sort of thing. They had an eating house, an old posada that stood in the main square, and they had an excellent relationship with the world of wine, with the world of manchego cheese, saffron . . ." He paused for a second to take a slug of whisky, his gaze losing itself momentarily in the empty space above the table. "As a child I was always interested in whatever my grandmother, my mother, my aunts were doing in the kitchen. All my family have always been good eaters, and I loved food, too. I began to realize that there were things you could eat that would make you happy: things from around the region. I learned what was meant by a good cheese, a good saffron; where there was good oil, good game meats, good vegetables. I have so many memories of the dishes of my childhood—memories of tastes, aromas, fragrances . . . The smell of cooking over an open fire . . ."

The restaurant was now deserted; its tables had been cleared and reset for the evening shift. From the kitchen came a sound of clanking pots and pans: people in there were washing dishes, whistling as they worked. It would be time in a short while for me to leave La Mancha and its idiosyncratic local cooking, and set forth like Don Quijote in search of new challenges. Manolo poured us both a final generous tumblerful of whisky, and lit himself a cigarette.

He leaned back in his chair, which creaked a little in protest. A silence fell. Perhaps it was just the traces on my fingers as I lifted my glass to my lips. But just then, for a second or two, I caught another whiff of that haunting fragrance. It was the genie of the garlic clove, the poltergeist of Las Pedroñeras, sneaking into my brain and switching the synapses.

8

Jaén

FROM A TABLE at a restaurant in Segura de la Sierra, a scrawny, stony village beside a mountain pass, I looked down at a distant plain colored dusty gray from the endless olive trees and the mist that hung above them. A thin river made its way awkwardly down the valley with a thread of bright green clinging to either side, and a neat forest of stumpy olives crept up the hillside almost to its craggy summit.

I was in Andalusia, but only just. Segura de la Sierra was backed into a corner of the country where four regions—Andalusia, Murcia, La Mancha, and Castile—meet in a wild and lonely place.

What the waiter brought me as I sat at that terrace table tasted unmistakably Andalusian, though I would be hard-pressed to explain precisely why. There were ajoatado, a hearty mash of potato and garlic; and ajopringue, a pork liver pâté with red pepper, pimentón, and spices; a roast leg of mountain lamb with a rust-red, smooth oily sauce (known as ajoharina) made with tomato and potato pureed with chili, cumin, and bay leaf; and a simple salad, simply dressed. And then there were enredos, a fried dough paste in syrup; panates; flores; and leche frita—variations on the Spanish theme of flour-and-water dough deep-fried and laced with something sweet. None of this would have been possible, of course, without the local olive oil, a limpid, green-yellow nectar which was brought to my table in a bottle, just in case I hadn't consumed enough of it as an ingredient of the food. I sloshed some on a hunk of bread, chewed on it, shut my eyes, and emptied my thoughts, and aromas came flooding in to fill my mind: freshly cut grass in a pile beside a lawn, the milky sap of a fig tree, and, surprisingly but unmistakably, the warm smell of tomato plants in a greenhouse on a summer day.

That morning I had visited the offices of the local denominación de origen, of which twenty exist in Spain for olive oil. I had sat and listened obediently to a woman in a white coat extolling the virtues of extra-virgin.

"Now, extra-virgin, it may seem expensive. But let me tell you, with extra-virgin you can fry seven or eight times with the same oil. And with sunflower, it's only two or three times; then you have to throw it away. So really, virgin olive oil is not only tastier; it is also much more economical," said the woman.

I found myself feeling entirely convinced.

My gaze wandered to a wall map of the varieties of olive in Spain, with colors for all types forming a jigsaw across the lower half of the peninsula. Every region producing olive oil has its favorite variety, and a few are exclusive to particular zones: Catalonia loves the Arbequina, with its small round berries and delicate oil; Toledo, Ciudad Real, and the central plain prefer the frost-resistant Cornicabra; Extremadura favors the Manzanilla, "little apple," whose oil is marvelously fragrant and long-lasting. Across the country, and especially in Jaén, the commonest variety is the Picual, which combines the natural advantages of high yield, high oil content in the fruit, and a wide spectrum of subtle flavors, often including a spicy "kick" as the oil makes its way down your throat.

Olive oil was, together with wheat, essential to the economy of ancient Iberia. The wild olive had always grown here and, according to the food historian Manuel Martínez Llopis, some of the earliest tribes of southern Spain may have made oil from its fruit. The cultivated olive *Olea europaea* (the name of the tree has given us the everyday English word "oil") was brought to the Iberian peninsula by the Greeks, or possibly the Phoenicians; but the entrepreneurial Romans, as ever, first saw the commercial possibilities of olive cultivation on a grand scale. During the first centuries of Roman occupation, *oleum* had to be imported into Hispania from the west coast of Italy; before long, however, the peninsula was self-sufficient in olive oil and even began to export to the rest of the empire. The olive tree was planted throughout the southern half of the peninsula, reaching its northern limit in the mountains near what is now Madrid. The plains of Betica, as the Roman province of southern Spain was known, produced fabulous harvests of olives from which was made an oil of high quality, and this oil was exported in enormous quantities to satisfy the sophisticated palates of Rome. By the second century after Christ the olive was so much a feature of the landscape that Emperor Hadrian (a Spaniard himself, let us not forget) chose an olive branch as the symbol of Hispania.

The Spanish word for olive oil derives from the Arabic *azeit,* which also gave rise, by a kind of reverse association, to the word for the olive itself: aceituna in Castilian. For centuries olive oil was held in the highest regard, and lent itself to countless culinary and medicinal uses, and an ancillary role as fuel for lamps, a base for soap manufacture, and so on. The quality of much food-grade olive oil must have been generally lamentable: foreign travelers in Spain in all epochs testify to the reek of rancid, overused oil that pervaded the atmosphere, and sometimes the food. In the northern provinces of Galicia, Asturias, Cantabria, and the Basque country, where the olive tree doesn't grow, "imported" oil would have been used alongside indigenous fats, mostly butter and lard. Generally speaking, however, the supremacy of olive oil as *the* Spanish cooking medium was never called into question—until the early 1950s, when it suddenly fell out of favor. As part of the United States treaty of cooperation with the Franco regime, which allowed U.S. military bases in Spain in return for economic support, huge quantities of American vegetable oil flooded the local market. This imported oil had to be consumed somehow, and an official campaign began a systematic denigration of olive oil. Rumors spread that it was more fattening than the new "lighter" oils. Consumption plummeted. Many almazaras (olive presses) fell into disuse. Eventually, in the early 1980s, the tide began to turn. The terrible rapeseed oil scandal of October 1981, in which 1,000 people died and many more were permanently disfigured by a vegetable oil that had been adulterated with poisonous chemicals, sent many consumers back to olive oil, which was once again perceived as natural and safe. Successive studies revealed that, far from being bad for health, olive oil was actively beneficial. Over the years, improved production techniques gradually removed the rancid "off" taste that had traditionally plagued it, so its subtle flavor and aroma could be appreciated as never before. For once in the history of contemporary eating habits, the story has a happy ending, and the juice of the fruit of the olive tree, one of the great achievements of European civilization, has returned to its rightful place at the center of Spanish food and life.

Olive oil production in Spain is not what it was. Traditionally, the olives were picked up from the ground, where they might have been lying for days, and packed into sacks for transport by donkey or mule cart. The almazara—the press—might have been many miles from the trees. Once there, the olives would be tipped into holding vats called trojes, where they might spend another few hours or even days before being pressed. There was often little regard for cleanliness. The whole process, in short, was guaranteed to produce an olive oil that modern palates would find simply repellent.

After lunch I took the car up the deserted roads of the sierra, winding up toward a crag with olives growing along one flank. I walked for a while among the trees, letting my hands drift over the rugged gray trunks. These were mountain olives, so hardy as to be virtually indestructible, squeezing their nutrients from a soil so poor and thin that nothing else will grow on it except the vine, that other master of economical living.

The province of Jaén is dedicated heart and soul to the cultivation and culture of the olive. There is nowhere else on earth with anything like the surface area given over to olive trees, and nowhere else on earth that works quite as hard to do things with them. Of the 220 million trees in the whole of Spain, almost a third are in Jaén. It is no surprise that the vast majority of Spanish olive oil comes from here, but the really impressive figure is that this single province of Andalusia accounts for almost a fifth of the entire world production of olive oil.

The olive in Jaén is called a monocultivo. This means that there is only one crop, and what you see is what you get. Almost 85 percent of the cultivatable land here has olive trees growing on it. The plantations of Jaén, covering more than 600,000 hectares, have been called the largest man-made woodland in the world.

The city of Jaén has its own cathedral—a neoclassical temple on such a huge scale that it dwarfs everything else in the city; the twin towers of its grand facade are a landmark for miles around. At ground level, just opposite the facade across the cathedral square, proudly stands an ancient olive tree, as if to say: I, too, have a claim on the souls of these people.

Taking the road out of Jaén toward Baeza I launched myself into the sea of gray-green, turning off at the sign that read: Cortijo de Nuestra Señora de los Milagros, "Farm of Our Lady of the Miracles." Earlier in the year, someone had given me an olive oil which had impressed me so much with its elegantly restrained aromas of cut grass and apples that I had copied the producer's address in a notebook before setting out for Jaén. Nuestra Señora de los Milagros was a rare example of a privately owned farm producing and selling its own oil, since most of the land around here was worked by faceless agribusinesses. Luis, who showed me around, was a scion of the Montabes family that owned the 850-hectare property. He was a big-boned, pale-skinned, energetic young man, a Spanish businessman of the most modern kind, shiny with the American patina of marketing and PR.

The cortijo was a plain white building with bright green shutters on the windows, in the classic style of the Andalusian country house. Ensconced in a niche in the hallway was a Barbie-sized figure of the Virgin of the Miracles, sitting pretty in a long silk dress. Upstairs was a living room with a beamed ceiling, antique lamps, colored tiles, and dark Spanish furniture against the whitewashed walls.

There might have been a better time to visit, if I had thought about the matter properly, than a month when the olive harvest is at its height, when farm managers are scurrying hither and thither and the air is thick with activity and stress. But Luis Montabes attended me with the affable courtesy I have become used to in the Spanish—particularly, for some reason, in those involved with the business of food.

Luis switched off his mobile phone and led me up a narrow metal staircase to a walkway where we stood for a while, looking down on a giant hopper in which the olives, a blur of purple and green, looked more like a liquid than a collection of solids, churning and bubbling as the multicolored mass moved slowly downward. On a day like today the factory was working at full capacity, humming in a controlled fury of trembling, rattling metal.

As an industry, Jaén's olive oil business is all about quantity and scale. From the reception area where the olives are washed and sorted, we strode over to the bodega, where thousands of liters of oil were stored in giant stainless steel tanks that reached to the roof like futuristic silver rockets. Then we went on to the almazara itself, where the old esparto-grass mats and hydraulic presses had long since been replaced by Italian-made machines that pulp the olives and extract the oil by means of a centrifuge. There was little romance in this streamlined, neoteric process. One would hardly know what was being made in this room, were it not for the smell that hung in the air among the stainless steel boxes that buzzed and whirred and the thick runnel of golden liquid just now emerging from one of the boxes, trickling out of a tube into the vat below. The olives used for the estate's finest oil, the one I had tried and loved for its grassy greenness, were being pressed at a temperature of twenty-nine degrees Celsius, which nowadays passes for "cold pressing." (The olives for most oil are subjected to much higher temperatures, for maximum yield.)

Jumping into the four-wheel drive, we set off at a great pace along the pitted dirt roads of the estate, twisting and turning into the labyrinth of trees. The cortijo has 85,000 trees, Luis told me nonchalantly. At the heart of this artificial woodland we passed a gang of pickers, laying their green nets under a tree whose branches were bowed with the weight of fruit. A yellow machine like a tractor with a long arm advanced robotically, clamping its arm on the waist of the tree, and the trunk began to vibrate; the whole tree shivered violently from top to bottom, and the olives rained down into the nets below.

Up a steep slope, through scrubby rock rose and lavender bushes, was the highest point of the estate, a little hill where wild olives grew—scrawny trees whose fruit was as hard and black as lead pellets. To the right was the barren ridge of the Sierra Mágina, sparkling chalky white in the winter sun. In front of us, down toward the valley, was another vast estate with some 210,000 trees, making it one of the largest olive farms anywhere in the world. From here to the horizon there was not a fig tree, not a vine, not a patch of vegetables or almond trees, nothing but an expanse of gray-green foliage. From a distance, a large olive plantation looks eerily like an restless ocean. The silvery leaves glitter slightly, and when the wind blows, currents sweep across the canopy of treetops.

"We're in a cold zone here, right on the edge of the sierra, and the Picual olive loves it here," said Luis. "Even in high summer there's a cool breeze. It means our olives are generally healthier than those down there—and the oil is better."

We tramped a little farther up the hill, startling a group of partridges into flight. Up here there were secret remains of an Iberian burial site; treasure hunters had found coins left behind by a Roman legion.

Back at the farm, we nosed about the installations, Luis showing me the little low whitewashed houses where the olive pickers stayed for the duration of the harvest. In the days before mechanization, 200 people lived on the estate, which became in effect a temporary village, with a school, a bar, a salon for socializing, and a lively party on the feast of Saint John.

Strictly speaking, the cortijo had been a latifundio. The term, a crucial concept in the history of rural Spain, implies a large property (*latus,* broad; *fundus,* estate) employing resident workers. In 1930, in the south of the country (essentially Andalusia, Extremadura, and La Mancha), estates of more than 100 hectares occupied as much as 52 percent of the rural space.

There is no doubt that the latifundio system has been responsible for some dreadful instances of social injustice. At its worst, it was nothing less than a form of slave labor, under which landless, unsalaried peasants depended on their masters for everything from sustenance to education. In the novel *Los Santos Inocentes,* by Miguel Delibes, everyone's favorite horror story of the latifundio system, the miserable lives of the ill-clothed, underfed, and illiterate employees are set against the lavish lifestyle of the señoritos (the owners), whose periodic visits to the estate to hunt and carouse only exacerbate the shocking inequity of the situation. However, Nuestra Señora de los Milagros was not that sort of latifundio. It was slick, efficient, and democratic. It was a thoroughly modern country estate, where the familiar "tú" was universal, the polite "usted" was almost obsolete, and there was no doffing of caps.

Luis shook hands with a grizzled elderly man who had a gap-toothed grin and wore a grubby white cap set squarely on his head. "This is Paco Yeguas, who makes the food for us. His best dish is a rice with rabbit. A nice rabbit from the finca. And he's an absolute master of migas." Migas, the national dish of the southern Spanish rural working classes. The triumph of artfulness over austerity.

"And what do you put in your migas, Paco? Apart from the bread? Chorizo, ham, garlic?" prompted Luis.

"That's right, a good few cloves of garlic," said Paco. "I don't peel them, just crush them with my hand; they go in whole—and some red pepper—and I fry it all up together, the bread crumbs and everything, and maybe a few eggs from our hens. My migas are the way migas should be. It's all in the movement of the pan. You've got to keep them moving; otherwise they'll burn."

"Good for you, Paco," said Luis, slapping him on the shoulder.

We repaired to the cortijo, where my host had provided an appetizer even simpler than Paco's fried bread crumbs, though the context was a little more refined. In the sitting room, silent apart from a ticking carriage clock, a table had been laid with a white linen cloth. A large white plate was filled with slices of acorn-fed ibérico ham, almost jewellike in their ruby color and so thin they were almost translucent. There were warm bread and cold fino sherry. The centerpiece of this miniature banquet was the family's finest olive oil, pressed a few days earlier. Luis poured it from the bottle in a thin, silent stream into a soup bowl, where it formed a puddle, the color showing up bewitchingly against the white china.

Before I left, Luis gave me a five-liter bottle of his oil, and over the following days and weeks, it would come to occupy an important role in my cooking and my life. The night I brought it home, I fried two eggs in the thick jade-green liquid: they were sublime. The next morning I dribbled it on hot toast for breakfast; butter held no charm for me now. From then on it was no holds barred: one minute I was cheerfully ladling it into a bowl of chickpea stew, the next I was mash-ing it with garlic and herbs to smother a leg of lamb, or beating it up with an egg yolk for a potent greenish-yellow mayonnaise. I made biscuits, rich pastry, a Spanish béchamel fragrant with olive, and a mint-green olive oil ice cream. Between times I caught myself drinking the occasional mouthful from a glass as if it were fruit juice—which in a way it is.

And the oil's uses didn't stop at the kitchen door. I found that it worked wonderfully as a moisturizer for scratched, chapped hands. When my neck hurt from sitting at the computer, I massaged it into my aching muscles. When someone told me the Gypsies put almond oil in their hair, I started combing a spoonful of olive oil into my hair as a natural conditioner—until one morning I woke to find that my pillowcase had greasy greenish stains on it, and that was the moment I decided this olive oil thing had probably gone far enough.

9

Granada

T HE WEEK AFTER the New Year, an arctic weather system
rolled in from northern Europe, leaving snow in all the right
places and some of the wrong ones. The festive season was
officially over, and there was a sense of dyspeptic exhaustion in the air,
a feeling that the whole country had simply crawled back under the
blankets to sleep off its digestive overdose of shellfish, turrón, cheap
Cava, and late nights.

At Christmastime Nacho had returned, bringing with him a Pales-
tinian friend, Haifa, who was also his landlady. Haifa's family, an

important dynasty of judges and intellectuals, arrived in Jerusalem in the eighth century, at around the time of the first Muslim settlement in the south of Spain. A natural cook in the purest Middle Eastern tradition, she found the simple, savory dishes of the traditional Spanish repertoire not merely dull, but puzzling in their very plainness. Apart from the fact that the local cooking relied intensely on pork, which occasionally repelled her (it was not the taboo so much, she claimed, as the excess of fat), what Haifa found hardest to understand was the studied avoidance of certain piquant and stimulating flavors which for her and her culture were as natural as breathing. Some days in my kitchen she would cook up a storm of falafel, hummus, tabouleh, and ground-meat *kubbeh,* drawing on a rich palette of spices which she had wisely brought with her from Jerusalem, correctly guessing that she might not easily find them here. When it came to my turn at the stove, she would ask plaintively as I prepared a tortilla de patatas, an oven-baked bream, or a baroque cocido with ten vegetables and five meats, "What spices will you use?," seeming to hope I would answer, "Allspice, sumac, black pepper, and coriander," instead of, "Just salt."

It was Haifa's first visit to Spain, and she wanted to see the historic remains left by her Arabic culture in the cities of the south. So we drove through Extremadura from north to south and through Andalusia from west to east, ending up in the Spanish city which has known best how to maintain the romantic splendor of its Islamic past: Gharnata in the language of its Arab and Berber colonizers or, as it later became, Granada. While Haifa and Nacho explored the patios and gardens of the Al-Hamra (the red fort, as it was known by its inhabitants), I roamed the city below, hunting for the roots of modern Spanish cooking in the rich and strange aromas of its Muslim past.

On the face of it, the cooking of Granada didn't seem very Arabic at all. In fact, granadino food seemed about as far removed as possible from the kaleidoscopic, highly spiced dishes that would have been common fare in the city as recently as 500 years ago. The books of traditional cooking I looked at in libraries and bookshops were endless parades of pucheros, cocidos, gachas, migas, sopas, and potajes, flavored with nothing more exotic than garlic, pimentón, oregano, and an occasional daring, faintly self-conscious foray into cumin, saffron, or chili pepper. In the restaurants of the city I tried habas con jamón, a sauté of baby broad beans with ham and garlic; and tortilla

Sacromonte, a rich omelet made with lamb brains and testicles, named for the famous district of Granada where hippies and Gypsies live in caves carved out of the hillside. During the scalding summers, I learned, Granada lived on refreshing gazpachos and crunchy salads. During the icy winters, it fortified itself with monstrous all-inclusive stews like olla de San Antón, prepared for the feast of Saint Anthony on January 16, with dried broad beans, dried alubias, rice, and a compendium of pork products ranging from salted ribs and fatty bacon to the bones of the spine, the tail, the ear, and the careta (face). Despite the alubias, it is hard to imagine a less Arabic dish than olla de San Antón—indeed, it almost amounts to a slap in the face, a deliberate offense against the code of Muslim sensibilities.

The Islamic adventure on the peninsula began in AD 711 with the arrival of 10,000 Muslim invaders under the leadership of Tariq ibn Ziyad, who set about founding Europe's first, and so far only, Islamic state. It ended with the final capitulation of Muslim Granada to Ferdinand and Isabella in 1492. The intervening years saw the flowering of a civilization, known as Al-Andalus, which may be considered Islam's most significant historical achievement to date.

When they first disembarked, the Moors can't have been impressed with the standard of living on the peninsula, which the Visigoths, never one of history's more dynamic peoples, had allowed to slip back to pre-Roman levels of penury. The land had been poorly managed in the absence of the Romans, so that the Visigothic diet, based almost entirely on cereals and meat, suffered from a lack of variety. In contrast to the Christians' triad of meat, wheat, and wine, the Andalusians had a far more sophisticated cuisine, in which vegetables and fruit were central, spices were omnipresent, and the arts of patisserie and sweets were raised to the heights of exquisiteness.

After the Nordic blandness of post-Roman cooking, the food of Islamic Spain appears to us now as a brilliant starburst of color and flavor. The newly irrigated land beside rivers—such as the Tagus, Guadalquivir, Guadiana, Turia, Júcar, Segura, and Genil—was planted with fruits like the watermelon (imported from Persia), lemon, lime, orange, apricot, quince, date palm, and pomegranate, transcendental symbol of the whole enterprise of Moorish Spain. Perhaps the most significant of all the new crops, however, was sugarcane, planted in the semitropical zones along the coast of what is now Motril, south of

Granada, where it is still cultivated today. (An acceptable rum is produced from its juice, by the firm of Francisco Montero Martín.)

At the height of its development, during the twelfth and thirteenth centuries, the cuisine of Al-Andalus was said to surpass even that of Byzantium in elegance and refinement. At its heart was the crucial importance of spicing, for, as the writer of an anonymous early-thirteenth-century Hispano-Arabic manuscript declares, "The understanding of the use of spices is the principal basis of all dishes." The most popular seasonings of the time were saffron, mint, lavender, cardamom, caraway, oregano, coriander, ginger, mustard, pepper, basil, nutmeg, rue, galangal, parsley, aniseed, thyme, cinnamon, cumin, and sumac. It's an impressive list; and one can't help reflecting on two facts: first, Spanish cooking of today has no use for more than a handful of them; second, pimentón, the best-loved Spanish spice of all, is absent from the list. The Moors had a good excuse for not including pimentón, since it didn't come into common use until several centuries after the discovery of the New World.

The Arabic influence on later Spanish eating is more a matter of suggestion, of resonance, than of particular ingredients or dishes per se. At least two specific dishes of the Arab-Andalusian repertoire have survived almost unaltered until the present day: albóndigas (meatballs), a comforting staple of tapas bars across the country; and alboronía, sometimes called boronía, a summer vegetable stew of eggplant, onion, pumpkin, and garlic—made in the province of Córdoba with the addition of tomato and red pepper.

During the golden age of Al-Andalus, in which the three great faiths shared and learned from each other's foodways, Muslims were said to be incorporating Christian food customs into their religious festivals, and vice versa. In the intolerant new world of the reconquest, however, this changed. A kind of ethnic cleansing was applied to the culinary arts: henceforth there was to be no more complex seasoning, no more titillating combinations of sweet and savory, no more perfumed sweets. Any deviation from the official Catholic diet could be, literally, the death of you.

Thus a barrier was placed between the Arab cuisine and its assimilation and continuance in Spain after 1492. It is not only the history books that are written by the conquerors, after all, but the cookbooks as well. What we are talking about is not so much a clash of civilizations as a gulf between culinary cultures. In a few places you might make the crossing. But the bridges were narrow, long-abandoned, and in poor repair.

José Luis Vázquez González, chef and researcher, was trying to make the connection. His restaurant, the Colina de Almanzora, occupied the top floor of a house in the shadow of the red fort, down by the meandering Darro River. The restaurant sat above a hammam and tea shop, which had stayed open when the restaurant had closed after a legal dispute over wheelchair access. Señor Vázquez now had another place just off Calle Recogidas, but the bourgeois patrons of the new town were not like the curious foreigners and free-spirited bohemians of the Albaicín. He would begin this new adventure with a classic Spanish menu, and bring in the old dishes stealthily, one by one, so that by the time his well-to-do clients realized they were actually eating, and enjoying, Arab food, it would be too late.

José Luis was born in Arcos de la Frontera, one of the famous "white towns" lying like snowdrifts over the mountains of Cádiz. His culinary memories begin with such curious and now forgotten foods as meloja, a dessert of melon cooked in honey; and queso en borra, a goat cheese rolled in bread crumbs and cured in the lees of last year's olive oil. He was trained as a cook in the city of Cádiz. When he married a granadina and moved to Granada, however, his perspective subtly changed. In a city with such a vast Islamic legacy, it made sense to consider the idea of serving traditional recipes from its era of greatest splendor—that of the Nazrid dynasty, which brought forth one of the wonders of the western world and promptly disappeared in a puff of jasmine-scented smoke.

I stood in the kitchen and watched him prepare for me a dish that would have been familiar in fourteenth-century Granada. Its two main ingredients were eggplant, then as now probably the most popular vegetable in Granada, and a "honey" that is really a kind of molasses, boiled down from the juice of the sugarcane. This miel de caña was used in both sweet and savory contexts: as a dressing and marinade for meat, and to drench sticky almond pastries.

The thin slices of eggplant had been soaking overnight in a mixture of milk, honey, salt, and pepper. Now José Luis drained them off, patted them dry, and coated them in a batter that turned an exotic shade of orange-yellow when a good pinch of toasted saffron threads had been added to the mixture. (Saffron, he explained, was limited to the houses of Gharnata's upper classes. Curiously enough, so was coriander, a much cheaper and more easily cultivatable herb.) Then he fried the coated pieces in thick green olive oil and heaped them on a multi-colored plate, the rich saffron yellow standing out photogenically against the blues and greens of traditional Andalusian ceramic ware. The sugarcane honey, produced in the village of Frigiliana by the last practitioners of a craft established by the Moors, was dribbled over the fritters in a thin stream that dripped into dark puddles on the plate beneath them.

"Fátima, turn on the lights in the dining room, would you?" he called to a waitress as he turned off the stove and we went in to eat.

10

Cáceres

T HE ANTHROPOLOGIST Marvin Harris has a theory that the human race can be divided into porcophobes and por-cophiles: those cultures that flee from the pig as a taboo animal and want nothing to do with it, alive or dead, and those that make pork a central element of their nutrition and cuisine.

If so, there can't be much doubt about which side of the fence Spain is on. This is a nation whose love of pork in all its forms comes close to worship. There is even a popular saying: Del cerdo me gusta hasta los andares, "I like everything about the pig, even the way it walks."

Yet the relationship is more complex than it seems. Even the most porcophile cultures have a trace of hate in their love for the pig, and the Spanish attitude verges on schizophrenia. Of all the many Spanish words for pig—guarro, cochino, marrano, puerco, cerdo—not one is free from the taint of something gross, disgusting, or filthy. Porquería is dirt or mess; una guarrada is an act of physical or moral vileness. For a Spanish-speaker the worst kind of envy, envidia cochina, is that which is supposed to be experienced by pigs.

When I first lived in Spain, I was surprised at how seldom I saw pigs, given the fact that the country has half as many pigs as people (22.1 million pigs and about 41 million people). I soon learned that you are actually never very far from pigs, it is just that their owners hide them away in hovels, caves, and holes in the ground, as if ashamed of their existence. In country areas, in the domestic context, the pig is nearly invisible. I have often been walking past a high wall when a sudden sweet stink and a low grumble betrayed the presence of a pig behind it.

One of my first neighbors kept a pig in a kind of underground cellar with no window. Her only contact with the animal was the moment, once a day, when she opened the door to hurl a bucket of kitchen slops directly into the ankle-deep muck in which it lived. This went on until the day of the matanza, when her attitude suddenly changed. Once dead, the pig was a thing of beauty, endlessly bounteous, and a source of delight. Thanks to the pig, the family would be nourished and fattened, deliciously, for the best part of a year. Why, then, had the animal deserved so little attention during its life? One Spanish writer talks about "public shame and private honor"; the pig is a guilty secret, feted behind closed doors but socially inadmissible.

I wonder whether Oscar Wilde's phrase about each man always killing the thing he loves is applicable to the pig.

In any case, the roots of the pig problem lie deep in Spanish history. For centuries, if not millennia, the pig was an object of cultish devotion. The stone verracos in certain Castilian villages, while their religious significance is not well understood, are supposed to be primitive Iberian representations of boars or pigs. Porcophilia raged during the Roman era; the words longaniza and morcilla have Latin roots, and the various botillos, botelos, and butiechus of Galicia and Asturias all proceed from the Latin word for large intestine, *botulus*. The invasion of the Moors in AD 711 brought a first wave of porcophobia to the peninsula, though the Muslims of Al-Andalus were never too strict in their interpretation of Koranic dietary laws. (In a village of the Alpujarras, last refuge of the Moors after the fall of Granada in 1492, I have heard it said these last Muslims happily ate wild boar, a forbidden food, with a sauce made of forest berries.)

It was among the Jews that the issue of pork became a matter of life or death. According to the ultimatum issued by the king and queen, the Jewish community faced a stark choice: conversion to Catholicism or expulsion from the country. Consumption of pork was then an outward sign of religious difference, and soon became crucial. Converts flouted the former taboo with an enthusiasm born of sheer terror. Perhaps if they showed their liking for pork in no uncertain terms, if they festooned their kitchens with chorizos and laced their (hitherto pork-free) adafinas with bacon and sausages, and especially with morcilla—which, being made with pig's blood, was doubly offensive to the laws of kashruth, the Inquisition might leave them alone. If their revulsion ran deep, they would have to do everything in their power not to show it. Of course there were Jews who, while outwardly observing the forms of Christianity, continued to practice their ancient rites in secret, sometimes for generations. These secret Jews were given a scornful, paradoxical name: marranos.

The annual ritual of the pig slaughter is of great significance in the social history as well as the culinary history of Spain. For a rural population living permanently on the verge of poverty, in which every calorie had to be worked for, the matanza had an importance difficult to overestimate. This was where people found the proteins and fats they needed for their lives of hard physical labor.

At some point in history, however, obligation began to be replaced by free will—and this moment is also the beginning of the history of gastronomy. The consumer of our own time can choose from a complete range of meats, yet pork will always occupy a special place in Spanish hearts. I once saw a straw poll in a magazine in which participants were asked to name the single food they found most delicious, the edible luxury they wouldn't want to be without. More than two-thirds of them said jamón serrano. (A good proportion of the rest, by the way, said tortilla de patatas.) But Spanish charcuterie goes a lot further than ham. Pork products in the form of embutidos, or sausages (from the verb embutir, "to stuff"), chorizo, salchichón, morcilla, botifarra, morcón, chistorra, botillo, sobrassada, and longaniza, among others, each with a regional heartland and enthusiastic local fans. For older country folk, particularly, there is something succulent and special about a lump of tocino or panceta, crisped in a frying pan or allowed to melt unctuously into a chickpea stew. Like Leopold Bloom in *Ulysses,* who "ate with relish the inner organs of beasts and fowls," many Spaniards still have a taste for what is known as casquería: what you might call the odd cuts of the pig—its feet, snout, heart, ears, and tongue. Though such cuts are losing popularity as the modern squeamishness with regard to food takes hold, there are still people in Spain who will go out of their way to eat pork muzzle in a gelatinous sauce; or a pig's ear, sliced up small and flash fried with plenty of garlic. There is also cochinillo—the suckling pig that in the Castilian city of Segovia is a branch of pork cookery in its own right, as well as a local industry that gets through no fewer than 68,000 piglets a year.

I LEFT GRANADA, and Andalusia, on the kind of bright, clear, sun-flooded morning that people anywhere else but the south of Spain would have trouble recognizing as a winter day. There was color in the landscape, and the afternoons were mild: it was shirtsleeve weather.

Back home in the far west, it was scarves and woolly sweaters. There had been a month's rain; then the temperature had dropped sharply, plunging the sierra into night after night of withering frosts. Nacho had left again for Palestine, and in our absence our little farm had taken on a sadly uncared-for wintry aspect. There were no more apples on the trees, no more olives, no more chestnuts. All that could be seen in the orchards were a few late persimmons, bright scarlet baubles lighting up the leafless trees. In the vegetable patch, rows of cabbages were the last crop to resist the relentless cold.

Here in this outpost of deep Spain, life and work are on a small scale. My neighbors in the village are mostly farmers working tiny patches of land, with a few vines, an olive grove, herds of goats and sheep, and fruits and vegetables for domestic consumption. But a minority of the farms operate on a much larger scale, with cattle grazing on wide estates in verdant valleys.

The Téllez family belongs in the latter category. The Téllezes run a ninety-hectare farm on the rolling plains a few kilometers outside the village of Villacolmena. Extensive beef farming is the family's main business, together with sheep, several thousand olive trees, and a guesthouse for the few intrepid tourists who make it to this western frontier country. Antonio Téllez is a villager who left for Bilbao to study and find work during the postwar period when times were especially hard. There, in the Basque country, he met his future wife, and eventually they returned with a son and three daughters to set up the farm on a property Antonio had recently inherited.

I left my house in the icy dark of a January morning, and arrived at the Téllez farm as the sun was coming up reluctantly over the sierra.

The Téllez parents and children were firm friends of mine, but unfamiliar faces loomed up out of the dawn light. The people who stood in the kitchen drinking coffee were villagers who had always helped out at matanzas in return for a daily wage or an armful of chorizos, or both. Felipe, the farmhand, was also the pig killer. Jesús would be the butcher, and his wife Petri was the main matancera, responsible for processing the meat. In the old days the expert countrywomen who came to work at matanzas were known as sabias— wise women—and were accorded a great deal of respect. One can understand why: if the matanza was mishandled, a year's supply of meat might be in jeopardy.

Petri was mopping out the matanza kitchen, a special room used only for preparing and storing the products of the day, and specially fitted out with a fireplace and a ceiling stuck with bent nails for hanging the sausages. Everything was still quiet; but not for long.

"For three days from now, everything is the matanza. Nothing else matters," murmured Petri. We were already on matanza time, and the routines and rhythms of normal life had ceased to exist. The matanza forms a whole world, a time and space of ritual and concentration. It has its own rhythm, a series of paragraphs that follow one after another with the mysterious, ineluctable logic of a dream.

Out in the countryside, the holm oaks wore a gray-green pallor, as if struck by the cold night, and a deeper gleam of green toward the trunk where the cold couldn't reach. There is no more noble Spanish tree than the holm oak, or encina: half the country is sustained by it. The pigs in their enclosure were already up, snuffling about in the short grass in the morning sun, vainly searching for any last remaining acorns, nuzzling the gate with their snouts. They were pure-bred ibéricos, floppy-eared and long-muzzled, with leathery skins of a dusty charcoal gray.

The ibérico pig is black and comely. It walks on the finest of elegant hooves, shiny and black and so delicately formed that it seems to go about on high heels. One somehow expects a semi-wild pig to look more like a wild boar: fierce and filthy, covered with thick matted hair and crashing through the undergrowth. In fact the ibérico pig is practically hairless and has a rather statuesque, refined build.

The cerdo ibérico is a descendant of the wild boar *Sus mediterraneus,* which once roamed the forests of the Mediterranean basin. For centuries it was the only pig breed of any importance in Spain, until the arrival of "white" breeds like the Duroc and Landrace from northern Europe, with their lean meat and adaptability to the new intensive farming. By the 1970s the pure ibérico pig was virtually extinct, surviving only on a few fincas that had failed to adapt to the changing times. The first denominaciones de origen in the late 1980s defined the breed as the source of the finest Spanish hams, and gradually the cerdo ibérico has made a triumphant recovery.

The ibérico pig is umbilically linked to its habitat—so much so that writers on this subject habitually use the French term *terroir* to refer to the environmental factors which make jamón ibérico de bellota what it is. The pig and the dehesa were, almost literally, made for each other. The whole process, from holm oak to ham, is in fact, as one Spanish writer wonderingly remarks, "a system so perfect that it seems almost impossible that it was achieved empirically."

The killers came out of the house, marching purposefully toward the pigsty. Toothy grins, glinting knives, a rifle loaded and ready, and a bucket to catch the blood.

"Let's go kill the pig," said Felipe, looking like Hollywood's image of a serial killer with a black rag tied around his head and a dazed, psycho smile.

"Make sure you get the blood," called Antonio from the house, "or my wife will kill you."

The next thing I knew, Felipe was inside the enclosure. He raised the gun and fired, and the first pig was down. But Felipe had picked a bad place, right beside the frozen pond. The pig tumbled straight in, smashing the ice and flailing about like a slaughtered whale, her blood dyeing the water bright red. "She's not dead yet," said Petri, in her green Carrefour apron, peering at the twitching body in the freezing water, while the menfolk swore blue murder. The second pig went better: shot clean through the brain, it dropped like a stone. Now, as her husband went for the jugular with his razor-sharp kitchen knife, Petri moved in with her bucket, stirring the bright hot blood with her hand. The blood and mud and cold of the matanza battlefield; this is the hardest moment of the day. When the others left to dispatch the third pig, I stayed on to watch the first one die, in spasms there in front of me, with a death rattle like a smoker's cough.

The three corpses were laid out on the green grass, crusted with mud and blood, ready to have the hairs burned off them with gas burners, and the first layer of epidermis blistered and scraped off with knifes and brushes. Jesús and Petri and Felipe and me, scratching and scraping the first pig's body, our nostrils full of the slaughterhouse smells of burning hair, shit, and warm meat. The depilation was leaving this gray pig ivory white, like an elegant woman at a spa.

"Better make sure we keep the cheeks," said Jesús, carefully shaving the pig's flabby chops. "They're better than the meat!" he exclaimed, declaring there and then he would grill these leathery delicacies on the barbecue and share them even with those doubters who could not see quite where their attraction lay.

He was gearing up for the day's major task: the deconstruction of the three pigs, and their classification according to body parts and types of meat: lean, gelatinous, fatty, and bony. From now on the matanza would have a new setting—a garage storeroom off the main farmyard, where the spare automobile parts, motorbikes, and power tools had been pushed back to make space for an impromptu morgue.

Jesús opened the pigs like treasure chests, revealing their caverns of pearly white lard, the steaming architecture of bone and muscle. He leaned into them and pulled out a succession of bits and pieces: the liver, a hot shiny floppy thing, seeming to cling like an octopus to the butcher's hand; the long snake of the loin, a meter-long tube of flesh; the heart, kidneys, ribs, lungs. The noble parts are handled with care: the hams and forefeet, carved away from the rest of the body and neatly trimmed, to be hung overnight and buried in salt. The ignoble parts are hauled out and flopped stinking into a sack, to be buried in the countryside and dug up by foxes.

What is this body part: spleen, thyroid, or pituitary? Distant memories of anatomy classes came swimming back into my mind; little did my teachers suspect the uses I might find for this subject. A constant stream of banter flowed around the room: what goes where, how much fat to leave, what do we do with the tails—and what about the ears? (Both tails and ears are used, in fact, for the chorizo de sábado, an embutido from southern Extremadura.) There is meat for freezing, and there are bones for stock, fat for rendering, and leftovers for the dogs.

Like any other collective creative endeavor, the matanza has a power structure and bureaucracy. Today the absent patriarch, the unseen CEO, was the farm's owner, Antonio. His wife, Ana Luz, was catering manager and *chef de cuisine*. Jesús was chief of butchery operations. Queen of the embutidos was Toni, a matancera in love with her craft and a cook of the old school who learned from her mother, worked firmly within the traditions of Extremadura, and wrote down her recipes in a girlish hand in an exercise book whose pages are now falling out.

Toni's frilly red-and-white polka-dot apron gave her a sunny southern look, like a Gypsy in Seville going off to the fair. This morning she had painted her lips bright red, to match her apron and the general bloody, cheerful redness of the day. She was a robustly handsome, good-humored Spanish woman, brimming with old-fashioned pride in her house, cooking, husband, and family.

"Remind me to give you the recipe for my lamb caldereta," she said to me confidentially as we worked side by side, knives separating lean meat for chorizo from fat for morcilla. "It's the real and authentic shepherd's caldereta. My recipes are village recipes, the ones you don't see in books. You ought to try my way with lamb chops. What I do is—I crush up garlic, parsley, black pepper, and a little bit of vinegar, and I cover the chops with this, and I leave them for a day. Then I cover the chops in flour and beaten egg, and fry them in hot oil. It's a dish for a day out in the country. I take them with me in a Tupperware box. You can eat them hot or cold."

Toni was now hard at work, trimming the fat off the long thick tube of the loin, slicing away with a practiced hand. The loin would be rubbed with garlic and pimentón and stuffed into a casing, air-cured along with the chorizos, eventually becoming what is known as lomo embuchado.

I sneaked a look at the recipe collection in her exercise book. It was an anthology of extremeño cooking the like of which, as its author had intimated, you wouldn't find in any published work. The perrunillas and dulces de chicharrones, traditional biscuits made with pork fat, olive oil, almonds, and anis, were not sweets that people ate much anymore, let alone bothered to cook. Here was a fine traditional dish made during Holy Week in Toni's hometown, Almendralejo, composed of chickpeas with chard and flavored with cumin, black pepper, garlic, vinegar, and pimentón. And here was Toni's famous caldereta de pastor. The caldereta was traditionally eaten in two parts: the thin sauce as a soup with slices of bread soaked in it, followed by the meat. Toni's recipe was a superbly authentic piece of local lore, and a powerful evocation of a farming society that has never quite forgotten its origins. The big, strong flavors of pimentón, bay leaf, garlic, and wine seemed to sum up the hard-bitten yet generous character of a region that, in the five years I have lived here, I have come to love zealously and possessively.

The name says it all: ferociously hot in summer and often miserably cold in winter, Extremadura can be an unforgiving place. For centuries its people, of whom there are fewer per square kilometer than anywhere else in Spain, have left the region in search of work, ending up in Bilbao, Barcelona, Madrid, France, Switzerland, or Germany. Most of the conquistadores of the sixteenth century, including Cortés and Pizarro, were extremeños who presumably felt they had nothing to lose by taking on the perils of the New World.

This is cattle country first and foremost. In terms of food that means three things: fresh meat, cured meat, and cheese. From the cerdo ibérico, the black-footed pig which feeds on the acorns of Extremadura's holm oak plantations, come the region's serrano hams, chorizos, and salchichones. The beef and lamb are of exceptional quality. And the cheeses are simply some of the very best in Spain. Torta del casar and its close relation torta de la serena are luxuriously gooey Vacherin-type sheep's-milk cheeses that you scoop out of the shell with a spoon, or with pieces of toast or bread in the manner of a fondue. Queso los ibores, from the hills around Guadalupe, is to my mind one of the three or four best goat cheeses in the country. Add to these the honeys of Las Hurdes, the cherries of El Jerte, olive oil, game, wild mushrooms, figs, asparagus, and some increasingly highly rated wines, and you have a larder well stocked with good things.

There is one local product, though, that eclipses all others. The fame of pimentón has crossed both national and international boundaries. When Emperor Charles V built his monastery retreat at Yuste, amid the fertile valleys of La Vera, Extremadura became a natural point of entry for the plants and products of the New World. None of these was to have such importance in the future development of Spanish cuisine (apart from the tomato, of course) as the pepper and its large extended family. Pimentón de La Vera is a spice produced by drying peppers over a smoldering fire of holm oak logs and grinding them to a powder. It has various gradations of heat, from dulce (sweet) through agridulce (bittersweet) to picante (hot), and gradations of color from fiery blood-orange to rust-red and ecclesiastical crimson.

Together with saffron, pimentón is a quintessential Spanish flavoring. (They are the colors of the flag, deep yellow and pomegranate red.) It is certainly the one that most Spanish cooks would not be without. It is ubiquitous in kitchens across the country, from Galicia, where life would grind to a halt without its presence in pulpo a feira; to the Balearic Islands, where I have used catering bags of the stuff to make the raw pork sausage sobrassada (pimentón is a powerful natural preservative).

In my kitchen at home I often use pimentón in summer gazpachos, chutneys, and pickles, and in a marinade for cured olives. My experiments have taught me that rubbing a leg of lamb with a pimentón, garlic, and olive oil paste before roasting gives the meat a tandoori-like fragrance and tenderness. Even a humble fried egg can be given a lift by whisking a generous pinch of pimentón and a little salt and pepper into the remaining olive oil and drizzling this sauce over the egg. A salad of cooked yellow French beans, chopped boiled egg, and yellow tomatoes is stunningly transformed by a blood-red pimentón vinaigrette—an idea I stole from chef Marcelo Tejedor at Casa Marcelo in Santiago de Compostela.

And pimentón, without a doubt, constitutes the soul of the matanza. When Saint Martin's tide comes around in Spain, the pimentón factories of La Vera see their stocks dwindle as matanceros all over the country buy the big bags they will need for making their chorizos, their sobrassadas, and their lomos embuchados.

A shiny two-kilo bag of pimentón stood on the sideboard in the matanza kitchen at the farm, ready for whatever use we might find for it. Now the wooden trough called the artesa came into its own. This traditional object persists in rural areas as a mixing vessel for large quantities of food, and in the cities it has already become a chic decorative item.

Now the matanceras from the village were down on their knees at the artesa, kneading the greasy sausage mixture as if it were dough. They were up to the elbows in it, their arms stained an unlikely orange. This would be the filling for the chorizos, flavored with pimentón and mashed garlic.

"You always add a little water. The pimentón is dry, it takes in moisture," said Petri, puffing after her energetic workout.

There are no recipes—it is all done first by eye, then by taste. How much garlic? How much salt? "Lo que pide," says Nieves: what it asks for. Nothing is prescribed. The measurements are a lot, less than that, a little, a handful more. Experienced mixers can tell by the color it leaves on your hands, when examined in the cold white light of a winter afternoon.

The proof of the pudding, or of the chorizo and morcilla, is in the eating. In Spanish it is called la prueba. A little of the mixture is fried in a small pan, and tasted for the balance of its seasoning. Is it short on garlic, pimentón, or salt? More of whatever is required is added to the mixture. If the prueba still has a purpose in the functional apparatus of the matanza, it has now also become a popular dish in its own right.

A little more of this and that. Humming and hah-ing over the various recipes. The prueba is always a rich seam of controversy and argument. This should be saltier. This can take a little bit more black pepper. This needs more pimentón; this has quite enough already! The sizzling, spicy orange mixture is sampled direct from the pan, forks together in the general eagerness to try a mouthful with a slice of bread. Somebody had brought homemade wine in a two-liter Fanta bottle with the label still on, and we took big swigs from plastic cups besmeared with grease.

What with all the talk of food, and the appetite you work up during a matanza morning, the prueba serves as a fine excuse for a late-morning snack.

But now the various mixtures were ready, and the time had come to wash our hands and arms, remove our orange-stained aprons, and sit down to eat a proper lunch.

In the old days, everything about the matanza was programmed with the precision of a religious rite—even the food, which in Villacolmena was served and eaten according to a cast-iron routine. The breakfast on a matanza morning was migas with glasses of aguardiente. Every porcophile village in Spain has its own plato matancero—the dish made at midday on matanza days. Here in Villacolmena it was kidneys and brains, with a pounded majao of garlic and bread crumbs. And in the afternoon, roscas fritas, an egg dough with lard and anis, fried crisp in virgin olive oil.

"Before, when we finished in the evening, we had chocolate with churros, like when we finished with the olives, and we used to sing songs," Petri reminisced.

"How the old things come back into fashion!" cried Antonio. "What I remember is the mojo de naranja, the orange salad with olive oil and onions, which nowadays you find in the best restaurants. I used to eat it for breakfast as a child, when my mother came back with the milk."

Cooking is a reflection of personal circumstances, a codified version of everything you are in genes, history, and taste. Ana Luz grew up in Bilbao, and the dishes she feels closest to are the classics of Basque cuisine: salt cod al pil-pil and a la vizcaina, hake in green sauce. A woman of substance, efficiency, and a rough-hewn generosity, the way Basque women often are, Ana Luz doesn't just use her kitchen; she inhabits it. If I think for a moment, I can summon up the memory of her piquillo peppers stuffed with crab . . . a sumptuous flan made with milk from the farm's house cow . . . and a phenomenal dish of veal with artichokes, based on a sofrito of tomato and onion, a dish that anthologizes all the organic, exuberant flavors of spring. Trays of pintxos emerge from Ana Luz's kitchen, as good as anything you might find at a bar-top buffet in San Sebastián. Her croquetas are sublime nuggets with a creamy filling, creatively deploying not only chopped ham and chicken, the essential traditional croqueta ingredients, but chopped mussels, bacalao, boiled egg, partridge, and—best of all—the shredded leftover meat from the Sunday cocido.

When Ana Luz married Antonio and made the move southward, her cooking naturally responded to the change. In her new home there was little seafood to be had, and the cuisine has none of the refinement of Basque tradition, but there was a tremendous quantity and quality of meat. Now she was making caldereta, and rich sticky stews from gelatinous cuts of pork and beef. Today for lunch she served liver with onions; slices of goat cheese in olive oil; cuttlefish in an inky-black sauce; and esparragao, a hearty country dish of cabbage and potato quick-simmered with olive oil, garlic, and pimentón. It was the first time she had ever made the esparragao—an extremeño dish—but the villagers approved entirely. They nodded their heads as they ate: Sí, señor, this was a good esparragao, even if Ana Luz's addition of thin-sliced fried panceta struck them as a sophisticated departure from the norm.

After lunch there were coffee and walnut turrón, but there was no lingering at the table. With weary steps we made our way back to the matanza kitchen. Outside, the afternoon was as cold and dark as lead. Our nerves were a little frayed, our senses a little dulled by the copious food and wine. But the last, longest, trickiest, and most important process of the matanza now awaited us.

We stood around the table, each with a role to play. While one turned the handle of the big cast-iron meat grinder, forcing the mix down a spiral and into the skins, another tied the strings in a double knot, another pricked the sausages with a cork stuck with pins, to release the air trapped inside, and a gofer fetched the curling lengths of shiny sausage from the heap on the table and hung them up in ranks from the ceiling. How thoughtful of nature to provide, as part of the generous package of the pig, not only the meat for sausages, but also the containers with which to make them.

These are repetitive, fussy tasks, and an atmosphere of quiet badinage develops, in which the subjects for discussion are the difference between women and men; illnesses; gossip in the village; and, most commonly, the various ways the matanza is performed in the villages of the region, and memorable matanzas of the past.

The timing of the event, earlier or later in the season, is a constant source of comment.

"Have you already killed? Yes, we killed last week."

"On Monday my sister-in-law is killing."

"We usually kill in the month of January."

After an hour or two of purposeful stuffing, tying, knotting, and pricking, we were finally done.

For the residents of the farm, there was still plenty of work ahead. The chorizos and salchichones were turning slowly darker in the air, shrinking, hardening, and drying. They would have to be checked on, smoked a little with the coals from the grate if the humidity went too high, and sprinkled with pimentón if a crack appeared in the skin. Walking into the storeroom a month after the matanza, when the roof is garlanded with sausages and filled with the marvelous aroma of the curing meats, one has a moment of surprise at discovering all the bounty that has appeared there, as if by magic. There would be hams to salt and dry, and bags of meat to freeze, and lard to clarify, and the best of all the Spanish sausages to make. Ana Luz's family has roots in Villarcayo, heartland of morcilla de Burgos, which she still makes at the farm according to the original recipe, with pig's blood, poached onion, cooked rice, and a generous amount of allspice, clove, and black pepper.

But for the support team, the helpers, the matanza was over for another twelve months—and thank goodness, really, that it happens only once a year. I climbed stiffly into the car with a Tupperware box full of prueba to try some other time. My hands felt soft and supple on the driving wheel. All those hours with the pork fat had served as a luxurious manicure.

I turned on the engine, the heater, and the music. A profound tiredness had taken hold in me, and I felt a powerful need to avoid animal fats for a while. I may be a practicing porcophile, but the matanza certainly tests the limits of your love for pork products, pigs, and so on. What with all the bean stews, gachas, and migas, the dense country foods I'd been eating in recent weeks, I felt like one of those ibérico pigs, fattening up for slaughter.

Then and there, as I sat in the car with the engine running, I modified my travel plan. In my journeying around Spain's wide interior I had picked up rural essences galore—most of them based on fats and proteins, the building blocks of rural food. Yet Spanish country cooking is not all pork and pork fat. It is also vegetables, and, depending on the region, these play as important a role as meat in the nourishment of the rural community. Now I promised myself a break from the hard-core culinary culture I'd been immersed in of late. I would wait for spring to bring in its first fruits, and then I would head for a place that really knows its onions, and its lettuces and artichokes: the vegetable paradise of Navarre.

Navarre

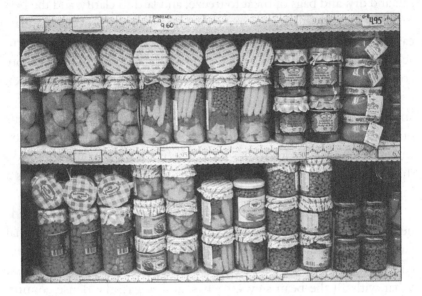

FOR MOST OF the winter in most of Spain, the range of available greens shrinks to a minimum of cabbages and other brassicas, chard, spinach, and leeks, plus anything the resourceful householder has been able to preserve over the summer. Then in February or March, a wave of early vegetables ripples across the country, beginning in the coastal zones of the south and east, where the first peas, beans, asparagus, and artichokes are celebrated like homecoming heroes.

Six weeks had gone by since the matanza. In the mountains of the west, winter clung on, determined to sit it out till the solstice, leaving its calling card of hoarfrost on the fields and hedges around my house.

Driving east cross-country was like watching the year in fast-forward. In Palencia it was still arctic winter; there was snow on the roofs of the old town, and passersby were swathed in fur and wool. Tractors were out in the arable plains around Burgos, sowing the first wheat under skies of a tentative blue. And when I crossed into La Rioja it was as though spring had arrived just that morning. As I waited at a traffic light in Navarrete, I noticed an old gentleman pricking out tomato plants in his back garden. The light turned green. And I thought: the whole of Spain will soon be turning green.

I HAD ONLY one contact in Tudela, but if you happen to be interested in vegetables, the king of vegetables is a pretty good contact to have.

Tudela is a good-looking medieval town with a distinguished cast of historical characters, chief among them being the twelfth-century mathematician and astrologer Abraham ibn Ezra, and the traveler Benjamin of Tudela, whose grand tour of the world's Jewish communities is recorded in his famous *Itinerary*. What had brought me to Tudela, however, was not culture, history, or famous names, but salad. A sad sign of the times it may be, but these days, Tudela is a good deal better known by the vast majority of the population for its cogollo, a sweet crisp lettuce, than for the life and works of its medieval thinkers.

I steered the car up into the dusty labyrinth of the old town, shuddered to a halt in a parking lot beside the cathedral, and called the only number I had at my disposal. Floren Damenzain was out, but his secretary answered the phone, and directed me to a bar where, she said, I was sure to find something interesting to eat. The bar in question was the José Luis, just around the corner from the town's main square, where I ordered a beer and a selection of the bar's splendid pinchos, which had all won prizes in a local contest. All were based on vegetables—as they would be, for Tudela is one of the great horticultural centers of Spain. I began with a miniature brochette, with tomato, prawn, and fried leek all wrapped in a spinach leaf on a wooden stick; a nugget of soft cheese rolled in a thin slice of ham and another thin slice of zucchini, the whole thing coated in bread crumbs and deep-fried; and a Swiss chard stem stuffed with thickly creamy béchamel and served straight from the kitchen, sizzling from the hot olive oil. I sat in the sun and watched the tudelanos go by, hurrying to get things done before the shops and offices clanged shut at two o'clock.

Now I needed a proper lunch followed by a proper siesta, to get me back on track. I made my way up to the Plaza de los Fueros and, finding a busy dining room where the lunchtime shift was well under way, headed straight inside with a dazed conviction that this, for sure, would be a good place to sample the rustic cooking of Tudela.

The Hostal Remigio was a straightforward establishment which turned out to have two main things to recommend it: the interior decor, and the food. It had been functioning as a simple lodging house since 1936, and was now in the hands of the Salcedo Zabalza family, who had brought the old place thoroughly up to date but had sensibly left its original wood-paneled dining room intact. The room was a fizz of activity on this Friday afternoon, with black-trousered waiters darting around like wasps. One of them brought me a plastic-covered menu, which I gazed at dumbly for a while, not quite able to believe what I was reading. Far from the standard Spanish eating-house fare—brimming bowls of lentil stew and slabs of meat with french fries and salad—the menu at the Hostal Remigio was a showcase for all that is best in the cuisine of this southern corner of Navarre. For anyone who loves vegetables, this was heaven: there were broad beans, peas, and artichokes five ways; little red piquillo peppers stuffed with spider crab, asparagus, spinach, and Swiss chard; cardoons in almond sauce; borage stems (borraja, a hairy-leafed vegetable unique to the communities of Navarre and Aragon); and scrambled eggs made with the season's first tender garlic. It sounded wonderful, and a wave of contentment rolled over me. I ordered a plate of cogollos, the crisp sweet lettuce hearts which had after all brought me to Tudela—they were draped with salted anchovies and dressed with olive oil. I also had a soup bowl of white baby onions a la tudelana, simmered in their own juices with olive oil and black pepper until they were tender enough to be swallowed after just one chew; and a medley of spring vegetables stir-fried separately and briefly bubbled up together: the menestra so characteristic of Navarrese and Riojano cooking. After all this, and most of a bottle of cold rosado, the wine that Navarre has always specialized in, I barely had the energy to pay the bill, inquire whether the hostal had a room for the night, and haul myself up to the third floor and the siesta I had been dreaming of all day. When I woke it was evening, and the day had embarked on the long preamble to a late, languid sunset.

Just outside the walls of the old town lay an expanse of flatland called La Mejana, where the Arabs and Jews who populated the city in its glory days of the twelfth century kept their vegetable gardens in the rich alluvial soil of the Ebro valley. The Ebro River is born in the mountains of Cantabria, and reaches the sea at the southernmost tip of Catalonia, where rice is grown amid the sluggish waters of its oozing delta. Between Logroño and Saragossa it runs along a wide flat valley, a thick ribbon of green between the dry hills to the north and south. The town of Tudela, the second most important in Navarre (after the capital, Pamplona) sits directly on the Ebro, with a stone bridge across. I walked halfway over and stopped to admire this handsome river, swelling with khaki-colored water, and thought about the benefits it brings to the vegetable farmers of the ribera, as this riverine region is known, who irrigate their crops directly with these waters. To my left lay the sprawling Mejana, a district of private huertas, all with neat rows of onions, lettuces, broad beans, and garlic; thickets of artichokes; fig trees flourishing in quiet corners; and quinces clinging to the fences.

The huertas were a series of intimate worlds made private by hedges and high stone walls. Some had little pavilions for lazy Sundays, as well as swimming pools and flower-fringed lawns. I found an open door and stepped inside, surprising an elderly man and his son who were busy watering their patch, directing the river water down long channels between the rows. There was a two-story little old house at the river end of the plot, with whitewashed arches and a weathercock turning creakily above the clay-tiled roof. Such casitas would have been used for storing potatoes, onions, tools, and other paraphernalia; their upper floors were an architectural response to the Ebro's periodic flooding.

Here was a scene of Spain at its most bucolic. The old man, with his shirt unbuttoned, stood leaning on the handle of his mattock. Beside him was an apricot tree, its branches bowed down with fruit. He handed me a couple of apricots as the water filled the channel around the tree: they were crisp and barely ripe but sweet, a foretaste of summer.

I wondered whom all this plenty was for: himself, or the market?

"For the family. We don't sell. All my daughters are married, so . . ." He left his explanation hanging, leaving me to form an idea of the demand for vegetables this situation naturally implied. His nearest and dearest would be well supplied, in any case, by this grand *huerta* in which everything was huge and healthy, from the giant cabbages that squeaked when the breeze blew over their fleshy hearts to the deep green glossy leaves of Swiss chard, wide and wrinkly as elephants' ears.

"In the old days we used to take all this stuff in to market. I had a cart with iron wheels. The roads were dirt tracks. You should have heard the noise! The carts full of artichokes. Vegetables mean everything to Tudela, everything. Why, this town was built on them! Nowhere else has artichokes like ours, or lettuces, or chard. It's the river, you see, the river. Sweet water. Good water."

He took up his mattock and swung it down into the earth, pulling open the channel that ran between two long rows of garlic plants. Their leaves were thick and fleshy; the white bulbs were still forming in the warm soil.

"José, keep that water coming!" he called to his son. "Never let it stop!"

EMILIA PARDO BAZÁN, in her prologue to *La Cocina Española Antigua* (1913), declares that the central virtues of Spanish cooking are "its strong clear flavors, without the ambiguity of sauces and dressings; its picturesque variety according to the regions; its perfect adaptation to the climate and the necessities of man," and, last but not least, its "vegetarian tendency, perhaps owed to religious ideas and heat."

I admire the concision of her phrase "religious ideas and heat," which nicely sums up two of the major determinants of Spanish eating over the centuries, and it seems to me she is right about the "vegetarian tendency"—even though vegetarianism in its literal sense is little practiced and still an object of puzzlement or hilarity among the older generation. Spain has no trouble whatsoever eating up its greens, and vegetable-based dishes account for a respectable percentage of the national repertoire.

If visitors to Spain are not often impressed by the range and quality of vegetable cookery, this is probably because they are not often brought into close contact with it. Vegetables here tend to be associated with the honestly nutritive virtues of domestic cookery, as opposed to the more elaborate or highly flavored food you might want to eat outside the home. I would suggest that, though they might be ashamed of admitting it, many Spaniards have a secret love of las verduras that goes above and beyond the thrills provided by more superficially exciting foods.

Vegetables in Spain are most commonly fried or boiled, but you also often find them baked, charcoal-grilled, or raw. The technique of rehogado—briefly sautéing a previously steamed or boiled vegetable with a little chopped ham or garlic—is often applied to Swiss chard or green beans. Chopped serrano ham is also a classic flavoring for broad beans (this is the essence of the granadino dish habas con jamón) as well as peas. Peppers, eggplants, and zucchinis are commonly stuffed with chopped meat, rice, or fish—especially in the Balearic Islands and the province of Valencia. The stuffed pimiento de piquillo is a classic of the Basque-speaking regions of the north (including Navarre). Root vegetables are most often found as ingredients of cocidos and similar pulse-based stews, or else in thick winter soups, purés, cremas, and potajes. The tenderest green peppers, such as Galicia's pimiento de Padrón, can be flash-fried in sizzling olive oil. When summer arrives and the body craves refreshment, the southern Spanish repertoire of ice-cold soups naturally and gratifyingly comes into its own. But the best way of treating summer vegetables is surely the charcoal grill, which both brings out their natural sweetness and overlays it with the scent of wood smoke. One of my all-time favorite vegetable dishes is the Catalan escalivada—the word derives from escaliu, meaning hot coals—which combines roasted peppers, eggplant, and onion, hand-peeled and shredded, dressed with olive oil and vinegar in a richly harmonious salad that sits perfectly alongside other grilled items such as lamb chops or fresh pork sausages.

An unmistakable aura of piety hovers over the vegetable kingdom, and this is partly a legacy of Catholic attitudes toward nutrition and morality. Put simply, whereas meat excited the sensual appetite, vegetables were thought conducive to virtue. As Reay Tannahill points out in her *Food in History,* for much of western history meat, eggs, and dairy products were prohibited by the church not only during the forty days of Lent, but also on Wednesdays, Fridays, and Saturdays—half the days of the year. For a great majority of the population, therefore, vegetables would have been a nearly constant presence on the family table, especially from Ash Wednesday until Easter Sunday. The grand vegetable dishes of the Spanish repertoire, such as spinach with pine nuts and raisins, and cardoons in almond sauce, clearly derive from the fast-day traditions of the Catholic calendar.

It is true that, while sometimes accorded a supporting role, vegetables are almost never the stars of the show. Most regions have at least one fetish vegetable, lusted after as something especially delicious: in Galicia it would be turnip tops, in Catalonia spring onions, and in parts of the Basque country, the long green chilies that are preserved in vinegar and are popularly known as langostinos de tierra ("prawns of the earth"). Only in a few places, however, is the vegetable kingdom as a whole given the respect it deserves.

One such place is Murcia, where, as we have seen, lettuces and beans are munched the way chocolate bars are eaten elsewhere—as a delicious and self-indulgent snack. Another place is the strip of land that runs along both sides of the Ebro River, especially in the 100 or so kilometers from Logroño to Saragossa, where the river is middle-aged and big-bellied and can afford to be generous with its waters. The Ribera del Ebro belongs essentially to two autonomous communities: Navarre and La Rioja. Here, more than anywhere else in Spain, vegetables not only aspire to the condition of meat or fish, but are actually valued more highly than either.

FLOREN DAMENZAIN was on a roll. It was a Saturday, and he was in his weekend mode—but then Floren's weekend mode was not, perhaps, very different from his weekday mode. He sat squarely at the wheel of his black Mercedes; playing music at top volume; cruising down the straight roads of southern Navarre as if they were American highways; and shouting into the hands-free whenever the thing went off, as it did every few minutes.

Floren was what in Spain is known as todo un personaje: quite a character. On the day I met him he wore a pink T-shirt with a pattern of Caribbean palm trees and scuffed black snakeskin moccasins with the backs trodden down. His hair was pulled back into a Status Quo style. His wide, wicked grin revealed teeth that appeared to justify the American view of European dentistry.

"Are you feeling cold? Thirsty?" he called. He flipped a couple of switches, and a panel in the backseat folded down to reveal a fridge stocked with beers and Cokes. He flipped another switch, and I felt a pleasant glow along my spine from the Merc's heated seats.

If Floren Damenzain tends to call a spade a spade, it must be because he knows better than most people just exactly what a spade is for. He was raised in a farming family in the village of Arguedas, on the edge of the desertlike landscape of the Bárdenas Reales, a popular location for scenes in movies whose production budgets won't stretch to real western deserts. There were six children in the family. Floren, the youngest, began a course at agricultural college, but his father's illness forced him to take over the family's 100-hectare farm with its mixed plantings of cereal and table vegetables.

"I had no idea about distribution or anything. I was a farmer, that's all. When the land started bringing in a bit of cash, I started up my business. At first it was all stuff from around here, peppers, artichokes, chicory, borrajas, cardoons, asparagus, cogollo. . . . I was going around in a van, just me, with a load of artichokes and salad. And that's how all this started."

He scrabbled in the side pocket of the car door and pulled out a thick folder lavishly illustrated with close-up photos of sexy veggies in appealing poses, a pair of hands cradling the dirt. As a sales catalog it was an impressive document, with various lists of vegetables, both local and imported: fifteen different peppers, forty different salad greens, azuki beans, arbutus fruit, and kumquats. The inside cover was a collage of photographs showing Floren with some of the important chefs who, in the eighteen years since the birth of the business, had become his loyal clients. I recognized Nacho Manzano, Manolo de la Osa, and Ferran Adrià. Some had added a tribute. Martín Berasategui, proprietor of the three-star Michelin restaurant of the same name in Lasarte, outside San Sebastián, was pictured alongside the king of vegetables. "Good cooking begins with the good raw materials of my friend Floren," chef Berasategui had written.

We pulled off the main road and went down a dirt track among fields of artichokes, waving prickly heads above the jagged fronds of their leaves.

A structure loomed ahead, a polyhedral building of wood and concrete. Construction was well under way for a splendid restaurant—no, more than a restaurant, a stately pleasure dome in which diners could sample the glories of the local produce as prepared by Floren himself.

His restaurant would be called, with a logic that was hard to refute, "The Temple of Vegetables." The menu would center on what was grown right here in the huerta: the giant red cardoons banked up with a miniature mountain of earth; the salad greens, beans, and borrajas; and, naturally, the artichokes, grown just beyond the plate-glass windows separating the client from the countryside. Diners at the Temple would be invited to pick the vegetables themselves before eating, just as you choose a lobster from a tank.

Next, we were on our way back to Floren's apartment, going through streets full of ritzy design shops and cover-girl hairdressers (Tudela seemed to be flush with money, much of it from agriculture). At home, he was planning to prepare for me a special menú degustación based on the produce of the ribera. Floren's skill in the kitchen is attested to by everyone who knows him—not least by himself. Of all his brothers and sisters, he was the one who paid most attention to their mother in Arguedas, and to her loving interpretation of Navarrese classics such as bacalao ajoarriero and vegetable menestra. He was a self-taught cook, but this fact had not stood in the way of his talent; nor had it lessened his covert influence on chefs of worldwide renown. How many times had he received a desperate phone call from some chef who was uninspired, at a loss, or bewildered by an exotic herb that had just arrived from Floren?

Half an hour later we were sitting in Floren's flat, which was nicely decorated with modern furnishings from Tudela's most fashionable design emporiums. My host disappeared into the kitchen and shut the door behind him, leaving me to chat with his girlfriend and an old friend, Fernando, from Saragossa who wasted no time in inviting us all back to his place for a feast of snails on Sunday afternoon.

The kitchen door opened, and out burst the chef, bearing the first two courses of his special menu: a partridge salad made with his own buttery, crisp cogollos; a nest of tender borage stalks on a creamy potato and olive oil puree; and a square white plate piled with the thickest, whitest, sweetest asparagus stems I had ever tasted, dressed with a fruity, uncomplicated local olive oil.

"You are eating the real, the genuine asparagus of Navarre. You'll remember this taste for many years," declared my host.

Then came a bowl of fresh artichoke hearts, steamed until they were so tender that they melted in the mouth. The flavor was intense, pure, and concentrated—as was that of the next dish, tiny peas stewed quickly in their own juice, with nothing more than a spoonful of finely chopped jamón ibérico de bellota to offset their almost dessert-like sweetness.

"Just what is it that makes the vegetables of the ribera the way they are?" I asked Floren.

He took up his catalog and jabbed his finger at what has become his company's selling line, slogan, or catchphrase: Tierra, Agua, y Sol ("earth, water, and sun"). It's obvious—the point is that nothing influences the taste of a vegetable more than its natural environment. "The soil might be clay-based, chalky, or sandy. Each has its advantages: chalky soil makes the best asparagus; clay the best tomatoes, borrajas, and peppers. Soil quality, plus fresh water. And there's something else: we have the best professionals. From the root to the flower and the death of the plant. From the foundations of the house to the pillars of the roof," said Floren. He was sounding rather mysterious now. Nonetheless, I got the point. It was a question of thorough understanding, of being close to the process from start to finish.

For the people of the Ebro valley, the vegetable kingdom is a fiesta all year round.

"If you were to knock on the door on a weekday lunchtime at any house in the ribera, what would you find on the table?" asked Fernando, the Aragonese, while Floren was busy in the kitchen.

"For sure, if it was winter you'd find chicory, broccoli, cauliflower, cabbage. If it was springtime, asparagus and artichoke. If it was next week, the first pochas." The pocha is a local phenomenon, a bean that is eaten neither fresh nor dried but somewhere in between.

"Everyone around here has his own huerto," said Floren as he came back with the coffeepot. "You might be a builder or electrician, but you're bound to have some little patch to grow your lettuces in, your borrajas, your beans." Only about 10 percent of all the vegetables consumed in the ribera are actually bought at shops and markets. The rest comes through a network of friends and neighbors who are happy to swap a kilo of borrajas for a bag of artichokes or a box of cogollos. We are talking not about economies of scale, cooperatives, or even business as such, but about a return to appreciating things for their taste rather than their monetary value—with the added thrill, irresistible to most Spaniards, of being delicately poised on the edge of illegality.

Back in the Merc, Floren put on a CD. It was his own group, Barricada, in the days when he used to play guitar with what was, in the early 1980s, one of Spain's most renowned heavy metal bands. "Track 1" came up on the screen, and from just behind my right ear emerged a blast of grinding heavy metal, the bass sounding like somebody moving furniture. Floren was up on stage again, his ponytail flying as he nodded in time.

We were heading out of town in the late afternoon. Our destination was a secret, but I had an idea Floren meant to take me to the house in Arguedas where his story began, the sprawling house where the family kept twenty mules in a stable on the ground floor, and Floren's mum gave him his bottle at intervals during her hard work in the artichoke fields.

Floren pressed a button on the panel and the sunroof slid open. He pushed up his wraparound sunglasses and slid the gearshift back into fourth, and we sped away through fields of artichokes turning turquoise-gray in the setting sun.

12

Catalonia

WHEN GENERALÍSIMO FRANCISCO FRANCO died in 1975 and his faltering regime finally crumbled, there were a lot of questions that needed answering. One of the most urgent questions concerned nothing less than the geopolitical organization of the country in a future democratic state. How to give back to the Spanish regions the sense of identity and political autonomy that had been so rigorously suppressed by the Franco regime, while safeguarding the unity of the country as a whole?

The solution reached by the post-Franco administration was a brilliant one. The new Spain would be a federal state composed of individual regions, each of which would enjoy a measure of autonomy—the comunidades autónomas. The great virtue of the system was its flexibility: provinces with little sense of their own identity, such as Castilla y León or Murcia, would be able to exist side by side with regions with a long, distinct history that felt themselves actually to be nations, such as the Basque country or Catalonia. The Catalan and Basque "statutes of autonomy" of 1979 were the beginning of an extraordinary process of national self-discovery. Regional languages and cultures, as well as political institutions, that had spent forty years in hibernation were quickly reborn in all their variegated glory.

By their very nature the various regional cuisines of Spain had been harder for the dictatorship to suppress—you could hardly have a guardia civil watching over every Basque, Catalan, and Galician stove —but they had certainly fallen into desuetude. Now they reemerged as a proud assertion of regional identity. The Catalan nationalist Ferran Agulló (1863–1933) once declared, "Catalonia is a nation because it has a language, a legal system, and a cuisine of its own." For Manuel Vázquez Montalbán, the novelist and gastrónomo, a major achievement of the devolution of power to the "autonomies" has been the effort expended by each region to rediscover and celebrate its own gastronomy. "The Spanish restaurateur has been obliged to bring back traditional cooking in response to the tastes of his avant-garde clientele, and it's thanks to this social pressure that Spain has not turned into a leathery hamburger, bordering on the quiche lorraine to the north and the couscous to the south."

Which of Spain's regional cuisines is the best? This question has caused almost as many arguments over dining tables as whether Franco actually did anything good for the country. This really has no answer beyond the equivocal, and boring, notion that each cuisine has its own strengths and weaknesses; each is remarkable in its own way.

Ask which cuisine is most highly developed, and the question becomes a little easier. Along with the Basque country, Catalonia surely possesses the richest traditional cuisine on the peninsula and, currently, is taking the most decisive steps to protect its heritage. Each of the four Catalan provinces—Barcelona, Tarragona, Lérida, and Gerona—has a distinct culinary personality, and that of Gerona, as we shall see, is especially idiosyncratic. Unlike most other cuisines in

Spain, this one has not just a rural background, but also an urban context of hostels, popular eating houses, and the homes of the bourgeoisie. Its range and variety are enormous. Pepa Aymamí, of the Catalan Institute of Cooking, estimates that there may be as many as 150 individual dishes in the local repertoire, although the majority of them are little known by the population at large.

Of all the regional culinary traditions of Spain, moreover, there is no doubt which has the most distinguished history. La cuina catalana was experiencing its first golden age when the great modern cuisines of Europe were as yet unformed. During the fourteenth and fifteenth centuries Catalan cooking occupied roughly the position in the international gastronomic league that classic French cuisine has today. Some of the most important cookbooks of the Middle Ages were written by Catalans in their own language; and the medieval Catalan cuisine enjoyed a reputation equaled only by the Italian (with which it shared a number of dishes and techniques, including pasta). *Llibre del Coch,* written by Robert (or Rupert) de Nola, the Catalan cook at the court of Fernando, king of Naples, was first published in Barcelona in 1520, and in its Castilian version it became a bestseller for the next 100 years. And the heritage of Catalan cooking goes back even further than this, to one of the earliest surviving cookbooks written in a European language, the legendary *Llibre de Sent Soví* of 1324, otherwise known as *De Totes Maneres de Potatges de Menjar* ("Of All Ways of Eating Pottages").

A few years ago I was lucky enough to see one of the two surviving original copies of the *Llibre de Sent Soví.* I carefully turned its parchment pages and attempted to decipher a few passages of its difficult language and calligraphy. It is bound together with several other medieval texts; has no title page as such and no apparent start or finish; and is such a mass of black inky script that you ask yourself whether this can really be the document that you have come to see. But then half-familiar words begin to swim out of the chaos. *Si vols fer*: if you want to make. *En altra manera*: in another manner. *Espinachs; macarrons; alberginies.*

The maddening vagueness and disorder of the *Llibre de Sent Soví* make you wonder how much genuine use it can have been to the cooks of the fourteenth century. Quantities seem arbitrary; timings are nonexistent. That said, it contains recipes which sound not only intriguing but perfectly plausible. *Brou de gallines* is a chicken soup, given a touch of the Middle East by the addiction of ginger and almonds. (Spices like nutmeg, mace, coriander, and hyssop were used more freely in European cooking during this period than at any other time until the late twentieth century.) You could use the recipe for rice pudding with almonds and cinnamon without altering a word.

More than particular dishes, however, it's the techniques that have survived. Fundamental to Catalan cooking both then and now, for instance, are the sofregit and picada, the beginning and end of most Catalan dishes. The sofregit is essentially a sauté of onions and tomato (the *Llibre de Sent Sovi* calls for onions and occasionally cansalada— fatty bacon) forming the base of a stew or casserole. The picada is a mixture of various ingredients, including nuts, herbs, and spices, fried bread, garlic, sweet biscuits, and even chocolate, which are pounded together in a pestle and mortar and added to a dish toward the end of the cooking time, to give texture and flavor to the sauce.

A great number of the 200 or so recipes in the *Llibre de Sent Sovi* call for sugar or honey, whether the dish happens to be savory, in our modern conception of the term, or sweet. The Catalan cuisine of today, too, particularly that of the province of Gerona (known as "old" Catalonia), nonchalantly confuses entrées and desserts. We find pears and apples stuffed with spiced ground meat—the rellenos of the Ampurdán region, around Gerona. The botifarra dolça, another Ampurdanese speciality, is a pork sausage made so sweet and sticky with sugar and spices that it almost crosses the line into a dessert. Compare this with the English mincemeat, which started as just that, spiced sweetened chopped meat, and ended up as a pudding.

WITH THE POSSIBLE EXCEPTION of Asturias, where every weekend of the year brings a fair or fiesta devoted to some aspect or ingredient of the traditional cooking, no region but Catalonia is so thoroughly convinced of the need to celebrate the excellence of its own gastronomy.

The four provinces of Spanish Catalonia are so rich in gastronomic fiestas that the Generalitat, the Catalan regional government, edits a special agenda giving details of everything from the Hazelnut Fair in Riudoms to the Gastronomic Days of the Potato in Palafolls, the Apple Fiesta in Barbens, and the Festival of Renaissance Gastronomy in Tortosa. The passing year in Catalonia is a whirl of celebrations of turnips, peas, mushrooms, chestnuts, snails, chocolate, doughnuts, sardines, sausages, and so on. Such a celebration is often referred to as an aplec—a uniquely Catalan concept, combining a vindication, workshop, and party. Almost every Catalan dish of note has its own aplec, usually in the town or village most closely associated with it.

The king of them all is the calçotada. This custom was born in Valls, outside Tarragona, but has now spread as far as Barcelona. It began, like many of the world's most appealing culinary inventions, as a way of making good use of an ingredient that would otherwise have gone to waste—in this case, the onions which were missed by the harvesters in the autumn, remained in the ground over the winter and in January or February, gave forth green sprouts from the old bulbs. In a wine-producing region where vine prunings were a traditional barbecue fuel, the idea of grilling these tender "stockings" would have seemed logical enough. The true stroke of genius was the sauce that, over time, became the accompaniment for grilled calçots. Essentially a kind of romesco, originally from Tarragona, calçot sauce is a rich picada of toasted hazelnuts and almonds, sweet ñora pepper, tomato, garlic, olive oil, and the flesh of a tomato roasted over the same fire on which the calçots are grilling. When the calçots are removed from the coals, their outer layers charred and blackened, they do not look especially appetizing. Peel off the burned skin, however, and the interior is pellucid, tender, and sweet. The idea now is to dunk the onion in the sauce and guzzle it by throwing your head back and dangling the calçot into your waiting jaws. The oily, nutty, faintly spicy sauce and the partly caramelized spring onion form a strikingly delicious combination. It almost comes as a surprise to discover that the recipe wasn't born in the mind of a clever modernist chef but emerged from the collective consciousness of a traditional rural society.

Masia Bou is where the calçotada began. The Masia was the farm-house of the Gatell family, who specialized in growing onions. The earliest calçotades were gatherings of friends or extended families, during the winter and early spring when the onion sprouts from last year's bulbs were at their juicy best. Over time the calçot fashion grew and grew, the Masia transformed itself from farmhouse into restaurant, and now the old place is a gigantic catering operation, a temple to the gluttonous delights of the calçotada.

To get to Catalonia from Navarre, I had roughly followed the Ebro River down its long, broad valley, from its vigorous middle age in Saragossa to its exhausted dotage in the sprawling delta where it finally meets the sea. In the hills around Valls, you could feel the closeness of the Mediterranean. In the first week of March a cold snap had gripped the rest of the peninsula. But here the ditches were alive with frogs, and fronds of new fennel gave off a sweet scent on the roadsides. Cherry and almond trees, in sudden full bloom, made snowdrifts of pastel pink and candy white.

On a Sunday during early spring, the Masia Bou has to be seen to be believed. When I drove up one day on the stroke of two o'clock, bumper-to-bumper traffic was forming on the road leading out of Valls. The restaurant was surrounded by parking lots. As at an airport, if you failed to remember in which section you had left your car, you might need to wander around for hours on your return while a gang of wardens directed the cars this way and that. When you reached the front door, a committee of greeters holding clipboards came forward in a smiling phalanx. Once assigned a table, you were guided toward it by one of the red-coated waiters barking into microphones attached to their faces. On a day like today, said a woman with a clipboard as we stood chatting by the door, there might be 1,500 people coming to Masia Bou, all expecting to eat and drink to their heart's content and possibly to its detriment.

The scale and slickness of the operation would be astonishing to anyone previously unaware of the Catalan lust for calçots. There was a fully equipped children's playground. There were gardens with tables and terraces. A monumental stone frieze by the front door paid homage to the pioneers who made the calçotada what it is today. At the back of the house was the engine room, a covered enclosure where fires of vine prunings blazed on an earth floor, and the calçots were piled up in rows on grills above the fire, filling the air with a thick, sweet smoke. I made a quick and easy calculation: if there were roughly twenty calçots per portion, and if 1,500 people would having lunch at the Masia that Sunday, we were dealing with a figure of around 30,000 calçots for the day.

It was easy enough to believe. The various dining rooms were packed with families, and each table had its pile of blackened calçots, served on a roof tile; its pot of reddish, glistening sauce; and its big carafe of local red wine. Some of the people were already finishing their lunch, the tables strewn with debris, the faces of their grinning children, like Victorian chimney sweeps, black with grime. (The Masia provides special paper bibs, for adults as well as children, or the dry cleaners of Valls would be even better off than they already are.) One couple had bravely ordered crema catalana, a caramel-topped custard that is the Catalan national dessert, but were struggling to finish it after their feast of calçots and grilled meats, dangling their spoons in midair as they gazed blankly into space. The volume of noise was prodigious. Even so, a grandfather figure at one long table had managed to sink into a postprandial snooze, his head slumped on his chest while the storm raged about him.

JOSEP PLA (1897–1981) was Ampurdanese, a man of the world, and Catalan—in that order. His prose is regarded by some as the twentieth century's most elegant use of the Catalan language; his opinions on food and cookery are some of the wisest. It seems to me that Pla's two-volume book of essays, *El Que Hem Menjat* ("What We Have Eaten"), is not only Catalonia's greatest work of gastronomical writing, but possibly the most important Spanish contribution to the genre during the twentieth century.

Pla was born in the town of Palafrugell, a few miles from Gerona, and grew up in a house with a beautiful, sizable, and beautifully maintained vegetable garden. Pla never forgot that garden, which was a permanent feature of his surroundings during his childhood; indeed, he was to claim that his adult love of order and logic derived from the hours he spent gazing at the perfect arrangement of the rows of vegetables in his backyard huerta.

The secret of Pla's art was to treat simple things with attention and respect, teasing out of them all the subtlety and poetry hidden behind their modest appearance. He defined cooking as "an art which consists in metamorphosing things in an amiable and discreet manner." Pla liked to eat with a knife, fork, and spoon, not with chopsticks or fingers. He fled from exoticism, freely admitting a preference for the cooking of his own land, however poor and unglamorous it might have been, and positively welcomed its lack of variety.

When Pla was compiling *El Que Hem Menjat,* his essays on everything from hare to mayonnaise and doughnuts to cigars, it seemed to him that the traditional cooking of his region had but a short time to live. "In the country in which I generally live—the Ampurdán—there is a certain familiar cooking which is, these days, surely and inevitably disappearing. This cooking was good—or at least, the inhabitants of the country thought it good. Now one eats well in a few private houses—very few. Before, everybody ate well, poor and rich. Now, this cooking, ever more rare, is shut in behind the four walls of a private house."

It's true that the twenty-first century has largely done away with the "certain familiar cooking" of rural Europe. Even in the domestic context it is rare to find Ampurdanese country cooking of the old school. But what Pla did not foresee was the role that restaurants, rather than private homes, would play in Spanish regional food in general, and Catalan cuisine in particular.

In the case of el niu, Palafrugell's most famous local dish, it could not be any other way. Indeed, only a few restaurants, and the occasional lover of culinary archaeology, had kept it alive at all. El niu—"the nest"—is a dish so bizarre, so archaic, and so rare that it has long since passed into shadowy legend. Few gastronomes, Spanish or other, have ever heard of it, and even fewer have ever tasted it. Colman Andrews, in his pioneering English-language study of Catalan cuisine, described it as "intense" and "mysterious," with "medieval overtones and a baroque sensibility." Pla includes a chapter on the dish in *El Que Hem Menjat,* describing it neatly, in a phrase that needs no translating, as una inexplicable i incomprensible combinació. With his love of the simple and genuine in food, he was unlikely to have much time for one of the maddest mixtures of disparate ingredients that has ever occurred to anyone, on any continent, at any time.

It is not the kind of dish you can walk into a restaurant and order just like that. For a start, it can be found in its true, authentic form only at three or four places in Palafrugell which still know the secret of its making—the guardians of the flame. Even there, you won't find it on the main menu. A restaurant might make it on only a few particular days each year, when the ingredients are all in season and the kitchen can spare the five hours needed to make the dish correctly. El niu is eaten only in winter and spring, preferably on a day when the Ampurdán's wicked north wind, the tramuntana, howls across the landscape, striking a chill into the bones of man and beast.

Together, Pere Bahí and Montse (Montserrat) Soler, of the restaurant La Xicra, probably knew more about the theory and practice of the niu than anyone else alive. Pere was the author of a book about food in the work of Josep Pla which, by coincidence, I had just been perusing in the library of the great man's house. He was a jovial, white-haired, robust man with a smoky voice, plainly a bon vivant, the sort of restaurateur they don't make anymore but you rather wish they did. He peered at me amiably through wraparound dark glasses which he never removed, inside or outside the dining room.

Like all the great rustic dishes, "the nest" is the expression of a particular landscape and culture. It is a signifier of Ampurdán life at a time when work meant something done with the hands, before tourism and industry ushered in new ways of earning and being. In the old days, the dense forests of cork oak around Palafrugell provided the corks for some of the great wines of France. The men who cut the cork from the trees and prepared it for export, known as tapers, worked in groups of six or seven, each taking a turn reading the newspaper aloud (including the advertisements, it's said) *pour encourager les autres*. It was the custom of the cork men to work irregular hours and, on their days off, to set traps in the forest for thrushes, pigeons, and other small game. In their free time the tapers linked up with another social group who also worked irregular hours: the fishermen of the nearby port of Calella, on the Costa Brava. When the time came to eat, each group contributed whatever it could to an impromptu but nevertheless extravagant meal. The fishermen brought dried stockfish and cheap cuts of salt cod (mainly the stomachs, which no one else wanted), plus the cuttlefish they caught off the rocks. The tapers brought their little birds (hence, perhaps, the strange name "nest"), and a few fresh sausages from the matanza. From this mélange the niu was born.

As Montse opened the door to the restaurant, her face was a picture of exhaustion and fury.

"Your niu has nearly killed us. Nearly killed us," she said.

Whereupon her grimace dissolved into a wry smile. A week or so earlier I had managed to persuade Montse, possibly against her better judgment, to have the kitchen staff prepare me a once-in-a-lifetime special edition of Palafrugell's major contribution to the world's gastronomy. A week, she had said, would give them only just enough time, since the pejepalo, or stockfish, needs to be soaked in water for five or six days to reduce it from the consistency of a baseball bat to something that can at least be cut with a knife.

I sat at the bar and drank a glass of beer, and Montse brought me an anchovy on a piece of pa amb tomàquet—the tomato-rubbed toasted bread that is practically the national dish of Catalonia. Outside in the street the good citizens of Palafrugell were hurrying home for lunch. Whatever they were having, it wouldn't be what I was having.

Pere and Montse ushered me into the kitchen where the chef, Anna Casadevall, had been supervising the niu—feathering my nest, so to speak—for most of the morning.

There it was on the stove, a wide metal casserole of something dark and indeterminately colored, still cooking after three hours on minimum heat. This was a serving for four people, said Pere brightly.

He reached out for a bowl that held some leftover sofregit of grated onion and red wine—an extraordinarily dark, thick, sweet-smelling mass with the consistency of olive paste. This powerfully flavored base, I surmised, would form the common ground on which the whole crazy edifice of the dish finally rested.

Following the sofregit, related Pere, a long parade of ingredients had marched into the pot. First the stockfish, soaked for a week; the cuttlefish, in pieces; and the salt cod stomach (the swim bladder, to be more precise), a flabby white flannel-like object with a frill around the edge. The tripa de bacallà was another of those items, like sea cucumbers and percebes, that were once discarded, unwanted, poor men's foods, and are now fashionable and expensive. It would prove to be an essential element of the niu, releasing all its rich gelatinous juices into the sauce.

Then came the pigeons, the sausages, the potatoes, and a little stock to keep everything moist during the further hour of gentle simmering needed to create a close relationship among the wildly disparate elements of the dish. We were on the home stretch. All that remained to be added, now, were some chunks of salt cod, desalted and briefly browned in flour and olive oil; and some halved hard-boiled eggs.

"It's a nest, after all, by God. And what good is a nest without an egg?" reasoned Pere.

El niu is a kind of platillo, or, as such things are known in the lower Ampurdán, un cachoflino—a throwing together of whatever you have on hand, however unlikely the mixture might seem. Next door, on the stove, Anna was making another ambitious-looking dish, a cachoflino of Dublin bay prawns, mussels, white beans, meatballs, and sausages, simmered into a rich stew with a final picada of hazelnuts, garlic, and fried bread. Yet another denomination of this peculiarly Catalan mélange is mar i muntanya, "sea and mountain": a combination of fish or shellfish with meat or game. In local lore, Catalonia was born of the union of a mermaid and a shepherd, which may or may not explain the national liking for surf and turf.

I sat down at my table. First came a plate of Catalan slicing sausages, from the matanza at a nearby farmhouse; then a dish of snails and prawns in a concentrated broth—thoughtfully small, bearing in mind what was to come.

Slowly, holding the plate in both hands, Anna approached the table, her head lowered in an attitude of reverence.

"Niu," she said simply.

It did look very brown. But that was normal. In Catalonia, you need to get over any problem you may have with brown food. This was a primeval soup of thick brown sauce from which the various ingredients could be seen to emerge as from a swamp: a bird's leg, a sausage, the piece of cod looking like a dirty iceberg.

With my first gingerly taste, my fears were dispelled. The niu was good. Not just surprisingly OK, but rich, concentratedly savory, extraordinarily good. What was fascinating was the degree to which the sweetness of the caramelized onion, the salty fishiness of the cod and stockfish, and the meatiness of the sausages and pigeons had melded into a single complex flavor, with the potatoes to provide unbiased proof, as potatoes do, of the balanced and powerful sauce. A cynic would say that any assortment of ingredients will blend together eventually, if you let them cook over a slow heat for long enough. Perhaps that's true. But there would be no guarantee that the final result would be worth the effort.

I gobbled up everything on my plate—even the salt cod swim bladder, which was so tenderly gelatinous that it melted in the mouth.

In the last analysis, el niu remains a curiosity, a museum piece. But the niu is also more than just a dish; it's a monument to the ingenuity of a rural community that called on modest resources to create something truly grand. It is a triumphant work of folk art; an example of subsistence cooking raised to celestial heights where the air gets a little thin, and earthbound notions of logic and good sense begin to vanish into the ether.

SILS, IN THE COUNTY OF La Selva, a few miles south of Gerona, is a village like thousands of others across the length and breadth of Spain. The population is 3,600, and rising. Formerly, like those other thousands of inland villages, this was a community that derived every-thing—wherewithal, sustenance, and values—from small-scale agri-culture. And now? Take a look at the village. The railroad cuts it in half, breaking up whatever physical cohesiveness it may once have had. Now it fizzles out for miles in two directions, into dull develop-ments of chalets with neat gardens, interspersed with halfhearted woodland. Many Chinese and Africans have moved into the area, attracted by work on the building sites and in a large abattoir behind the village.

If Sils is on the map in any sense other than the strictly topographi-cal, it is largely thanks to the grannies.

Their story begins in 1992, during a dinner held by the town hall for the elderly people of Sils. On the menu was a dish of stuffed pimientos de piquillo. The conversation turned to the various local recipes for stuffed peppers, and by the end of the dinner there were plans afoot. A group of the women agreed to meet over the course of a year to record impressions, memories, and recipes relating to the tra-ditional cuisine of the region. When the year was up, they had so much material that it seemed like a good idea to compile it into a book. The next stage was a tasting of regional dishes prepared by the women themselves. And, as often happens, the movement grew and grew. The initial group of seventeen increased impressively as more and more women joined. By the turn of the twenty-first century there were sixty. Five years later there were over 100. (The average age, by the way, is steady at seventy-five.)

Llucia López had a big house in a residential neighborhood some distance from the village center. It was extremely clean, neat, and new, like a model home, but comfortably furnished with big soft sofas and design-store lamps, a ficus in the hall, and paintings in the style of Van Gogh on the walls.

Of my four hosts today, Rosa, Llucia, and another Rosa were actual grannies from Sils, and the fourth was the organizer of the group, Xicu Anoro. Xicu was just the kind of placid, imperturbable guy you would need to keep 100 excitable elderly women under control. Rosa, Llucia, and Rosa had prepared in my honor a magnificent lunch, drawing on their years of expertise to produce three dishes, one made by each.

For most of these women's lives, the village of Sils was a community that, while not grindingly poor, got by on modest rations of food, almost entirely home-produced and home-cooked. There was a repertoire of day-to-day dishes—rather monotonous, since it was based on the Catalan all-inclusive soup-stew escudella, with its protein-rich combination of pulses and meat. There was also a hierarchy of special dishes, prepared on Sundays, on certain Catholic feast days, and during village fiestas. It was in these plats de festa major that the true excellence of the regional cuisine took flight. The important platillos of duck with salsify, rabbit with snails, octopus with potato and peas, and meatballs with prawns were time-consuming dishes that required a great deal of skill and dedication. They could not be cooked, eaten, or digested in a hurry.

Plainly, some of the villagers lived better than others. Rosa Brugué, on my right at the table, grew up in a big house in town. She was a forthright, straight-backed woman, somewhat grander than the other two.

"Even though we lived in the village, we had a nice big patio, and my parents kept two pigs—one to sell, to cover the cost of feeding the second, which was for the family," she told me. "We also had rabbits. Before, in the villages, every family had its own huerta. And so did we. My father walked out in the morning and watered everything. He used to bring back grass for the rabbits. There were five of us, and the parents."

Llucia cautioned me, "It sounds like we lived like kings. But there were bad times, also. Some of us did go hungry. There were days when there was nothing. We talked about that once, in one of our first meetings. One woman said that during the postwar period, she had a speciality: tortillas for the whole family, made with just one egg!"

I joined Llucia in the kitchen, where she let me nose around the cupboards while she gave the finishing touches to her chosen dish.

Llucia had reddish hair, bright eyes, and a warm smile. She wore a black blouse with gold bits. She seemed like an ideal grandmother, with her big house, her smile, and her cooking; but then all three women seemed ideal.

"I've made an escudella," said Llucia.

I might have known, from the unmistakable, evocative smell of long-cooked chickpeas, meats, and vegetables that had been wafting through the house ever since I arrived, that something of the sort was on its way. The escudella is the sister dish of the cocido madrileño: both are based on chickpeas. They differ principally in that the Catalans always add a large meatball, the pilota, and use no chorizo, so that the dish stays pale in color. It has always seemed to me that the escudella is more comforting and the cocido more robust (and the fabada, the Asturian contribution to the debate, more powerful still)—but these differences may be purely illusory.

Llucia's version was an escudella such as I have never tasted before or since: opulent but not overpowering; subtly flavored but certainly not bland. I could taste the five hours it had slowly cooked, and the melding flavors.

"You wouldn't believe it, but in the old days the dish we're eating now was eaten every day," Llucia murmured between mouthfuls.

"Not with all this, though, dear," said Rosa Brugué. "Not so much of anything." She turned to me. "You used whatever you had. My aunt made the meatball with tocino. I would have just a little bit, with potatoes."

We sat around the lunch table, the five of us, chatting away like old friends. The grannies chirped in Catalan, sometimes remembering to translate for my benefit, but sometimes forgetting, carried away by the undertow of memory.

The second Rosa—Rosa V—told me, "Before, I was just sitting at home, and that was it. The cooking, the group, and everything, gave me a new lease on life." For years she had been the cook at the village school, dishing up huge pots of lentils and macarrones for 200 pupils.

Rosa V's dish of the day was a platillo of beef with wild mushrooms, cooked in a terra-cotta casserole with a substantial picada of almonds, hazelnuts, garlic, and fried bread. The sofregit, she explained, was done with green pepper, tomato, onion, leek, and garlic. The meat was first roasted with vi ranci—a maderized wine that is still drunk as an aperitif—and was then sliced and slow-simmered. It was such a purely, authentically Catalan creation that you could sample it blind-folded and know from the taste alone that you were in Catalonia.

When the dish arrived on the table, Rosa Brugué hugged herself with pleasure.

"Quina meravella," she breathed. What a marvel.

The front door opened and a young woman breezed in, carrying a bag on her shoulder.

It was Montserrat, the daughter of Llucia, who had just finished her morning's work at the hospital. Like many Spaniards in their thirties, she still lived at home. What with people coming in from Gerona and Barcelona, prices of houses in the dormitory town of Sils had risen way beyond her reach.

"Montse, come in here," called her mother. "Have you eaten?"

The young woman sat down at a spare chair at the head of the table. She was pretty, fair-skinned, modern, wasp-waisted, smartly dressed.

"Not really," she said with a shrug. "I didn't like what they had in the cafeteria. Canelones. I'd rather not know what they were filled with."

"She doesn't eat much," Llucia apologized for her.

"Mum! I eat little, but often. I'm trying to lose weight. At the hospital we're all on diets." She patted her waist. I tried to picture her in forty years' time, with the low stature and thickset figure of the three grannies around this table.

"Have a glass of cava and a piece of Rosa's cake, at least."

Rosa Brugué had made a superb sweet coca, more like a rich sponge than the thin-based savory Catalan coques I was familiar with, which are more like pizza. It was studded with early strawberries.

Montse took a tiny sliver and nibbled it approvingly.

We sat side by side and exchanged opinions about the grannies and their cooking club.

"I think it's fantastic!" she said. "It keeps them busy. Because, as we know, the devil finds work . . ." She winked at me knowingly. We are of the same generation.

"She doesn't cook. It's a shame," Llucia was telling Rosa V.

"Ah, my daughter does. She's a good cook. She makes everything. Y eso que trabaja—and she works, too. She makes an escudella almost as good as yours, Llucia, except that she uses a pressure cooker, which I don't use. She leaves work at half past one and goes straight into the kitchen."

I wondered how many mothers in Sils could say the same.

"Not many, for certain, not many," mused Llucia.

"No, it's true. We need to start teaching our grandchildren. We've done what we can, but we need to pass on the message."

"Ay, señor," sighed Xicu.

We drained our coffee cups and pushed back our chairs. By unspoken consent, lunch was over. We dropped off Rosa Brugué in the village, then took the road out of town again, towards Rosa V's small bungalow on the outskirts.

Rosa's husband, Jacinto, had long since finished his lunch and had spent the afternoon working in the vegetable patch. For years he had worked in a paper factory. Now retired, he could do whatever he felt like, and he had, in a way, reverted to type—"type" being a human paradigm of Spanish country life, predicated on the values of simplicity, hard physical work, and a profound understanding of the ways of nature.

Rosa and Jacinto showed me around their little paradise. In the backyard, they kept chickens and rabbits in cages. Across the street, on a patch of rough ground, you could see cabbages as big as soccer balls, turnips, and rows of bright green calçots. In the front garden were lettuces, carrots, artichokes, Swiss chard, salsify, broad beans, and peas. Rosa never bought vegetables; they ate only their own, and lived according to the seasons. In late summer, when there was a glut of tomatoes, peppers, and eggplants, she made tomato sauce and samfaina to last through the winter. On special occasions Jacinto would kill a rabbit and Rosa would make one of her plats de festa major, with pears, prawns, mushrooms, or snails.

"We are country people, and we understand the country," said Rosa. "Our children, of course, have a different life. They do things differently. They eat different things."

She gave me a look with her soft gray eyes. "As for us, this is the way we always lived. And we still do."

City

CITIES REPRESENT DEMAND; the countryside represents supply. If cooking equals ingredients plus skill in preparing them, the city knows only about the skill in this equation. It produces nothing. What it is good at is processing and transforming the raw materials that come in from the country. There is no doubt that cities are the seat of modern creativity, where taste and fashions are invented, traded, paraded, and subsequently discarded. Most important, cities are where we find the greatest concentration of disposable income, for without cash, frankly, there is nothing doing in the world of haute cuisine.

I have never lived in a Spanish city for any length of time, though I have frequently fantasized about living in one. I have spent the last fifteen years as a country bumpkin with e-mail, and my visits to cities have been, in Joni Mitchell's phrase, safaris to the heart of all that jazz. I only duck into cities now, feeling awkward in clothes that looked clean enough when I put them on in the dark of the early morning, but that now, under the neon lights of the metro, show dog hairs and the ghosts of oil stains. There are calluses on my hands from digging vegetables, and there is dried dirt at the edges of my fingernails.

Where would I go, if I ever got bored with clear skies and an empty diary? Perhaps to a medium-size provincial city—Lugo, Pamplona, Murcia, Cádiz. Or perhaps to a big busy metropolis like Barcelona or Seville. Either way, my food life would undergo a major change. In my fantasy, I see myself as an urban foodie, flitting like a hummingbird from cheese shop to bakery and fish store to wine store. On Sunday mornings I would join the aperitif round, grazing on regional tapas and sipping cold beers long into the lazy afternoon. In the evenings I might meet friends for dinner in the casual-chic restaurant of the moment, or invite them around to my place, having previously shopped for a particular recipe rather than, as in the country, merely looking for new ways to use up a glut. I would be sure to have access to ingredients that don't exist within a 100-kilometer radius of my country home: soy sauce, ginger, grain mustard, green tea. Would my life be more satisfactory as a result? Possibly not. But I would relish the city's prodigious variety and *embarras de choix*.

I had spent the winter looking inward and downward—at the soil and the customs that arise from it, and at the society that depends on it. Now it was time to look outward and upward—at the Spanish city and its peculiar way of life. Up to now, the object of my attention had been ingredients, raw materials, and the traditions that govern their use. Now I craved a taste of the metropolitan virtues: innovation, image, and technique. I wanted to see chefs at the coal face of contemporary cuisine. I began by following this creativity back to the source: San Sebastián, least Spanish of all Spanish cities, but the city which, in the twilight years of the Franco regime, witnessed the birth of a new kind of Spanish cuisine. I knew where I needed to go thereafter, in order to find out what Spanish food did next: to Barcelona and Madrid—or Madrid and Barcelona, if you prefer—the great rival cities where, in very different ways, the food revolution is polished and packaged for the world.

13

San Sebastián

A SK ANY SPANIARD, and he or she will tell you what San
Sebastián is famous for: its festival, its jazz festival, and its
crazy fiesta of the Tamborrada, during which for twenty-
four hours the whole place rocks to the thunderous sound of drums.
Donostia—to give San Sebastián its proper name—is also known as a
hotbed of Basque nationalism, and as one of the few places on earth
where the Basque culture and language are able to flourish un-self-
consciously.

But its major claim to fame, many would say, is food. San
Sebastián's proud boast is that it has not only the best food in the
country but the most sophisticated food culture of any Spanish city
(and that includes Barcelona). No other city in Europe, with the obvious exception of Paris, has San Sebastián's constellation of Michelin

stars. Bryan Miller, erstwhile food critic of the *New York Times,* once declared that only Manhattan can top it for great restaurants per capita.

Moreover, San Sebastián's food culture goes much further, and runs much deeper, than the bourgeois glamour of the fancy restaurant.

As a food-loving city San Sebastián is nothing if not democratic, and this is true of the Basque country in general; there is good food at every level of society. Quite apart from the star-spangled temples of gastronomy, the range of eating places also includes roast-meat asadores; rustic cider houses (sagardotegiak); and simple menú-based eating houses where a three-course meal of plain, proper local dishes such as zurrukutuna (cod, garlic, and potato soup, onomatopoeically named to suggest slurping it, piping hot, from the bowl), piperrada (scrambled eggs with peppers), and porrusalda of leek and potato, will set you back no more than a few euros. The city is also known for its gastronomic societies, or txokos, some a century old, where members go to cook, eat, and talk about Basque food. There are more than sixty such societies in the old town alone, many of them historical foundations dating back to the early 1900s, and a good few of them obstinately resisting the admission of females to their ranks.

Perhaps most significant are the pintxo bars. The pintxo is essentially a variant of the tapa, the difference being mainly in the way these amusing *amuse-gueules* are spread out on trays at the bar, to be grabbed at will, washed down with a glass of something, and paid for when you leave. The bars of San Sebastián have made the pintxo into a culinary art in its own right, a superlative and splendid fast food, available to anyone who cares about such things, which in the city means pretty much everyone.

Every eating place here, every eating event, has its own menu and agenda. At a cider house on the outskirts of town, you will typically be given salt-cod tortilla and char-grilled lamb chops, the traditional vehicle for tangy local cider served foaming straight from the barrel. At the village fiesta, pots of marmitako—the Basque fishermen's stew of tuna, potato, and tomato—stand bubbling on outdoor stoves; and stands sell bocadillos stuffed with tender pork loin and roasted red peppers. For anyone lucky enough to have access to a txoko, there will be rich old-fashioned dishes like bacalao al pil-pil—salt cod in an

olive-oil emulsion sauce, fiendishly tricky to make—and serious delicacies such as kokotxas de merluza: highly prized morsels of gelatinous flesh extracted with some difficulty from the cheeks of the hake.

Donostia–San Sebastián is a place that cares about good eating and
doesn't care who knows it. For donostiarras the excellence of the city's
gastronomic life can be a curse as well as a blessing. I have heard people here ruefully declare that they hated traveling, because wherever
else they went in the world the food was always worse than at home.

Marisa, the landlady at my pensión a few streets away from the
beach, knew whereof she spoke. Taking a pencil and paper, she made
me out a list of the places that, in her considered opinion, were worth-
while. I was to avoid like the plague the new wave of fashionable,
avant-garde, minimalist, nouvelle places. She couldn't abide that sort
of nonsense. And I was to head for the sort of place that made a big
deal of traditional Basque cooking with first-class raw materials—such
as one well-known restaurant in the parte vieja, the old town. It was
absolutely de toda la vida, insisted Marisa. I said I'd give it a try. Of
course, traditional was best. But though I dared not tell her, I was far
more interested in the avant-garde stuff, the restless creativity that had
made this resort city a standard-bearer of gastronomic modernity,
effectively transforming the food life of Spain.

I left my luggage with Marisa and set off along the promenade,
making my way around the curve of the beach toward the parte vieja,
a maze of narrow streets with buildings all in the same crumbly limestone. If anywhere has a serious claim to be the heart, or perhaps the
belly, of good food in Spain, it's this square mile of medieval streets in
which every other doorway seems to lead to a seafood restaurant, a
simple casa de comida, a high-class restaurante de autor, a pintxo bar,
or the discreet headquarters of a gastronomic society.

On this cold March morning the north wind came in bracing gusts
off the sea. A few solitary figures hurried past me on the promenade.
Down on the sand a woman was running with two dogs. It felt strange
to be here, in these well-washed streets full of polite, well-to-do people, after the earthy charms of the Ampurdán. I puzzled over the street
signs with their runic X's, K's, and Z's. (Basque is like a Scrabble game
in which everyone gets to use the high-scoring letters.)

The Luis Irízar School of Cooking occupied the basement in a grand apartment building a few steps from the old harbor. It was run by a man who is often regarded as the founding father of the new Basque cooking and one of the patriarchs of the Spanish culinary scene, Luis Irízar. This maestro of maestros, as his numerous admirers call him, has inspired several generations of cooks, including Arzak, Subijana, and Karlos Arguiñano, who have since become Michelin-starred master chefs.

Luis, a sprightly, amiable gentleman who looked a decade younger than his seventy years, was sitting in a glass-walled office with his two grown-up daughters, who work at the school. He had a neat gray mustache and a kind face with gentle eyes. He got up from his chair and shook my hand warmly.

Beyond the office, there was an appealingly chaotic atmosphere; attractive young people joshed in the corridors. "When we first started, the pupils were mainly Basque. Now they come from all over Spain. But we also have French kids, Americans, Mexicans, Japanese. The foreigners tend to come with a point of reference, some Spanish cook they've heard about—usually Ferran Adrià," said Luis, I thought a trifle ruefully. In the small kitchen classroom a teacher in whites was preparing to give a class on fine baking, with particular emphasis on the croissant. The pupils hurriedly found their seats, while their director looked on benignly. At the back of the room a tall boy with curly black hair was flirting with a small girl in a bandanna, playfully pushing her with his hips against the stainless steel walk-in fridge.

Luis and I walked out along the harborside in search of a bar that might provide us with a plate of good jamón ibérico and a bottle of fresh white txakoli. When we found it, Luis sat down gratefully, puffing a little.

When he was a boy, Luis said, his parents ran a restaurant in San Sebastián called the Buenavista. The place had been in his mother's family for years.

"I was practically born in the kitchen," he told me, gratefully sipping his tumbler of white wine. "My mother and my aunts were very good cooks; they had learned the trade in Casa Nicolasa, which in those days was the best in the city, and I of course learned from them." At age sixteen Luis started as an apprentice in the kitchens of the María Cristina, the grandest old wedding-cake hotel in San Sebastián, and so began a distinguished career that would take him to Biarritz, Paris,

London, and finally Madrid, where he worked with the great Clodoaldo Cortés at what is still one of the city's poshest, plushest restaurants, the Jockey.

Irízar is one of the last surviving witnesses of an era in Basque food, and by extension in Spanish food, that dates back to the late nineteenth century and the earliest days of San Sebastián as a resort town for the European nobility. There was no such thing as a native haute cuisine in Spain; it went without saying that for elegance and refinement in food, there was no one but the French. So when the new hotels and casinos wanted chefs de cuisine and maîtres d'hôtel, they naturally looked on the other side of the border. But the lower places in the kitchen hierarchy were occupied by young Basques, who learned the art of cuisine from their French masters. Over time a Basque-French culinary tradition came into being, and it was in this context that Luis Irízar, too, received his professional training.

Born in 1935, he grew up in the postwar period, when half of Spain was on the breadline. Even for the rarefied world of haute cuisine, this was hardly an easy time. Many ingredients were rationed, and still more were simply unobtainable. Foie gras, then as now an indispensable element of the menu at any grand restaurant, was unknown in Spain. "We used to pop over to France. There was a border, and it was closely guarded, but we bought our foie gras on the French side and brought it back. Here it hadn't been seen for years—if ever."

What was to be the new Basque cooking of the 1970s sprang from a combination of various factors, the most important being the historic significance of good food, and discourse about good food, within Basque culture itself.

Euskadi, the Basque name for the Basque country, is effectively wedged between sea and mountain—like Catalonia—with rich pastures and a mild, rainy climate: Atlantic along the coast, Mediterranean toward Navarre and La Rioja in the south. Partly as a result of this variety, its cuisine has a wider, richer repertoire than that of any other Spanish region (though Catalonia runs it close).

The cuisine starts with history and geography and moves into sociology: the custom of the koadrila (cuadrilla), a group of friends for life who meet regularly to eat and drink together, is crucial to the Basque way of being. The gastronomic societies grew up as permanent meeting places where classic Basque dishes could be cooked and eaten in a casual masculine atmosphere, away from the structures and strictures of the domestic (female-dominated) environment.

The final impulse toward the revolution was nouvelle cuisine. Gastronomically, San Sebastián was umbilically linked to France, and so its chefs were careful to pay close attention to a movement that aimed at purifying and simplifying regional cuisines, which had become so bastardized and cheapened as to be almost unrecognizable. Many luminaries of nouvelle cuisine—Michel Guérard, Paul Bocuse, the Troisgros brothers—were well-known figures in San Sebastián, and before long the shock waves were beginning to ripple across the border. In 1975 a group of young Basque chefs set about creating a radical culinary movement of their own.

The year is significant. In 1975 Franco died. After forty years in which he and his government had done everything they could to prevent the expression of Basque national identity, the time had come for Basque culture, language, and politics to break out into the open. In a way, therefore, the new Basque cooking can be seen as one of the first acts of regional self-assertion to take place during the period following Franco's death.

Luis Irízar, who was one of the revolutionaries, remembers well the euphoria of those heady days. "There were twelve of us. Let me see: there was Arzak, Arguiñano, Ramón Roteta, Pedro Subijana, Patxi Kintana. . . . I think of all the dozen, about ten were pupils of mine. We were all a bit fed up of seeing restaurants all over Spain that claimed to offer cocina vasca, cocina vasca, when really they had nothing to do with genuine Basque cooking.

"So we started trying to do what the French had done. Working together. For two years we held a special dinner once a month, taking turns in each of our restaurants, and we invited journalists and knowledgeable clients, and after each dinner we held a forum and talked about the food we'd eaten. The idea was to preserve the authentic roots of the Basque repertoire, using genuine recipes, but giving them a touch of lightness and modernity. As we went on, we realized that we were indeed inventing a new kind of cooking; which was a paradox in a way. And that was really the start of the modern movement in Spanish food: everything that's going on now can be traced to what happened in San Sebastián in the middle of the 1970s."

Luis Irízar is right: the effects of those monthly meetings are still being felt thirty years later, and not only in the realm of food. In the old days in Spain, which is to say nearly until the late 1980s, the profession of *chef de cuisine* had none of the glamour it has today. The chef was never seen in the dining room: Juan Mari Arzak remembers that his father was once dismissed from the room by a client who felt it was beneath his dignity to deal with such a humble figure and asked instead to see la señora de la casa ("the lady of the house"). To be a cook was to be part of the working class: there was no social status attached to the job, and the salary was poor. Luis and his friends gave the profession a cachet and respect that it had lacked before. The only thing lacking now was the possibility of a decent education in the trade—and this wouldn't be long in coming, thanks to the pioneering example of Irízar's own cookery school.

It was midday, and Luis had people to see before lunch. "I have an important date with my granddaughter," he said with a twinkle in his eye.

We took our leave outside the Bar Txepetxa in the Calle Pescadería and I dived inside for a pintxo and a glass of wine. The Txepetxa is known locally as the "temple of the anchovy" and its creative treatment of this little fish—cured in vinegar with a huge range of accompaniments, from sea urchin eggs to olive pâté, crabmeat, and papaya, regularly wins prizes in the city's annual pintxo contest. There was quite a crowd inside the tiny bar, a mixture of businesspeople in suits and ties, dressed-up girls and boys, and a tourist couple shyly nibbling in a corner. I tagged along after a group of students from the city university, with Basque Nationalist leanings and the cropped hair of militants, and followed them on their pintxo round. Together we covered Calles Fermín Calbetón and 31 de Agosto, the two main streets of this snack heaven, plucking pintxos from the counters as you might pluck cherries from a tree. Today at Ganbara, on Calle San Jerónimo, there were hot crab tartlets, deep-fried asparagus, and chunks of marinated tuna roe with onions and peppers on cocktail sticks. At the Bar Martínez, around the corner on 31 de Agosto, there were miniature croissants stuffed with fried baby artichoke hearts and a morsel of ham; grilled cèpes with olive oil on toast; and pickled green chilies, long, thin, and excruciatingly hot. I was pleased to see that La Viña, an age-old watering hole on Calle 31 de Agosto, was still serving its age-old especialidad, a crisp cone of flaky pastry stuffed with fresh goat cheese. But there was new blood coming in, and there were new-wave pintxos I had never seen before. In the dank, dark corner of two sun-less streets gleamed a designer pintxo bar, a place of stainless steel and polished concrete, brightly proffering salt cod tempura, baby squid stuffed with spring onion, and chilled crab soup with tomato com-pote.

My new Basque friends took it all in their stride. Their country had always been in the vanguard of everything, from industry to culture; it made Spain (they spoke the word España with a wince of disgust) look primitive and old-fashioned. When they marched off to a meeting in the nearest Herriko Taberna, "village tavern" and hotbed of ETA's sympathizers, I invented a lunch appointment and said farewell to the whole gang, with kisses on both cheeks and promises to meet again someday in the future independent republic of Euskadi.

THERE IS A CASE for saying that the truly important restaurants of Spain, the ones that will outlast the foams of fashion, are those that have been in the family for generations, where there is continuity in the business and a well-established heritage. The paradigm is the humble or not-so-humble eating house where the son goes off to cookery school and comes back to run the kitchen with all his new energy and modern ideas, but still with family and local tradition as an anchor. Of the great Spanish restaurants of our time, it is rather sur-prising how many have followed this pattern. Las Rejas, Echaurren, Ca' Sento, Café de Paris, and Celler de Can Roca are a few that come to mind. And the mother of all the restaurants of this type, which we might call "generational," "evolutionary," or simply "family-run," is surely Arzak.

The Arzak saga stretches back to 1897, when Juan Mari's grandpar-ents opened a wineshop, tavern, and eating house in the village of Alza, now a suburban barrio of San Sebastián. The restaurant is still to be found in the same house, on a busy road leading out of the city, and is now in its fourth generation of the same family: Elena Arzak, one of Juan Mari's two daughters, is the brilliant young chef who now runs the kitchen with her father and will take over the reins when he even-tually retires.

The place is sui generis. The main dining room is small, overstuffed, and cramped by modern standards, with the tables rather close together and lots of varnished wood and antique furniture. The waitresses are matronly women who have been with the family since the dawn of time, or at least the dawn of democracy, and wear curious gray uniforms with a minimalist, Yohji Yamamoto look. The menu was based on classic Basque cooking as served by Juan Mari's parents and their parents: marmitako, chipirones (baby squid) en su tinta, hake in green sauce. But the kitchen has taken note of all the newest tendencies, partly thanks to the influence of Elena; and now there is a research department upstairs where new techniques and flavors are cunningly developed. The old restaurant is amazingly ahead of the game. When I was last there I ate prawns cooked in apple juice steam, poached egg with squid ink and parsley sprays, lamb subtly flavored with coffee, and apple and black olive sponge with fresh cheese, turmeric, and orange powder. All this was tremendously and memorably good. The effect of the modernity, given the heritage of the place, is rather like the feeling you get when your parents are seen in public dressed in the latest fashion, and looking surprisingly good. At first it's embarrassing, but you end up admiring them for moving so agilely with the times.

Andoni Luis Aduriz represents another aspect of the scene. He is a man who had no background in food, no family tradition, and no early aptitude for the kitchen. He was born and grew up in a suburb of San Sebastián, where his parents were simple working people. It had never occurred either to them or to their son that he might end up doing what it is he does now.

I first saw Andoni's photograph on the cover of a magazine, in an issue dedicated to the new culinary sensibility at work in Spain. Andoni was shown with a toothy, faintly nervous smile, cradling in his arms a giant orange pumpkin and looking like the boy next door dressed up in chef's whites.

Just a week earlier the food critic of the same magazine had given Mugaritz, Aduriz's restaurant outside San Sebastián, a glowing review in his weekly column. The critic described Aburiz as a "real hot-shot of contemporary Spanish cooking" and said, "He possesses the sensibility of an ecologist, the rigor of a cultural investigator, and the soul of an idealist with his feet on the ground. He has the sensibility of a gastronome and the elegance of those who make simplicity into a way of life." The critic awarded Mugaritz nine points out of ten, a score only surpassed by Adrià and Arzak.

I knew then that this was someone I would have to meet, if I wanted to take the pulse of modern Spanish food in all its scintillating novelty and brio. And now it seemed the time had come: I was within half an hour's taxi ride of the restaurant; a spare table was available for lunch; the chef was in the kitchen; and Andoni Luis Aduriz was looking forward to meeting me.

The history of the Basque country over the last century and a half is, at least in part, that of a rural society forced off the land by its own push for prosperity, yet still hungrily attached to its own, now partly idealized, rural origins. Euskadi is the most densely urbanized corner of Spain, its valley floors scarred with heavy industry (the Basque country was the cradle of Spain's own industrial revolution), crammed with smoke-stained factories, warehouses that look prefabricated, and dark slabs of apartment buildings of an almost Soviet grimness. Yet the hillsides above this urban landscape have luscious green pastures and bolts of dark pinewood, picked out here and there with the architectural forms of an earlier time: the rough dome of a haystack, a triangular stone farmhouse that may remind you fleetingly of Switzerland. Nowhere else in the Spanish state do industrial and preindustrial, urban and rural values, so intimately coexist.

The word caserío describes the traditional Basque country property, where the big stone farmhouse and its various inhabitants, animal and human, constitute a practically self-sufficient socioeconomic unit. In one of these pitch-roofed farmhouses, just beyond the scrappy hardworking town of Rentería, I found the place I was looking for. The house I was looking at now occupied such a sprawling surface area that two very different enterprises were able to fit comfortably under its low roof; a dwelling occupied by the elderly bachelor who had been born in the house and still farmed the land, with cattle, chickens, vegetables, and corn; and a restaurant said, by the few people who truly understand such things, to be among the four or five most fascinating and important phenomena in the world of Spanish food. The facade of the caserío—one side postmodern rustic with plate-glass windows giving onto the dining room, and the other half proper old-fashioned rustic, sharing the space under the wide arms of the clay-tiled roof— was neatly indicative of the curious convergence going on inside.

In front of the house a mighty oak tree marked the boundary between two suburban centers, once bucolic villages: Rentería and Oiartzun. This oak was the trademark of the restaurant, a tree in leaf straddling two halves of a rectangle, black and white, reflecting each other.

Outside in the garden a group of white-clad figures crouched over flower beds, carefully plucking leaves and putting them into jars of water. The hillside above the restaurant was a green sward crowned with oak woods; the hedges were fringed with hazel trees and apple orchards. Along the track that led beside the parking lot, a line of brown cows plodded heavily through the mud.

The restaurant's interior was decorated in a "rustic minimalist" style, with beams, rough wood paneling, and big windows framing a voluptuous expanse of green. A long line of m's, for Mugaritz and deliciousness, trailed MMMMMMMMMMMMMMMMM around the walls.

Andoni Luis Aduriz, a small, quick, shy person in his mid-thirties, came out of the kitchen and introduced me to my lunch companion, a Basque girl called Nagore who wore her hair in long shiny dark-brown tresses. She had known Andoni and Mugaritz ever since the confluence of man and restaurant; she had observed their development with admiration. A writer on Basque food, Nagore had grown up in San Sebastián.

"My mother lives in a big apartment overlooking the sea. She likes to shop at La Bretxa market and cook lunch for me once in a while. My ex-boyfriend runs the Urepel, just near the bridge where the river meets the sea." What a coincidence: that was the old-fashioned Basque place my landlady had recommended. Maybe I should give it a try after all.

Aduriz had prepared for Nagore and me a menú degustación, which he hoped would provide a window on his world. The list of dishes, translated for my benefit into eccentric English, was itself an extraordinary document. The "whipped mock lard," "chilled lilia-ceous soup," and "split crayfish royale upon a bed of plant roe" were pure Lewis Carroll. The "squid and bread fisherman's gel with orchard shoots and simple grains of paradise" had a fantastic sound, like something you might dream of seeing on a menu, and then forget the minute you woke up. A paragraph of his own writing, printed on the cover of the menu, loftily proclaimed the tenets of Aduriz's natural philosophy: "Cultured and refined spirits are called to rediscover their relationship with nature. To this end, no better way exists than through the raw material, the only thing upon which, over time, human beings have never been able to improve. All the grasses, flowers, seeds, and elements that you may find in any of our dishes are edible; the generous gift of a new world of emotions."

Two small envelopes lay on the table before me. One read, "150 minutes: submit"; the other, "150 minutes: rebel." I thought of the cake and the drink in *Alice in Wonderland*: one made you grow, and the other made you shrink. I chose rebellion; the card inside the envelope exhorted me to "feel, imagine, remember, discover."

The first dish to arrive was a mad mixed salad of "raw and roast vegetables, shoots and leaves, wild and cultivated, dressed with walnut butter, dusted with seeds and petals and generously seasoned with Emmental cheese." The dish was clearly influenced in part by the wild-salad creations of Michel Bras, who shares Aduriz's romantic back-to-nature philosophy. It was lovely to look at, in any case, and cleverly constructed, with bitter and sour notes from all those roots and shoots.

Next came a tempura-like fritter of artichoke pieces with a foamy sauce compounded of some kind of shellfish essence, grapefruit peel, and the juice of the mangosteen. And a dish of potatoes cooked in a crust of white clay, served with an "unctuous cream" of chipiron (baby squid) and various squidlets roasted over coals. And a comforting, almost homey creation with a strange and slightly sinister touch: eggs with crushed potatoes, perhaps a reference to the famous huevos estrellados at Casa Lucio in Madrid, and "vegetable charcoal": pieces of purple potato smoked and dried until black and mummified. And a concoction of salt cod stomach and kokotxas in a gelatinous sauce given a lift with parsley and tomato: in essence a traditional idea pared down to its soul. And a fantastically fresh meaty fillet of red mullet with an elegant fumet tinctured with juniper, with a comedy fish bone on the side, all its ribs and vertebrae intact, fried in viciously hot oil until brown and crisp, a fire-scorched skeleton.

"You may eat the fish bone after the fillet," graciously allowed the smiling waiter.

It was all very exciting, as well as wondrously original, mysterious, and witty. Bursts of drop-dead flavor—the piquant herbaceous blast of curry leaves; the cool bitter crunch of earthnuts; and that strange-sounding fisherman's gel, which turned out to be an extreme reduction of squid ink, black and sticky as beach tar—punctuated the meal like the piercing notes of a trumpet. But Aduriz's isn't the kind of high-wire cooking that induces you to gasp in delight or dissolve into giggles. Ferran Adrià's cooking is often described as surrealistic, and this seemed almost hyper-real: it had an intensity born not so much in theatrical whimsy or conceit as in a concentrated study of where things come from and just what they do to each other.

There were fourteen dishes in all. The card on the table had promised 150 minutes of feeling, imagining, remembering, and discovery, but 250 minutes would have been nearer the mark. Even Nagore, who was used to the creative fireworks of the chefs of San Sebastián, was touched and impressed by the show her friend was putting on for us.

Under the neon lights of the kitchen, Nagore and I gave him our effusive congratulations—perhaps we were slightly drunk from all the food, wine, and talk—and he blushed pink, shyness bringing out a tic at the corners of his mouth.

Later, we sat in the stone room where the chef and his team entertain their guests. The chef sat before me with a cup of green tea, talking quickly and quietly, leaning forward on the sofa. There was something monkish and ascetic about his rounded, delicate-boned face, pale from the hours spent in the kitchen, and his boyish haircut with its short bangs.

"I grew up in Egia, a suburb of San Sebastián. My parents had nothing to do with food, except that my mother was and is a marvelous cook. She is one of those women who always were proper housewives, one of those women who cook twice a day at home, waiting for their husband—the sort of role that these days is almost unthinkable for a young woman. What did she cook? Simple things, good things: a lot of vegetables, pasta, stews, meat."

Aduriz has done all the right things and spent time with all the right people. One of them is Martín Berasategui, the businesslike but brilliant chef whose flagship restaurant in Lasarte has three Michelin stars. Another, of course, is Ferran Adrià, probably his true creative maestro. Adrià's influence is undeniably present in his cooking, but he now finds Adrià's work fussy and alienating. (He last ate at El Bulli in 1998, and hasn't been back since.)

Partly under the influence of the alchemist Adrià, Aduriz became drawn to the idea that scientific analysis could usefully be applied to the art of cooking. His research into the nature of foie gras, for example, led to a period of study in association with the pathology department of the University of Granada. Over the next few years, there would be further research into salt cod, and into the nature and behavior of meat. The conduit, in this case, between scientists and chefs was the gastronome and savant Raimundo del Moral, who specializes in opening the kitchen doors of famous restaurants to the curious world of modern science. The newest chefs on the scene are hardheaded, meticulous to the point of obsession; they are intellectuals, fascinated by technique and process. At Mugaritz a new dish typically passes a rigorous process of research and development, being rejected up to twenty times before it is presented to the public.

Yet there's another side to Aduriz. He is attached like a forest fern to the rock of his origins. A child of Euskadi, with Basque as his mother tongue and his headquarters in a Basque farmhouse, how could he deny them? Bizarre and perhaps pretentious though it may sound, he even believes he is working in the tradition of Basque cuisine in its widest, most spiritual sense. Aduriz looks at a dish like merluza en salsa verde, with its emulsion sauce of parsley and wine—a totemic dish in Basque tradition—and decides that it is naturally avant-garde and that he will keep it on the menu as a paragon of modernity. The boundary oak brings together two sides, tradition and zeitgeist, under the same overarching branches.

Casting about for sources of supply, he looks at the caseríos in the vicinity, bringing eggs from one farm, onions from another, potatoes from a third. In his stunning dish of espresso coffee grounds with chilled cocoa juice, chicory cream, and a skin of farmhouse milk, the farmhouse milk is provided by his neighbor's cows, those slow brown cows I saw going by as I parked my car.

Then there are the wild things. The historian Jean-François Revel defines the dominant character of contemporary gastronomy as "the return to nature." Aduriz has found inspiration in the woods and meadows around the restaurant, and many of his ingredients now come straight from the natural environment. For instance, *Polipodium vulgare,* one of his favorites of the wild herbs, is a diminutive fern that grows amid the forest moss and rocks, in the cracks of garden walls, and among the stones of cemeteries. In his book *Clorofilia,* a treatise on the cooking of herbs and grasses, he gives a recipe for foie gras escalope in a wood-perfumed stock with a licorice and polipodium root infusion, Jerusalem artichokes, and muscovado sugar.

As much as a willed return to nature, Aduriz's work is a necessary redefinition of the idea of luxury. When much about modern-day food has been cheapened, homogenized, and spoiled, the leaf of a forest grass you gather at dawn with the dew still on it might be considered the greatest indulgence of all.

The chef leaned forward on the sofa, his fingertips touching each other to form a ball in the air.

"That's it. That's just it," he said, conviction giving his quiet voice a tremble.

"Society's values have changed. The man next door might think we're crazy, giving importance to these wild grasses he has known all his life. But for the man from the city, those things might seem like the greatest treasures in the world."

14

Barcelona

I T WAS GETTING LATE, and I was beginning to feeling awkward about taking up so much of the chef's precious time. Nagore had left for San Sebastián, cursing the afternoon meeting that was tearing her away from Mugaritz. The office was almost dark and the lights had come on in the empty parking lot. In an hour or two a new set of cars would be pulling up, bringing in smartly dressed customers for dinner. And the day after tomorrow, I knew, Aduriz had a challenge on his hands: a banquet at the Hotel Ritz in Barcelona, part of a four-day festival of fashion, design, and the Sabatier-sharp cutting edge of modern European cuisine.

The chef led me back to the kitchen, where he was ready to bring out of the oven a piece of beef that had been cooking for the last thirty-five hours at a constant 70 degrees Celsius.

The kitchen was deserted. Its surfaces shone under the neon. It had the neutral smell, the non-smell, of absolute cleanness.

Andoni stood by the stove. He put a finger to his lips, turning over an idea in his head.

"Listen," he said quietly. "As you know, I'm giving a dinner in Barcelona the day after tomorrow. It is a special celebration, something I have been working on for months. A lot of our friends will be there. I am sure there will be room for you. And if not, we will make room. Come. It will be a fiesta."

An invitation to Barcelona is never easy to refuse, and this one was impossible. The next day I was on the road again, crossing the peninsula at its slenderest point, skimming the southern slopes of the Pyrenees, via Pamplona and Huesca. And by the following evening I was in the Spanish city that is the world's favorite as well as my own, the most vibrant, the most questingly modern, and the one in which, together with San Sebastián, the new Spanish cuisine has, arguably, reached its highest development.

The banquet Andoni Luis Aduriz served for fifty friends at the Ritz in Barcelona has stayed in my mind as an expression of contemporary culture at its most challenging and exquisite. Some of the ten dishes Andoni presented were things I had eaten just forty-eight hours ago at Mugaritz. I recognized the crazy mixed salad; the toasted fresh foie gras with rosemary-infused soy cream; and the coffee grounds with cacao juice, chicory cream, and the skin from the milk of the cows that share the building with Andoni's restaurant. But the context had changed, and so, oddly, had the nature of the food. Taking it out of the Basque countryside and placing it in a velvety, low-lighted, plush nineteenth-century hotel had made it seem even more radical, more dramatic, and more sophisticated than it had looked in the sylvan setting that inspired it.

If the food was memorable, the drink was perhaps even more so. One might have expected a parade of fine Spanish wines, leading us through the meal with the comforting logic of sparkling, white, red, sweet. But Andoni as usual was one step ahead. He had created for the occasion a series of infusions, juices, and decoctions, each meant to accompany a particular dish. The drinks were poured from glass jugs into a series of specially designed cups and containers, some of them held in origami-like constructions that seemed to suspend the crystal in midair. We sipped, tasted, and murmured our surprise and approval. Instead of providing an alcoholic crescendo, Andoni's banquet progressed in a hushed and reflective manner, and our senses were as twitchingly acute at the end of the feast as they had been at the start.

THE FIRST TIME I went to Barcelona was as a student, during the summer vacation. This was a decade or more before the annus mirabilis of 1992, when the Olympic Games transfigured the city into what it had always dreamed of being, a sparkling European capital and a design center to rival Paris and Milan.

The idea of Barcelona in my mind as I stepped off the train was a murky harbor city, more like Marseille than Milan, a hotbed of anarchism, bohemianism, and low-life. Jean Genet had given Barcelona his seal of approval (notably in his novel of 1949, *The Thief's Journal*), and that was all I needed to know.

The reality was certainly decadent, but not quite in the way I expected. I arrived during Holy Week to find everything shut: shops, banks, museums. I had so little money, however, that having nothing to spend it on made no difference. In the house of a friend who lived near the Sants railroad station, we ransacked the kitchen cupboards and sat down to a spartan Good Friday dinner, my first meal in Barcelona—canned sardines, boiled spaghetti, and a handful of dried apricots.

Things could only get better. On my next visit a few years later I stayed with Susan, another adventurous English friend, who had found herself a top-floor apartment with a roof terrace on Carrer Joaquín Costa, in the Raval, for the not unreasonable rent of forty pounds a month. The Raval was Barcelona's old red-light district, an area described by the Catalan essayist Josep Maria de Segarra as one of "great poverty, great dirtiness, a resigned and desolate humility." In the late 1980s the barrio was a bohemian dream: atmospheric, cheap, and with an exhilarating undercurrent of sleaze. Immigration hadn't yet begun in earnest: there was just one Pakistani restaurant, the Shalimar (now there are dozens), and just two or three halal grocers selling basmati rice and drums of ghee.

The streets below hummed with life. One night there was a house fire a block away, and we leaned over the balcony to watch the roaring flames. In the evenings we went out for absinthe at the louche Bar Marsella, founded in 1947 and apparently undecorated ever since, followed by dancing at La Paloma, the working-class dance hall where an orchestra plays and couples turn under a huge chandelier.

Susan was a smart cookie, and there was no cheap restaurant in the barrio where she didn't know the price of the daily menú by heart. Together we sampled most of these places, and we never spent more than 600 pesetas on a three-course meal with a bottle of red wine so thin it was more like rosé. These were family-run restaurants, noisy with clattering dishes and boisterous customers. At Cal Estevet, I see from my diary, I ate oven-roasted artichokes and salt cod with samfaina, the Catalan summer sauce of tomatoes, eggplants, and peppers; Susan had macarrones and fricandó of beef. "Not bad," pronounced my friend. "But Can Lluis is cheaper." So the next day we duly tried Can Lluis, on Carrer Cera, then one of the darkest, grimiest streets of the old Raval. It was even more rough and raucous than Cal Estevet, but the food was just as good: gazpacho, grilled rabbit with garlic and thyme, gambas a la plancha. For dessert we usually had one of two things—either flan, the eternal pan-Spanish favorite, wobbling above its pool of caramel; or crema catalana, the Catalan national pudding, yellow and creamy with a hard crust of burned sugar to crack, satisfyingly, with the side of a spoon.

One of our few daring sallies out of the neighborhood was to eat arroz a banda at a beachside chiringuito called El Merendero de la Mari, just below the fishing district of Barceloneta, above the beach. The merendero was one of a line of shacks that served absolutely fresh seafood and rice dishes at bargain prices, in an atmosphere of cheerful indifference to modern standards of construction and hygiene. Partly for reasons of health, partly because the chic new Barcelona of the 1990s found them embarrassing, the shacks were eventually cleared away, and nostalgists for old Barcelona still lament their passing.

What would I have found to eat in the city at large, if budgetary constraints hadn't prevented me from moving very far beyond the cheap, cheerful ghetto of the Raval? The late 1980s were not, perhaps, a very remarkable era in Barcelona restaurants. The excitement of the new Catalan cooking was chiefly to be found elsewhere in Catalonia: at the Hotel Ampurdán in Figueres, and at Big Rock in Platja d'Aro. In Barcelona the restaurants of note were classy places for the upper classes. Reno, Via Veneto, Windsor: the names almost say it all. For posh seafood there was Butafumeiro, a Galician place where the food was famous, as well as famously expensive. The interior of what passed for a fashionable restaurant would have been carpeted and curtained, tending toward the frilly and overstuffed. Colman Andrews—whose book *Catalan Cuisine,* first published in 1988, turned a generation of English-speaking food lovers on to the fact that here in northeastern Spain was a coherent, idiosyncratic cuisine which had hitherto been overlooked—mentions Reno, Via Veneto, Florian, and Petit Paris as among "Catalonia's . . . best contemporary-style restaurants." At the time, this meant that they were serving canelones, bacallà, stuffed pigs' feet, and mongetes amb butifarra (sausage and beans "raised to an art form")—hardly what one would describe today as state-of-the-art fare.

Another ten years were to pass, however, before I got up to speed on exactly what modern food in Barcelona was all about. In the spring of 2001 I was sent on assignment by a magazine to research its restaurant scene, which was beginning to be talked about as one of the most varied and excellent of any European city.

Needing a second opinion, I called a Catalan friend, Joan, who had been exiled for many years in Alicante but nevertheless kept in close touch with the food in his hometown. Yes, yes, he confirmed, what they were saying was true: Barcelona was experiencing a restaurant boom. He had been there recently and had been amazed by the quality and sophistication being offered, a huge improvement on earlier decades, and a world away from the old-fashioned rice dishes and cocina marinera of his adopted city.

Joan was the first to tell me about the restaurants that really mattered in the early years of the new millennium, and I was happy to follow his instructions to the letter. In the course of my four-day stay in 2001, I ate at Cal Isidre, where Isidre Gironés and his wife, Montse, have been dishing up impeccable Catalan food for nearly forty years, and at Alkimia, where at the time chef Jordi Vila was offering rice with ñora peppers and salt cod and sautéed banana with ice cream of yogurt, cinnamon, and lime in a ragingly fashionable haut-industrial setting. At a place called Abac—"it might be the best in town," Joan had told me—I ate a strange but unforgettable tarte tatin of eel with apples and foie gras. I also recall a restaurant, Espai Sucre, that served only desserts—but what desserts! There was so much variety, so much fizzing creativity, that it was hard to get a handle on this scene.

When I began planning my two-year immersion in the foods and food habits of Spain, I knew for sure I'd be coming back to Barcelona. And here I was, with the memory of last night's banquet fresh in my mind, and the prospect of another few days in a city that, whatever it offers you to eat, almost always leaves a good taste in the mouth.

I left the car in a parking lot and spent a few days revisiting old haunts, some of them more haunted than others. From everything my senses told me as I walked its familiar streets, Barcelona was still in its twenty-year cycle of convulsive change. It was cleaner, neater, shinier, and faster than I had ever known it, and its inhabitants were more expensively dressed. It was no longer the shabby southern harbor city I had once known; it was functional and efficient, prices for everything had soared, and it had smart hotels with trendy interiors.

As for restaurants, there was more disseny about than ever, and in the most unlikely places. In the dark, narrow Carrer Carretes, one of the last really dismal streets of the old Raval, a fusion-food restaurant had recently opened. Over several days I lunched on Japanese-Hispanic fusion food at Invisible, Catalan tapas in a converted convent called Carmelitas, and "new global cuisine" in a design workshop that had once been a church. Deejay (DJ) restaurants—where a man in headphones puts on electronic music while you attempt to make yourself heard across the table—were all the rage. Salsitas, on Carrer Nou de la Rambla, had been around for years. But now this latest incarnation of the "restaurant de disseny" had gone forth and multiplied, and within a few square miles there were DJ restaurants with names like Iposa, Rita Blue, Nova ("Cuisine + Musique"), and Lupino, a "restaurant lounge" with a terrace at the back for schmoozing and boozing into the early hours.

I spent my first morning on a tour of the city's best food shops, fulfilling my out-of-towner's dreams about urban eating. My wanderings took me out of the Raval and all over town, into neighborhoods I barely knew, each with its own distinct culinary personality. The Born, an old-town area near the port, was Barcelona's new high-fashion zone, its hypermodern restaurants serving wild fusion cuisine with an emphasis on oriental flavors. Gràcia, a former working-class neighborhood, now boho, was strong on Middle Eastern bakeries and souvlaki bars. Deep in the Barrio Gótico, the city's medieval heart, I found cheese shops, coffee merchants, and new-wave bodegas specializing in the potent new wines of Priorat and Penedés. I spent a happy half hour in an old-fashioned grocery called Gispert, close to the church of Santa María del Mar, where I bought dried ñora peppers and dried mongetes and watched a batch of toasted hazelnuts emerge from an ancient oven at the back of the shop.

Fired up by the morning's adventures, I had a quick lunch at a falafel shop on the Ramblas and then returned to the metro, letting myself be guided by instinct, curiosity, and the recommendations of various observant friends.

This afternoon, the theme of my investigation would be sugar. Barcelona had always had a notoriously sweet tooth, and its pastisseries (pastry shops) had always been an important part of its city's gastronomic life. No saint's day or other religious fiesta was without a special biscuit, cake, or sweet. At All Saints' Day there would be panellets—round almond macaroons studded with pine nuts; for the Three Kings, people rushed to buy tortell de reis, a cake filled with marzipan which often hides a dried fava bean and a tiny figure of a king. (Whoever finds the bean in his slice must pay for the cake the following year, whereas the finder of the king is "crowned" with a party hat of gold cardboard.)

It was only two weeks before Easter, and already Barcelona was preparing for one of its most important fiestas. On Easter Monday, according to a tradition dating back to Roman times, godparents are supposed to give their godchildren a mona de Pascua—originally a loaf of bread with a whole hen's egg, shell and all, encrusted in its surface. Such primitive mones can still be found, but in Barcelona the ritual, like so much else in its food culture, has taken a radical departure. The modern-day mona is based around chocolate, either in the form of a rich chocolate cake or, in the grandest pastisseries, a figure molded entirely out of chocolate.

Steering a course through the crosshatched streets of the Eixample, I went to have a chat with Christian Escribà, of the city's most important pastry-making family, and to take a look at this year's mona.

The Escribàs are the aristocrats of pastissers in Barcelona. The business was founded in 1906; and Antoni Escribà, the patriarch of the firm, is as famous in Catalonia as Ferran Adrià, and even has an entry to himself in the Catalan national encyclopedia. ("A man of great culture and sensibility," declares the text.)

The window display at the family's flagship shop on Gran Via was a stage set crammed with elaborate confectionery. I saw pairs of high-heeled shoes modeled in white and black chocolate, spun sugar flowers at 150 euros a box, multilayered chocolate cakes as gorgeously decorated as abstract paintings. In the midst of it all was the mona: a meter-high representation of Harry Potter, complete with wizard's cape and wand, all molded from an almost obscene quantity of chocolate couverture.

Inside the shop, Barcelona women with stylish hairdos patiently waited in line to be served bread, cakes, and other sweet fripperies, all beautifully packed up to take away.

Christian is the Escribà brother responsible for the important business of custom-made fantasy cakes, which he has produced in honor of Pedro Almodóvar, Bruce Springsteen, and the pope. If something is truly worth celebrating, it is worth discussing with Christian. When Ferran Adrià got married a year or two ago, it was Christian who planned the extravagant wedding party, using actors and lighting effects to create a cake-centered "happening."

"My job, really, is to make people's sweetest dreams a reality," said Christian, with conviction.

Together we stepped up a flight of stairs to a room that the family keeps as a kind of museum of the mona, where some of the masterpieces of Easters past are preserved for posterity. Around the room, on podiums under atmospheric lighting, stood chocolate sculptures of Gaudí's Sagrada Familia, and of Mick Jagger's guitar; there were dinosaurs and dolphins in chocolate, and a quarter-scale model of a Formula One racing car, made for Spanish driver Pedro Martínez de la Rosa.

The author of all this artistry stood and watched as, awestruck, I took in this shameless display of sugary kitsch.

"We in Barcelona always liked chocolate, but we never understood chocolate," pronounced Christian. "Now, finally, we are becoming experts. We have artisans doing really interesting things, and a whole world of xocolata de disseny: designer chocolate."

He gave me an itinerary for a chocolate-based tour of the city. As I followed the list that afternoon, I found that, indeed, cacao was being put to some fantastic uses in Barcelona. A chocolate boutique called Sampaka was sleek and beautiful inside. It sold chocolate in the form of truffles with balsamic vinegar, with olive oil, with anchovies, and with hazelnuts; and a chic little café at the back served such novelties as chocolate sandwiches and toast spread with tomato-and-chocolate jam. At Xokoa I bought chocolate CDs in proper CD cases, and hot chocolate lollipops flavored with chili. And at the headquarters of master patissier Oriol Balaguer, where you are admitted through an industrial iron portcullis after announcing yourself at an entry phone, the high-design creations had names like substance, intensity, pleasure, and paradigm. They were displayed like jewelry, in exquisite black boxes on squares of plate glass. They had no price tags, and I got the feeling that Balaguer's place was like a fashion boutique not only in appearance but also in the sense that if you had to ask the price of something, you probably couldn't afford it.

The next day was another bright March morning, and I had more food shopping to do. Crossing the Raval from south to north, I came out directly on the Ramblas, dodging the living sculptures, the pamphleteers, and the British tourists in their shorts and sandals, and turned right toward a grand entrance set back from the street. This portal excitingly presages the splendor that lies within.

First-time visitors to Barcelona are often surprised to discover that, along with the buildings by Gaudí and the Picasso museum, the city also possesses a food market that is practically a work of art. Of the two greatest Spanish markets—Barcelona's Boqueria (properly known as the Mercat de Sant Josep) and the Mercat Central in Valencia—I would be hard-pressed to say which I prefer. Perhaps I'd have them share first place, with Bilbao's Mercado de Abando or Madrid's Maravillas coming in second. Valencia gets a high score for its glorious building, and for the brisk authenticity of its functioning, so genuinely valenciano. Barcelona is more exquisite and more expensive, and comes perilously close to a kind of super food hall, but wins out overall on sheer good taste and passion for food.

La Boqueria was a convent of Carmelite monks until the convent burned down in 1835 and a fine new market was set up in its place. In 1914 it was given a roof and a stained-glass modernista front entrance, which, as in the Mercat Central of Valencia, gives the building a touch of ecclesiastical grandeur.

In an age of hypermarkets and convenience foods, there is something heroic about a food market where everything is of the finest quality imaginable, almost everything is locally produced, and the place is busy—and not just with tourists, though they do gape with understandable awe at the spectacular displays. Equally, it's a cause for celebration that this huge, vibrant market—at 6,000 square meters the largest in Spain—is still alive and kicking at the heart of the city center and hasn't been hauled out to the suburbs to make way for ritzy shops and apartments.

I plunged into the fray, starting with Marisc Genaro at stand number 743, where I took away half a kilo of Palamós prawns. At Especialitats Salaons, round the corner at number 737, I bought a big slab of salt cod loin, pearly white and virtually boneless. The sales clerk wrapped it up in wax paper and added a complimentary can of anchovies, thereby ensuring my continued patronage of Especialitats Salaons. From there I worked back toward the vegetables, taking a detour through the fish section, where the merchandise was spread out theatrically on raised marble slabs and the fishwives waited behind the slabs like music-hall actresses about to start their number.

The sunlight flooded in through the glass roof, picking out the colors of the exotic fruit at Marisa's stand near the front entrance. Marisa brings in fruit that had never been seen in Spain until it appeared on her stand: durian, star fruit, jackfruit, kumquat. A group of Spaniards from some other community stood before the display chatting and pointing, amazed by this kaleidoscopic collection of novelties. A few steps away was a tiny, nameless stall selling snails in various sizes—autèntics cargols de Lleida ("real Lérida snails")—hanging in clusters in fat string bags. There were more wild things hanging from the roof at Salvador Capdevila, the Boqueria's great expert in game meats, where I fantasized about buying a whole hare and making liebre a la royale for dinner; and at Llorenç Petràs, fungi king of Barcelona, who has his stand at the very back of the market beside the Plaça de la Gardunya. Petràs is one of Spain's great authorities on fungi of all kinds. He remembers that twenty years ago there was only one species the Catalans would touch: the rovelló or níscalo (*Lactarius deliciosus*), known in English as the saffron milk cap. Nowadays there is no limit to their lust for any and every edible species: on the stand today Petràs had chanterelles, parasols, and Saint George's mushroom, as well as a selection of local rarities in dried form, wrinkled and gray-brown, with unappetizing names like orelles de gat (cat's ears), potes de rata (rat's legs), and pets de llop (wolf's farts). I noticed a tray of dried moixernons, the fabulously aromatic little mushroom that some Catalan cooks add to their beef fricandó. I picked up a handful of them and raised it to my nose, breathing in their essence of earth and wilderness. I bought 100 grams and put them in a box in my kitchen at home, where they are still awaiting a moment of culinary glory that may never come.

It was now nearly midday, and all this sensory stimulation had given me a powerful appetite. Fortunately the market bars of the Boqueria would be there when I needed them. These bars are a vital element of the market's body politic, serving hearty breakfasts of pigs' feet and fricandó for market workers at a time of the morning when most of Spain is only beginning to contemplate a cup of coffee and a croissant. They are all good places to eat but only one is really good: the Bar Pinotxo, just inside the market from the Ramblas side, just at the point where the froth of passersby gives way to the serious foodie action of the interior.

The Pinotxo belongs to the Bayen Asin family, who have run it for years. The bar's patriarch and visible head is Juanito, a Boqueria personality with his trademark bow tie and permanent smile. While Juanito chats with customers over the counter, preparing coffee or pouring drinks, members of the younger generation cook up a storm at the back of the tiny galley kitchen. The steaming casseroles they dish up at midday reflect their morning's adventures around the stands. Never was "market cooking" more precisely that.

I claimed an aluminum bar stool, leaving my bags of purchases on the floor, savoring for a moment my return to one of my favorite places on earth. Here was Juanito, looking the same as ever in his vest and red bow tie, smiling genially as he loomed up to me to tell me that today the chickpeas were very good, and that also there were langoustines a la plancha, new-season peas with morcilla and ham, breaded lamb chops . . . I ordered a plate of chickpeas—they were rich, oily, and perfectly tender—and a crisp bread flauta rubbed with tomato and dribbled with olive oil (pa amb tomàquet, the greatest of all Catalan contributions to human happiness). "¿Y para beber?" Juanito suggested a glass of cold sparkling Cava, and it did seem like a good idea. Barcelona is almost the only place in Spain one can drink champagne in a bar without feeling pretentious. So I sat on my bar stool, flicked through the newspaper that the Pinotxo keeps bound on a pole, and lost myself in a bubble of quiet contentment while the noise and color of the Boqueria swirled around me.

The cut and thrust of the market had taken the edge off my urge to shop. Besides, I was now well ensconced in the aperitif phase, the delicious downward slope toward lunch.

I would jump into a taxi and visit a few of my favorite bars, taking a drink and a tapa in each, before crash-landing at a certain "restaurant de disseny," where I had booked a table for two-thirty.

The car sped off down the Ramblas in the squinting sunshine, heading for a one-room bodega in Poble Sec where the house speciality is a miniature feast of wild mushrooms in oil, tuna escabeche, pickled baby onions, and slices of mojama. Some of the best foods in Barcelona are the tangy, appetizing snacks composed of cured and pickled ingredients, traditionally taken with a glass of vermouth. From there I moved on to Txampanyet, beside the Picasso museum in Carrer Montcada, for a plate of green olives and another of pickled garlic cloves, cool, crunchy, and surprisingly mild.

What would Spanish food be without tapas? More to the point, *where* would it be without tapas? Nibbling on something savory along with your drink is an idea as old as the hills—because, as every drinker knows, a little something salty helps the booze go down and also stops you from getting tipsy quite so quickly. But the Spanish have made the custom a central part of the experience of life.

In the meaning of the word tapa ("cover") lies its secret history. The tapa was invented as a way of keeping the flies out of your glass of wine, in the days when drinks were taken in the dark, dank bodegas where the wine was stored. First a piece of bread would be placed over the glass; then the bread came with a slice of cheese or ham, or perhaps an olive or two on the side; and before anyone knew it, the tapa was born.

If the tapa did not exist, however, it would be necessary to invent it. In a society where breakfast is so perfunctory a meal that for many people it simply doesn't exist (a recent survey found that almost half of all Spanish children had nothing to eat before school), and where the midday meal is often at three in the afternoon, the idea of nibbling something savory and salty with some bread and a drink at the end of the morning is not so much a luxury as a lifesaver.

Any decent bar from Cádiz to La Coruña, from Gerona to Jerez, will be able to offer the drinker at the very least some potato chips, some olives or almonds, perhaps a slice of cheese and a few rounds of chorizo and a basket of bread to make these items into something resembling a meal. Beyond these basics, over the years a standard, pan-Spanish tapas menu has developed, including tortilla de patatas, fresh anchovies in vinegar, chicken or ham croquetas, meatballs, patatas bravas (brave potatoes!) in spicy sauce, prawns al ajillo, "little Russian salad" of cooked vegetables in mayonnaise . . .

Then comes the great divergence. Every Spanish region, every city has its own take on tapas culture. Seville, historical heartland of the tapa, is strong on fried things, and also on traditional guisos like chickpeas and spinach, bull's tail, and so on; but (and the same goes for other areas of sevillano life) it has not made much of an effort to update its repertoire. Madrid, as the city where every Spanish region is represented, has an unrivaled variety of tapas as well as its very own callos (tripe) a la madrileña, and Madrid still respectfully observes the ritual of the midday aperitif. The pintxo of the Basque country is a sophisticated offshoot of tapas, forming a culinary genre of its own.

As for the tapas of Barcelona, the question of whether, and if so what, is vexed. There is no real tradition, as in the south, of whiling away the hours before lunch over endless glasses of beer or wine. This has a lot to do with the Catalan character, which places a high value on the work ethic and is not prone to wasting time. Unlike the andaluz or madrileño, the Catalan worker traditionally preferred to eat sitting down. He had his midday meal at home, and didn't dillydally on the way.

Of course, all this is changing fast. The Catalan aperitif tradition is still alive, though only just. But other Spanish regional traditions are making their mark: Basque bars have recently sprung up all over town, with fascinating pintxos on trays on the counter. Galicians were probably the first immigrant community to settle in Barcelona, and many of their bars offer regional tapas such as pulpo a feira and tuna-stuffed empanada. Meanwhile the new-style cervecerías—beer halls with more than a touch of Madrid—cheerfully mix and match local traditions with whatever takes their fancy.

When I last looked, the newest wave in Barcelona tapas was the tapa de autor. The addition of autor, as in cine de autor, was significant. It implied this tapa had a creative genius behind it, not just a short-order cook doling out patatas bravas and croquetas. There were three or four hot spots in town for tapas de autor, but Comerç 24 was the center of the genre. When it first opened in June 2001, it was a pioneer of the playful new Spanish cuisine, then at an apogee of fame. As the years have gone by there have been imitators, but nothing has quite dislodged Comerç 24 as the coolest restaurant in a town that takes the notion of coolness with touching seriousness.

Comerç 24: the name is also the address. When letters arrive at the restaurant, the writing on the envelope reads: Comerç 24, Comerç 24.

This was the place to be, a restaurant that summed up in a single experience the sunny optimism of modern Barcelona regarding food, interiors, and clientele. It was in the Born, the city's art and fashion neighborhood. I walked the mile or so from the Picasso museum, arriving a little short of breath and flushed from almost half a bottle of Cava.

If you weren't in the mood for high design or were feeling shy, you might find Comerç 24 an intimidating sort of place for a solitary lunch. The dining room was sunk in a penumbra of moody gloom, lit up by spotlights on walls colored deep wine red and rich mushroom gray. Iron columns, left over from some former industrial incarnation of the building, grimly stalked the room.

I sat on a high chair looking out over this broodingly minimalist landscape. To my left was a plate-glass window behind which lay the all-white kitchen. Within a meter of my table, an Asian chef was hard at work with raw fish—sniffing it, slicing it, and arranging it on curvy white plates. Two giant vases of bright-colored glass held a stook of massive calla lilies. The Germans at the next table were snapping away with their digital cameras. I heard English, Japanese, and French conversations. There was barely a Spaniard in the room.

"Marchando un festival," someone called in the kitchen. This is the term at Comerç 24 for the long, thin menú degustación, so in vogue in Spain. A number of small dishes are brought to the table in rapid succession, rather in the manner of El Bulli—where, to be sure, the chef at Comerç 24 earned his stripes in the 1990s. The menu included "Surprise Kinder Eggs," asparagus with Parmesan and mandarin, and "our onion soup."

Carles Abellan had thought deeply about the theory of tapas and its application to the modern restaurant. What was interesting to him was the custom of tapas, the atmosphere surrounding them, and their democratic character. He found it fascinating that, for example, by the mere fact of serving tapas, a restaurant became somehow more informal, more comfortable, more fun.

"You would never wear a jacket in a tapas bar. Anything goes. It's more like being at home," said Carles. He was dark-haired, strong-faced, and handsome, with a dark countenance more andaluz than Catalan. Looking at him, you could see how the Spanish got their reputation for devilish good looks.

An Indian waiter in a black suit was coming toward our table, bearing a tray laden with interesting objects.

"OK, now first I want you to try this," said Carles.

On the tray was a selection of cans in the ovoid forms of old-fashioned sardine cans: you pulled back the ring to reveal the nuts, olives, caper buds, and potato chips that you might find at a classic aperitif bar like Txampanyet. A glass of sweetish, spicy vermouth foamed up with soda from a canister.

"It's a classic. It's the essence. The idea of starting with vermouth and snacks. Vermouth and appetizer. One goes with the other. It's a Barcelona thing," said Carles.

The chef sat down opposite me and watched my reactions as the festival progressed. His dishes were all small, but perfectly formed, and ingeniously presented on Japanese lacquer and slate slabs and white porcelain squares. There was a tiny sándwich of jamón serrano, mozzarella, and black truffle—a little homage, perhaps, to the mutual admiration society that exists between Spaniards and Italians. And then there were two cold soups: cherry gazpacho and melon with grapefruit and mint.

Then came a strip of raw salt cod with two small puddles of sauce—pil-pil and samfaina—a witty mix-up of two regional traditions, poking fun a little at the solemn culinary nationalists who say that never the twain shall meet. As if to add a little Oriental spice to the mixture, I had seen it being prepared a little earlier by the Japanese chef behind the plate-glass window.

"Of course we must vindicate the traditions from here and there, but they can live together perfectly and no pasa nada," said Carles with a nonchalant movement of his hand. "Maybe it can't happen in politics, but in cooking it can. Everything mixes; everything enriches."

Carles grew up in the working-class barrio of Gràcia, where his parents still live. He was one of five children. His mother's cooking was straightforward traditional Catalan, of a kind that few Barcelona households are still familiar with. Proper stews with a base of sofregit: macaroni in the Catalan style with ground meat, onion, sausage, and ham; fricandó of beef; rabbit with samfaina; chicken with prawns— and, every Sunday, the eternal escudella with its full complement of meats, vegetables, and pilota. Salt cod with peas, or a la llauna. A lot of traditional casseroles, because a nice guiso was a good way of feeding a big family.

"Per mullar pa. It's a Catalan expression. Good enough to dunk your bread in. It means the dish is succulent and tasty." I had a quick mental picture of the whole family around the dining table, mopping up the last of a rich sauce with hunks of crusty white bread. "And this is what our food was like. Per mullar pa."

It made me smile to think of this supercool chef in his supermodern restaurant de disseny, secretly lusting after the home-cooked dishes of his childhood. This reminded me that, although the energy and confidence of Spain's contemporary cooks has brought about a food revolution, it could never have happened without the psychological anchors of tradition, family, and regional identity. The glittering edifice of the new Spanish food is built on the solid foundations of the old.

"You know what's happened? We have changed very quickly," mused Carles. "We have taken to creative cooking with tremendous speed. And now we're missing a different kind of food. Look at me. I'm an example. I still want to do modern things. But more and more I'm interested in things that just taste good. I do a black rice with cuttlefish ink and garlic. And I've had customers who said, 'You can't have this rice on your menu.' I say, 'Why on earth not?' And they say, 'Because you can't have this dish next to a Surprise Kinder Egg.' And I say, 'Yes I can.' Finding a rice like this—it's like putting your feet on the ground; you're on home turf. And anyway, if everything were modern it would be boring. Don't you think?"

15

Madrid

O N THE TUESDAY after Easter, when the Holy Week processions had all gone by, I took a train from my home to the mainline station of Atocha. The countryside was in bloom; there were cherry blossoms in the gardens, and thickets of broad beans in the vegetable patches that lined the fringes of the railway tracks. The city itself, too, was caught up in the euphoria of spring. Even its gray stone tenements, so gloomy in the rain and snow, seemed to be making an effort to look picturesque.

Madrid is the center. When Philip II made it the capital of a united

Spain, wresting the title from Toledo, this dusty one-horse town had little to recommend it beyond its position at the geographical heart of the nation. And ever since, what Madrid has done best is to concentrate, bring to the center, the cultural currents of the country at large, as well as add a special flavor of its own.

Unlike Barcelona, which is sure it wants to be modern, Madrid has not quite made up its mind. But when it does, Barcelona had better watch out. For the energy of Madrid, once it gets an idea in its head, is irresistible. Even more than Barcelona, Madrid has been the focus of an extraordinary process of social change. In just over fifty years, the city has gone from being the war-torn capital of one of Europe's poorest countries, where the inhabitants were dying of starvation, to being the prosperous hub of a wealthy nation.

RICARDO MIRANDA AND Amparo Camarero were born in 1928 and 1929 respectively and witnessed at close quarters some of the most turbulent years of Spanish history. They were born at opposite ends of the great Castilian plateau: Ricardo in Valladolid, and Amparo in Alcubilla de Avellaneda, on the high plains of Soria. Even in those days the metropolis exercised a powerful attraction over the rural population, and their families duly ended up in Madrid, where Amparo's father eventually found a job for life with Telefónica and Ricardo's father was a telegraph operator in the army.

I first met the couple in a bar in the Valdeacederas neighborhood, at the northern end of Paseo de la Castellana, where I'd been browsing in a bookstore on Calle Tetuán. When the bookstore closed for the evening, I walked into the bar next door and ordered a café con leche (early evening being the only time other than the morning, by the way, when Spaniards will countenance drinking coffee with milk). Ricardo and Amparo were sitting at the next table, also drinking café con leche.

I think we started talking about the luxury of milk; how we all tended to take it for granted these days; and how the center of Madrid had actual dairies, with cows, right up until the 1960s. Where Ricardo first lived when they arrived from Castile, there were open fields, the houses stood on their own, and his mother had night frights at the emptiness around them.

"During the war, of course, there was no milk for breakfast," said

Ricardo. Then he paused, unsure of the direction the conversation should now take. There are subjects that are still not very much discussed, chief among them being the three-part Spanish tragedy of the democratically engendered Second Republic, which briefly offered hope for a brave modern Spain; the civil war, which snuffed out that hope; and the thirty-six long years of joyless dictatorship that followed the war.

"During the war, of course, there was a great deal of hunger," Ricardo ventured to add. "One really would eat almost anything. There was money, but there was very little supply. You exchanged things—clothes, shoes, whatever you had that anyone else might want—for sugar, rice, lentils, coffee. We ate things we hadn't seen before."

"You got used to making the most of everything," said Amparo, a bright-eyed woman with a timid smile and a piping grandmotherly voice.

"It lasted for three years," said Ricardo.

"We slept fully clothed, in case there was a bombing raid and we had to get down to the basement," said his wife.

The Spanish civil war broke out in July 1936, when an uprising began among Spanish troops in North Africa and quickly spread to the area around Cádiz. Almost from the beginning, the majority of Spain's arable, cereal-producing lands were in the hands of the so-called "nationalist" side, while the cities remained under the control of the republic. During the three years of the war the nationalist zone never suffered any serious problems of food supply. But in "loyal Spain," especially in the cities and above all in Madrid, famine and malnutrition reached unspeakable and, from the contemporary perspective, nearly unthinkable levels.

In August 1936, when Madrid was not yet even on the front line, the city began to see the first signs of trouble. By September there were shortages of eggs, potatoes, and sugar. There were lines in the streets for even the most basic foodstuffs. By the autumn, ration cards were being issued. Each citizen was allowed, per day, a total of 100 grams of lentils or beans, one-fourth of a liter of milk, half a kilo of bread, 100 grams of meat, 25 grams of tocino, half a kilo of fruit, 50 grams of soup, and one-fourth of a kilo of potatoes.

The problem was as much poor organization and lack of planning as scarcity per se. Those parts of the country that were Madrid's principal sources of supply—namely Galicia and the two Castiles—had fallen into fascist hands before the siege began. But the city authorities did not foresee a protracted and difficult war, and there was little attempt at a rational distribution of what limited resources were still available. In the Sierra de Madrid, which became a lifeline as far as food was concerned, huge numbers of cattle were slaughtered during the first few months of the war. At a time when railroad links with the outside world were still open, large amounts of food and coal could have been brought in for stockpiling. Yet this was not done, and by the following winter the city was shivering with cold and hunger.

On January 23, 1937, the governing junta of Madrid announced in one of its periodic briefings, "Today, we can be sure that the population has almost nothing to eat. It will be of no use to have weapons if Madrid dies of hunger."

Madrid did not die of hunger, though many of its people came agonizingly close, and according to a report, perhaps partisan, in the *London Times* in February 1939, between 400 and 500 people were perishing every week. How did the survivors survive? By a combination of resourcefulness and ingenuity. Rice and oranges came in by train from republican Valencia, at least until the battle of Jarama, when the supply lines from that city were broken. There was very little meat, at least not of the commonly available sort. In Calle Lista there was a private house where horsemeat was sometimes sold. Whenever a horse broke its leg at the old Hippodrome near the La Coruña road, and had to be put down, the carcass was shared out among the employees. The Spanish phrase vender gato por liebre—"to sell cat as hare," meaning to cheat or fake—probably originated in the civil war. Survivors of the siege of Madrid remember that the city was virtually emptied of cats, most of which undoubtedly found their way onto the table.

Necessity was the mother of invention. Some families kept a chicken or two in the attic. If there was not much in the way of vegetables to be found in the markets of the city, there was always plenty of purslane for salads—it grew on the rooftops, and was harvested and sold in bunches. When lentils ran out, a substitute was found in the seeds of the carob pod, which resembled them in everything except taste. Above all, one learned to be flexible.

Amparo had finished her coffee and was fiddling with an

unopened packet of sugar, laying it like a tiny pillow on the tabletop in front of her.

"My mother used to save potato peelings and fry them," she told me. Her voice had taken on a wistful, faraway sound. "We made croquetas with plain white rice. The pods of broad beans . . . they tasted of green peppers. My father smoked a lot. So when there was no tobacco, he used to dry orange peels, and smoked that instead."

Generally speaking, war is bad for the art of cookery. War tends to concentrate the mind on the basic facts of existence, such as whether or not one has enough to eat, so that the subtleties of taste and aroma suddenly seem like ridiculous frivolities. During the three years of the civil war almost nothing was published in Spain in the way of a cookbook; but a slim volume of recipes for hard times, *Cocina de Recursos: Deseo Mi Comida* (roughly, "Resourceful Cooking: I Want My Food") was written in Barcelona and published after the end of the war. The author was Ignasi Doménech, a Catalan who had worked as a cook in the houses of the Spanish nobility and in various embassies, and who was well known before the war for his *Nueva Cocina Elegante Española,* a recipe book cleverly interweaving the Spanish culinary tradition with the famous dishes of French and Italian cuisine.

In the winter of 1938, as the war entered its desperate final year, there was little room for elegance in the eating habits of the divided nation. The list of recipes in Doménech's book says much about the reality of wartime Spanish cuisine: we find such curious paradoxes as "eggless tortilla," "fried calamares without calamares," and "bouillabaisse without fish." The book also suggests cunning ways with stinging nettles, chrysanthemums, and the leaves of wild thistles.

If the civil war brought hunger back into Spanish life, the postwar period made it common currency. Even today, the word posguerra carries a connotation of misery and despair. These years brought new hardships, subtly different from the old. The postwar daily bread ration of 150 grams was supposed to last all day. Lentils came to be the central ingredient of the national diet—but they were often contaminated with insects, and it was common to see black weevils floating on the surface of a bubbling pot of lentejas. People who had no fuel for cooking ate their potatoes raw. According to a popular urban myth of the time, there was a figure called el sustanciero, a man who went from house to house with a ham bone which, at a small price, was left for a while in each pot of chickpeas or lentils, to add sustancia (substance) to what would otherwise have been a weakly flavored stew.

This was the era of the estraperlo, the black market: and the estra-perlista, a Dickensian character who made a fortune from the misery of others. Almost anything could be bought from the estraperlistas, if you had the money (but not republican money, which was now invalid), and the authorities mostly turned a blind eye to their activi-ties. The most visible signs of this immensely lucrative and wide-spread business were the women who hung around the markets, offering loaves of bread, bags of flour, and liters of olive oil, for either cash or barter.

The low point came in 1941, known ever since as "the year of hunger." Rationing was harsher than ever. A series of savage droughts had reduced the country's ability to feed itself.

"We were left with nothing more than the day and the night," said Amparo.

"You had to find ways around the problem. In our family we had sixty kilos of chickpeas for the whole year, at five pesetas a kilo. On the black market, you understand. If you went to have a glass of wine, there were no aperitivos. I used to carry a lump of salt cod in my pocket, and I would gnaw on that," said Ricardo.

"I remember a product called huevina, a substitute for eggs, a kind of powder," said Amparo.

"And the meat that came in from Russia, in big cans. How delicious that was, madre mía!"

If any single thing kept Spain alive during the dreadful 1940s, how-ever, it was probably gachas. In the years following the civil war, when its calorific and stomach-filling qualities were needed more than ever, this savory slurry became once more a staple of the national diet—along with other "prehistoric" foods like migas, chestnut stews, milled acorns, and altramuces.

As though to dignify an embarrassing fact, this greasy porridge was now known by a euphemism: puré de San Antón. Gachas were most often prepared with the flour of the almorta, *Lathyrus sativus,* a relative of the lupine. Almortas are squarish little beans, which are still culti-vated in some rural areas of Spain; in the Balearic Islands country peo-ple know them as guixes, and prepare them with wild greens for the

Lenten dish cuinat. The problem with the almorta is that it actually constitutes a health hazard. It contains a toxin which if consumed excessively over long periods can lead to muscle weakness, trembling, and paralysis of the limbs. A pathology known as latirismo was described by Roman medical authors but had been a rare phenomenon in succeeding centuries—until the year 1943, when it reappeared. Apart from the big cities, where it was rife, along with dysentery, typhus, and tuberculosis, the epidemic was especially severe in the provinces of Ciudad Real, Cuenca, and Toledo, where the postwar diet frequently consisted of little more than gachas de almorta, week in, week out.

"There were so many of us in my family. . . . Seven children, nine people including my parents, and my grandmother made ten," continued Ricardo. "We lived in Calle Santa Isabel, down toward Atocha station. Before the war my mother made cocido almost every day of the week, with chickpeas. And on Sunday, paella. But my favorite was always gachas. In winter we ate them a lot. As a child I thought they were delicious."

"A mí me hacen gracia las gachas—I'm fond of gachas. Ricardo's mother made them very well," said Amparo, smiling at a memory that had bubbled up from nowhere.

Clearly the technique, or the aptitude, had been handed down from mother to son, because Ricardo was also quite a specialist in cooking this ancient porridge. It was his party piece, the dish he prepared when he wanted to make an impression. His current version, it seemed to me, was a good deal more sophisticated than the oily gruel that sustained the nation during the grin-and-bear-it years of the posguerra.

"You make them in a frying pan like the ones you used to see in the old days, with high sides," he explained enthusiastically. "You fry pieces of tocino, chorizo, and liver, and slices of sausage; and with the fat left over from the tocino you add the almorta flour; you toast the flour a little—and you add water, little by little. And you see how it begins to get thicker and thicker, and you keep on stirring, and you know when it's almost done when it starts to bubble, plup, plup, like the lava in a volcano. It's at this moment that you add the fried things: the chorizo, the liver, the sausage and tocino, whatever you like. You can also add some caraway, some cumin, some parsley, ground up in a mortar and pestle with a little water. A little salt. Y ya está. It's winter food, with plenty of calories. A bowl of gachas on a cold morning, and you'll be set up for the rest of the day."

"More like the rest of the week," quipped Amparo. She shot me a mischievous glance across the table.

With regard to food, Madrid has a double personality. The capital of Spain, perhaps like the nation as a whole, seems caught between a rush for modernity and a comforting slow undertow of tradition. It harbors a secret passion for the old-fashioned life and food of its forefathers: vermouth at midday, tapas of tripe and tortilla in the creaking taverns of the old town, cocido madrileño with its interminable soup, meat, vegetables, and chickpeas. But it also likes to show the world that it, too, can be avant-garde, and that anything New York and London can do, it can do just as well.

I took the metro to the Puerta del Sol, climbing the staircase into a dazzling Spanish spring morning. The semicircle of the Puerta del Sol was a cauldron of dust, noise, and humanity. Pile drivers thundered behind a labyrinth of barriers; frustrated drivers leaned on their horns.

I took off down Carrera de San Jerónimo, my senses attuned to the uneasy coexistence, in this schizoid city, of the obstinately old-fashioned and the racingly, bracingly new. Here was the grand door-way of Lhardy, founded by a Swiss in 1839, where you could still take your cup of consommé from the silver samovar at the back of the shop, and the upstairs dining-room served a cocido madrileño that would shut down your digestive system for the rest of the afternoon.

A little farther on was Casa Mira, renowned since 1855 for its luxurious and expensive turrón. Doubling back to Sol, I worked my way along Calle Mayor toward the old market of San Miguel, housed in a delicate construction of ironwork and glass dating from 1914, and somehow clinging to life in the twenty-first century jungle of super-markets and hypermarkets, its clientele now reduced to a dwindling congregation of old town residents. Down a narrow street that juts off Calle Mayor, I recognized the church of San Ginés. Next door was the famous Chocolatería San Ginés, where I remembered going on a Sunday morning in the late 1980s, straight from the discoteca, stumbling in with a gang of friends for a restorative breakfast of crisp fried churros dunked in cups of hot chocolate as thick as custard.

On a street corner someone handed me a free newspaper, and I ducked into a quiet cafetería to read it. In the restaurant pages was a review of a place I had never heard of before, a curious-sounding hybrid of tapas bar, fast-food joint, and designer eatery. Fast Good, as it was called, was the brainchild of that grand master of modernity in Spanish food, Ferran Adrià. It was in the Salamanca neighborhood, Madrid's version of the Upper East Side.

When morning rolled around to midday, I took the metro again, getting out at Goya. Life in the scuzzy old town had ill prepared me for the elegance of an uptown neighborhood with tree-lined avenues and tall houses. The air here smelled of money and clean sidewalks. The people looked thinner, blonder, and whiter than the folk downtown; their skin was clearer, their hair more lustrous. On this weekday at lunchtime, the men were in suits and ties; the women brandished designer handbags and wore big sunglasses pushed up over their hair.

Fast Good had a retro feel, an atmosphere of pop art and nostalgia for the future. I sat at a window where three giant plastic lamps colored bright blue, purple, and emerald green cast the light from the street on the floor like stained glass. Well-groomed young mothers sat in white leather armchairs while their friends and husbands lined up at the cashier's desk, taking sips from big glasses of mineral water as they chatted idly into mobile phones. White vinyl arches divided the space, with white vinyl baubles suspended in curtains beneath them. You might easily have been in a groovy nightclub in London at its swingingest during the 1960s.

The idea of the working lunch, American-style, has finally been subsumed into Spanish life, but in the process it has lost something of its Protestant urgency. Here in Madrid, it seemed less about being in a genuine hurry to get back to the office, and more about needing to demonstrate to the world that, as a modern person, you were fashionably short on two faintly embarrassing traditional commodities: appetite and time.

I looked around the various counters, where you could choose from a range of tiny goodies in space-age portions tightly wrapped in cellophane. Miniature sandwiches of chicken, lemon, and rocket, or black olive and mushroom, or soy-marinated tuna with sesame paste;

a tapa of roasted vegetables with hazelnut dressing. A separate section
held kits for making modern food at home. A cutely packaged box
included two organic eggs, a block of Parmesan cheese, a packet of saffron and some hazelnuts, together with a recipe for a kind of savory
flan. There were good wines by the bottle (the new Spanish working
lunch by no means precludes a glass of wine), cold beers, and the kind
of teas and tisanes that never had much of a presence here, until health
and hippies brought them into circulation. Everything was clean,
small, neat, and bright. By two o'clock, zero hour of the Spanish
lunchtime, neat clean people were lined up, snakelike, across the floor.
Balearic chill-out music murmured in the background. It was a vision
of a contemporary urban lifestyle that would have astonished anyone
who had known Spain in its "black" version, grim, dark, and primitive.

But Fast Good was merely an aperitif before the day's main meal:
the restaurant La Broche, modern gastronomy personified by the
Catalan chef Sergi Arola. Both Fast Good and La Broche bear the
imprint of Ferran Adrià: the former because the idea of a designer
snack bar was his, and the latter, because Sergi Arola is, of all the various alumni and followers of the master, the one who has brought his
philosophy to the widest public.

I walked the few blocks across the barrio de Salamanca to where
Hotel Miguel Angel sits beside the squalling Paseo de la Castellana.

One can understand the appeal of minimalism as a reaction against
the dark, cluttered Spanish interiors of the past; but La Broche was a
cool box in which color had been banished from everything except the
bright assemblies on the big white dining plates.

Sergi Arola was the very model of a media chef, a phenomenon
that, in the early twenty-first century, was still a novelty in Spain.
Handsome and fashion-conscious, he was known among magazine
editors as a good sport who would happily pose undressed in the
kitchen for a feature on naked celebrities, or reminisce about the alternative rock band Los Canguros (the Kangaroos), with which he played
guitar in Barcelona during the early 1980s. It was television that
cemented the foundations of his fame. I had seen him recently on two
occasions: as guest chef on a game show in which two teams of cooks
competed with each other to produce a meal in the shortest time, and
as the star of an advertisement for crispbread. In the ad, Arola was
shown in a domestic setting with his two little daughters, offering one

of them a dish of "ciabatta crisp with fillet of beef" to which she appeared to consent in the manner of a haughty client. "Crispbread Espiga de Oro: so that my best little customers are satisfied," was the tagline, followed by a kiss from Daddy and a gruesome forced laugh, to the camera, from the debonair chef.

Since its opening in February 2000, La Broche had soared to the height of fashion, galvanizing Madrid's food scene, which had hitherto lacked a little sparkle. When the Reina Sofía art museum opened a gleaming new wing designed by Jean Nouvel, it went without saying that the new building would include a matching, fabulous café-restaurant, and there can have been little doubt in anyone's mind about who would be hired to create the menu.

Today I was lucky enough to catch him at home in the kitchen of La Broche, and he served me a menú degustación that fairly took my breath away. It included a deconstructed escudella of beans and meatballs with foie gras; confit of cocks' combs; and a surrealist combination of sea and land snails roasted in lard with a mad salad of tiny violet potatoes, capers, marinated onions, and chanterelle mushrooms, all arranged on a square of fine phyllo pastry. I wished I could have tried the loin of horse with tomato bonbons, if only because seeing it on the menu reminded me forcefully of the civil war and postwar period in Madrid, when the eating of horse was more a matter of desperation than of scaling the summit of exquisiteness in food.

WHEN I FIRST LIVED in Spain there were no restaurants like La Broche. There was little general awareness that anything else existed besides la cocina de siempre: the cooking we've always known. Bookshops, if they had a food section at all, would carry only a feeble selection, nothing like the large-format glossy cookbooks that fill the shelves today. Most Spanish newspapers had no restaurant critic, and chefs were rarely in the news. Gastronomical writing was a furrowed-brow genre dominated by male writers (in the Anglo-Saxon context, interestingly, women have flown the flag) who solemnly pontificated about the correct recipe for suckling pig or the origins of mayonnaise.

Every revolution needs a person with the clarity of vision and expression to convey its message to the wider world. For the new Spanish cooking it's José Carlos Capel. Capel writes a column in the newspaper *El País*, which has for ten years acted as a register for every-thing new—appetizing and not so appetizing—in the national gastro-nomic life. Today he had found me half an hour in a schedule even more hectic than usual, since he was organizing a three-day food fair in Madrid, to be opened the following day, at which most of the lead-ing Spanish chefs would be present, as well as a healthy representation of the world's gastronomic media.

"I've been writing about gastronomy for—what?—twenty-four or twenty-five years, so really you could say I've been a witness to the evolution of what's been going on in Spain since at least, oh, 1976," said this elegantly spare gentleman with a shock of wavy gray hair.

While he took a phone call I browsed through a book of his that lay on the table before me, a breviary of the tortilla de patata, in which a galaxy of modern chefs—such as Sergi Arola, Joan Roca, Pedro Subi-jana, and Manuel de la Osa provided artful reinterpretations of the plainest and most universally loved of all Spanish national dishes. I was especially taken with Andoni's egg poached at seventy degrees Celsius in a consommé of onion, potato, and green peppers—in essence a deconstruction of the Basque tortilla of his youth.

"The movement begins in 1977," he said as he put down the phone. "Well, the 1980s were a tremendous time. We had no idea where we were going; there was a sense of perpetual change in the air. Zalacaín opens in 1974, and three or four years later gets its third Michelin star. Subijana, Martín Berasategui have their moments of greatness. Then, in the early 1990s, there is a pause. After the Olympic Games in Barcelona and the Expo in Seville, there is a crisis. Many restaurants are forced to close; those that stay open must lower their prices. Zala-caín is sold.

"Until that moment, of course, what had been happening was a bringing up-to-date of traditional cooking. But there had never been entirely new techniques. What happens in 1993, or 1994, is that we begin to hear about a new figure on the scene, a Catalan chef who is astonishingly innovative. He is creating a new cuisine with concepts and techniques that no one has ever thought of before. How should we cook shellfish? Should we cook them at all? In the old days, to make a French-style mousse, you needed some kind of fat, or whipped cream. He discovered that you could create a foam with car-bon dioxide, and it would have a delicacy that no mousse had ever had.

Health, and lightness. Both were fundamental. And it's at this point that the seed is sown—the seed of creativity and change. The techniques of this new man are the ones to be copied, which all the major chefs in Spain are naturally inclined to do. There is no doubt that he is the revolutionary figure. He is the Robespierre. And he is proclaimed a genius.

"There had always been fashions in restaurant food. The 1980s were the era of salmon, lobster, and piquillo peppers stuffed with everything under the sun. But nothing like this. Now everyone was creating foams; people were deconstructing every dish that crossed their minds. When the fad for liquid nitrogen came along, everyone started making dishes with nitrogen."

José Carlos has seen it all. The chefs he still rates highest are those of the first wave: Adrià, Arzak, Roca, de la Osa. But there's a new generation coming along. He mentions Quique Dacosta, Dani García, and Nacho Manzano. "And a young man who has a restaurant in a farmhouse outside San Sebastián, fantastically talented. He'll be one of the greats, no doubt."

Not Andoni Luis Aduriz? Yes indeed, the very same. José Carlos was at the Barcelona Ritz when Andoni Luis served his famous alcohol-free banquet there. How wonderful that was, we agree. But how very surprising, and how very strange.

"It's madness," he said mildly, seeming to refer not so much to Andoni's experimental cooking as to the restaurant world in general—its chefs, its fads, and the sheer amount of work it puts him to. "Madness," he said again. His gaze became momentarily vacant, losing itself for a second in midair.

He glanced at his watch: my time was up. Half an hour of this man's time on a day like this was already a great favor. But José Carlos had another favor to offer, as we wound up the conversation: a VIP pass to the big show tomorrow.

A phone call to his assistant, and I was set up with a plastic-coated security tag to hang around my neck or clip to my shirt pocket. The event had sold out long ago, and José Carlos's secretary was fending off calls from frustrated food folk all over the world who had left their requests until too late. I tucked the card in an inside pocket of my briefcase, feeling like a lucky man. There would be people outside the conference center begging for tickets. The show was in all the newspapers, and on the national television news. Madrid Fusión: the name had resonances of "fusion food" and "fashion," and also suggested a coming together of heterogeneous elements, a blending into a whole. It sounded modern, optimistic, and somehow inclusive: you too could be fused, if you could afford the price. I felt it to be the culmination, in a peculiar way, not merely of my own experiences in the world of Spanish food, but of the history of Spanish food itself.

On a clear day, Madrid is a mountain town. The sky is piercingly bright. The air is refreshingly cold, and so dry it cracks and chaps the lips. The horizon is ringed with sierras where patches of late snow still cling to the shadier slopes. De Madrid al cielo, runs the saying: from Madrid to heaven.

The next morning I'm sitting in a big white taxi on the way to a conference center on the outskirts of town, a strange outpost of society in a landscape of plate-glass glitter, a suburb open only during office hours.

Women in neat short skirts and high heels, men in dark suits, filing in fast through the big chrome doors. Legions of attendants, checking passes, talking into walkie-talkies, handing out programs. The echoing whiteness of the foyer, filled with the noises of expectation and organization, like the entrance to a gleaming new railroad station. From the ground floor a white marble staircase ascends to the upper level, where a theater stands on a central island, under a high glass roof. Bridges radiate out to other zones, other departments of the show: a product fair, a room for tastings, coffee bars, beer bars, and sherry bars. Some of the bars have serrano hams on stands at the front, with a professional slicer furiously carving away.

Food in Spain is production, consumption, tradition, and the humdrum business of cooking and eating. Over and above all that, it's an industry that moves millions of euros and gives employment to millions of workers. Anyone who had been used to thinking of Spanish food merely as a pleasurable adjunct to the good life on the costas—a plate of tortilla and some olives to go with your glass of wine—would be amazed at the power and influence of the industry that exists to present such food to the world. Twenty-two percent of Spain's gross domestic product is made up by the food industry in its various forms, compared with the 10 percent accounted for by tourism. From restaurants themselves, the human resources necessary to staff them, the tourist industry that provides a large percentage of their clients, and the suppliers of the necessary raw materials, its sphere of influences radiates outward into many ancillary industries. They all are here. The suppliers of glassware, crockery, cooking equipment, uniforms, cookbooks . . . A number of the autonomous regions have their own stands at the fair, and well-dressed young women are smilingly handing out handsomely produced literature—books, recipe leaflets, and DVDs. The most forward-looking Spanish regions are belatedly realizing that visitors are able to make a close association between food and sense of place. Sell them the gastronomy of Tenerife, therefore, and you're selling them Tenerife. Build the food into the core brand: it's basic marketing.

There is plenty of fun to be had. Food as entertainment, food as pastime. If you had the stamina and time, you could spend three days making the rounds of the seminars, tastings, roundtables, and demonstrations. There are workshops on tapas, the art of the grill, cocktails, desserts; on the properties of dried fish scales and eyes and bones; on the uses of aloe vera in haute cuisine. Tomorrow there will be cookery demos by Sergi Arola, Joan and Jordi Roca, and a legion of Basque chefs with unreproducible names.

For now, the fairgoers have an appetizing morning ahead of us. At ten o'clock sharp, the whole place shuts up to listen to the mayor of Madrid, who gives a short speech to open the show. He talks about the value of "interculturality," the breaking down of barriers, the opening of frontiers, the sharing of experience, and the importance of his city on the international restaurant scene. What he doesn't say is what I'm thinking: that a city which now prizes itself as a producer of audacious avant-garde cuisine, was, just sixty years before, a city where people were reduced to eating dogs and cats.

First on the cookery stage is Martín Berasategui, three-star general of the new Spanish cuisine. Born and bred in San Sebastián, Martín grew up in his parents' wine cellar in the old town. He walks onto a set that gleams with stainless steel and bristles with gadgets. Behind him on the kitchen wall are the names of the sponsors, never out of sight: Maggi; BMW; El Corte Inglés; the Madrid Olympics bid; Mahou, the beer of Madrid. Martín is a solid professional and a businessman, but a man of great taste. His raw-pea puree is a classic of contemporary cuisine; I have eaten it myself, at his restaurant in Lasarte. "My cooking begins with the product. My first loyalty will always be to the farmers, the fishermen, the winemakers of our land." The ponytailed Floren Damenzain, king of vegetables, flashes into my mind; I remember Martín's tribute in Floren's catalog. Martín prepares a dish of soybean sprouts and oyster with coffee, pepper, and curry, and tells us the importance of cooking vegetables without water. "I'm not the kind of chef who throws much of a shadow," he says modestly, almost to himself, leaning over the countertop to slice a beet into paper-thin sheets. "I'm more the older brother who's here to help."

Then Juan Mari Arzak takes the stage. We applaud like mad as he bumbles onstage, genial and beaming.

"People talk about cooking as technology, as art, as raw material. Well, today I want to talk about cooking as diversion," he announces.

"Cooking is a game: a serious game, but still a game. I have never in my life cooked anything without enjoying myself. It's so important to think like a child, to develop the capacity to amaze and delight. You need to get out and about, into the street. Discover the world."

Then he says, "Look at this dish," showing us blown-up digital images on a screen behind him. It's that poached egg with parsley and squid-ink sprays; I ate it last year at his restaurant. The origins of the dish are in Basque home cooking: when there were leftovers from the squid in its own ink, they'd be eaten the next day with fried eggs and parsley. But then came the twist. Arzak was inspired, he says, by a graffiti artist he saw working on a wall one day: those sprayed starbursts of color. He's a man of nearly seventy, but as open-minded as a twenty-year-old. The old rocker, he calls himself. He shows us the making of his cordero con café cortado, the process of rolling a tender piece of lamb in a sheet of coffee as thin as cellophane, peeled from the base of a frying pan, so that when the sauce is poured into the tube it gently disintegrates. "Wow, I love this; it's a fantasy; it's like a game," he chuckles as the sauce goes in and the translucent brown tube falls in on itself like a fairy-tale tower. It is difficult to understand, and curious to see, how anyone at this moment in the world can be so brimful of optimism.

"The young generation is so much better prepared than we ever were," says Juan Mari from the edge of the stage. "Which is why I can't see that there's a problem with Spanish cooking. On the contrary: things are getting better and better."

At the end of the morning I leave a sweater on my front-row seat, hoping this will be enough to dissuade anyone else from stealing my place, and roam the stands in search of something to eat. My program says there's to be a tasting of regional tapas, with local wines to match.

From my place at the bar I watch a parade of waiters emerge from their field kitchen.

"Let's see what they think of this fancy shit," mutters one as he balances a tray on one hand and strides out into the fray.

The canapés are distantly inspired by the cooking of Navarre. This means that there is chistorra in a crisp pastry case, and menestra served in tiny pots, and Swiss chard stalks fried with béchamel and roncal cheese.

As the Navarrese wine begins to flow, however, culinary considerations begin to take second place to the need to eat. The waiters' route takes them from the kitchen door across the bridge separating the stage area from the rest of the hall. The cleverest and hungriest of the fairgoers, I see, have quickly learned to position themselves at the end of the bridge, in order to pick off the best morsels before they reach the desperate masses on the far side. Now the battle is on to seize as many canapés as will fit in a hand, on top of a program, or wherever else the booty can be conveyed. As tempers fray, the scene degenerates into a free-for-all. Raiding parties can be seen looting entire trays of tapas from the agitated waiters. One woman, a smart executive in Blahnik heels, holds aloft a paper shopping bag, shoveling half a dozen pinchos into it from on high, calling to her friends behind her, "OK, guys, I've got something. Now we can eat."

I stay at the bar to watch this comic scene and settle for a plate of acorn-fed ham, some green olives, and a free big glass of Mahou beer.

Now a voice comes over the Tannoy: the next master class will begin in five minutes, *five minutes.*

A shiver of excitement runs through the conference center, from the ground floor all the way up to the back row of seats in the theater.

The atmosphere is suddenly akin to a busy foyer in a concert hall where a charismatic pop star is about to perform, with people hurriedly grabbing their hot dogs and Cokes, checking their tickets, and chattering. The last of the wine is swigged, glasses are dumped on tables strewn with abandoned leaflets, and the throng can be felt to move, gradually but purposely, toward the theater.

The stage now resembles a television set, blazing with lights, buzzing with cameras. The foot of the stage seethes with audience members, some trying to get to their seats; others peering at the setup onstage, which includes a giant industrial gas bottle that looks like an unexploded bomb, but is actually a siphon; still others simply milling about, perhaps hoping for a glimpse of the man who is a living incarnation of the transformation their country has recently undergone. From my seat he is just a few yards away, adrift in the crowd in his white chef's jacket, fending off questions that come at him from right and left. Some Japanese journalists surround and trap him, making little nods and bows, assembling themselves around him while one of them backs away with a camera. The journalists pose for the photo op with delighted grins—if their friends could see them now!—but the star's smile is merely friendly and a little distracted.

At the seaside on that evening last summer I found him affable and sure of himself, but in a self-effacing way. Here in Madrid he looks different: a bigger, wide-screen version of himself, with not a trace of nerves. He seems energized, enthusiastic. I would never have suspected it, knowing what I know about his mistrust and rejection of celebrity. But up here in front of the world's media and his peers, he is in his element. In the atmosphere, I sense affection, admiration, perhaps a dose of gratitude toward a man who has done at least as much as anyone else alive for the power of Spain as a brand. At least as much as Plácido Domingo, Montserrat Caballé, Pedro Almodóvar, King Juan Carlos II, Antonio Banderas, or Penélope Cruz—though not quite as much, heaven knows, as Julio Iglesias.

A man in an olive-green sports jacket bounds onto the stage. It is José Carlos Capel, the summit's master of ceremonies. José Carlos begins saying something inaudibly into a microphone. The crowd disperses: the hubbub fades into a murmur. It's time.

"Por favor, ladies and gentlemen, por favor . . ." he says three times, until the noise has subsided and he can just be heard.

The mise-en-scène is impeccable. It feels like an apotheosis, a consecration. I can see down below: there he is; the man is waiting to go on, smoothing down his jacket, checking his mike. What is he going to do? We don't much care. It'll be enough just to see him up there, strolling onstage, chatting to us about food, life, the restaurant, and his inspirations. It might not even be a demonstration by any conventional definition; it might be more of a rambling disquisition on originality in art and the meaning of electric milk. But that's fine with us. We just want to see him.

Thousands of watts of spring sunlight pour through the roof. The stage is a whiteout.

José Carlos is speaking in measured tones, conscious of the charged nature of this moment. But he's smiling, too. There's sweetness in the moment, a sense of triumph.

We know what is coming; he can't shut us up anymore. Some of us are already on our feet, cheering, hands clapping, loose papers fluttering from files over the heads of the rows in front.

Now the decibel level is rising again. It flashes across my mind that this is the noisiest country in the world; the authorities have done surveys, measured the shouting in the streets at midnight and the motorbikes that roar by in the squares. Our massed voices echo off the glass roof, booming around the lower floors. It looks as if José Carlos was going to say something more. If he was, he now gives up, letting his hands fall to his sides in mock exasperation. The only thing left for him to say now is the inevitable show-business formula, the words that raise the curtain.

"Señoras y señores, Ferran Adrià."

Epilogue

>≼≽<

I AM SITTING IN our small stone house with the generator humming. A gentle mist is flooding the valley, muffling the sounds of dogs barking farther up the hill. Then comes the rain: at first a soft pattering, now a furious downpour, drumming on the roof tiles, picking off the moss from the stones. A black cloud has squatted like a giant sulky toad at the head of the valley. On an afternoon like this there is nothing to do but read, think, write, cook, and eat.

After the cities, it was good to slip back into home and routine. The farm and its produce resumed their rightful place at the center of my life. In springtime there were peas and beans, the first spring onions, lettuces of all shapes and colors. When the hens started laying again, I made little omelets with fresh peas and garlic, and habas con jamón with shreds of our own home-cured ham. In May I planted potatoes, French beans, cucumbers, corn, and the rest of the hot-weather stuff. On June 15 a hailstorm pulverized it all, and the following week I planted it all again.

I spent the summer quietly, my routine a slow round of mornings up at the farm, afternoons at the river with friends and books, and late nights in the kitchen. Spanish summer eating is about measure and modesty: we want energy and refreshment in easily manageable forms. I made liters of gazpacho and kept it in a flat glass jug in the fridge door, for those dog days when I want nothing more for lunch than a glass or two of cold gazpacho along with a piece of goat cheese or an anchovy fillet, some bread with olive oil, and a ripe peach for postre. Toward the end of the summer, when the eggplants and peppers kicked in, I made huge quantities of pisto, Spain's answer to rata-touille. My summer nights were spent processing boxes of fruit and vegetables before the heat could rot them. Luckily there are always people glad to take a box of zucchini off your hands in return for a cheese, a loaf of homemade bread, a bag of lemons.

After the autumn rains come the last tomatoes of the season, as precious and special as the first. While they were coming in bucketfuls, all through the hot summer, I held them almost in contempt. Now I realize that a long winter beckons without their familiar acid-tinged sweetness and musky aroma, and I decide to treat these late specimens with a little more respect. I bring them out, these October tomatoes which have been slowly ripening on newspaper on the kitchen table, in careful slices on white plates, with an announcement at the table that this just may be one of the last two or three tomato salads of the year.

It has been a good year for quince, and my trees are still laden with big knobbly fruits that, once you wash off their grubby felt, become bright shiny yellow boulders, hefty in the hands. Now is the time to make dulce de membrillo, the Spanish sweetmeat par excellence, essentially a fruit jam poured into molds and allowed to set until firm enough to be cut into slices. I have made ten kilos this year, and more is to come.

Nacho got back from Palestine last week, full of stories of orchards in Jericho with year-round vegetable patches and wondrous fruit. While it is still raining, there is a lull in our agricultural routine. But soon there will be important tasks to consider: winter tasks. The pig must be killed. The olives must be picked and taken to the mill, the wine racked off into clean glass demijohns. On a bright, short, cold day when there is nothing else to do, we might spend the afternoon making aguardiente—literally "burning water," the Spanish equivalent of grappa—in a copper still set up in the open air, distilling it from the skins and stalks left over from the grape harvest. When the oranges are at their best, in January, I make a dark, bitter marmalade without which breakfast at my house could never be the same.

It is no exaggeration to say that most of what I know about food has been taught to me by the people and landscapes of Spain. But the rest I have discovered myself, through an apprenticeship as a small-time farmer who doesn't mind getting dirt under his fingernails. When food production is taken out of our hands by industrial processes and global economies, we lose out in understanding, in the effects on our health, and in the loss of true flavor. Taking back control of the process can be empowering. Until I made butter from the cream of my own cow, I never understood that butter could be a rich oily paste, almost as yellow as saffron, smelling of pasture and flowers. Until I ate slices of loin from my own home-slaughtered pig, I never realized that if the animal has eaten figs and apples all summer and foraged for acorns all winter, the meat will be incomparably fine-textured as a result. Life in the country gives me daily lessons in the way things ought to taste.

PETRA CAME UP AGAIN this afternoon, bringing food and conversation. Everybody should have neighbors as good as she is.

My friendship with Petra sums up most of what I have learned from these years in Spain. The particular rhythm of passing time, the texture of life, and how that which is of value is celebrated.

As a cook and as a farmer I model myself on her, because she understands better than anyone else I know that growing food and cooking food are two sides of the same coin. She does all the country things I try to do, but does them very much better, with an unassuming brilliance born out of natural aptitude, and after years and years of hard experience. From the milk of her husband's goats she makes a cheese so true-flavored that if it were available on the open market, it would win prizes at every cheese fair in the country.

This afternoon we stood among the cabbages, talking about what can be done with them. She had brought me a clutch of oranges she had picked on the way up.

Before lunch, she tells me what she intends to cook; in the afternoon, she tells me what she and her family have eaten at midday. There might have been a nice hot caldo, a Spanish consommé, to which people here attribute miraculous powers of defense against the demons of cold and damp. A big pot of costilla con patata, the savory winter stew of pork spareribs and potato with garlic, onion, olive oil, and pimentón. Or on Sunday, a proper cocido of beans and meats, to send her husband stumbling to the armchair while the rain falls harder and the afternoon darkens into evening.

My talks with Petra are proof that the rustic cooking of the region, though suffering under the onslaught of convenience, still has plenty of life left in it. Sometimes when I am walking down from the farm at lunchtime, through narrow streets of modest stone houses, I can hear the sound of pots and pans, smell the fine odors of frying and simmering on either side of the street; and it makes me happy to think that there is a corner of old Europe that still cares about proper home cooking and regional dishes, and hasn't sold its soul for bottled sauces and just-add-water noodles.

Where I live, the supermarkets have a special shelf for sacks of salt, sausage casings, kilo bags of pimentón, and the paraphernalia of the matanza. Street markets sell not just the fruits and vegetables themselves, but trays of seedlings and fruit-tree saplings so that people can grow their own. I take these as signs that the traditional rural idea of food—which is to say, that it is entirely normal for the consumer to produce at least some of it himself—is here alive and well, if losing a little currency with every passing year.

NIGHT HAS FALLEN; the stream is rushing in the darkness. Inside the house the fire is lit; Nacho is asleep in front of it.

The church clock rings the hour: it is just ten o'clock. A good time to eat a simple Spanish dinner. I list in my mind the available ingredients: half a pumpkin (the other half we ate yesterday, in a rice with saffron), a head of purple garlic, half a dozen eggs. I will venture out with a flashlight if need be for some parsley, an onion, a head of lettuce. A pair of precious late tomatoes, to be rubbed on toasted rye bread, and a bottle of our own olive oil. Salt and pepper and pimentón. I lay it all out on the kitchen table, an old master's still life of rich and appetizing color. Just at this moment, the soul of Spanish food is all around me— out in the fields, in the olive groves and orchards, and right here on the table in front of me.

I ponder the possibilities as I put another log on the fire. And in half an hour we are sitting down to a revuelto de calabaza, the yolks with their warm maize yellow tinged a deeper shade by the pumpkin pieces, which have softened and melted a little around the edges. Somewhere in there is a garlic clove, bashed and roughly chopped, to be sizzled in the heating olive oil. And parsley, the greenest thing I've ever seen, torn with the fingers over the top. There is bread rubbed with tomato and our own aromatic, smoky white wine. And for dessert, Petra's gift of oranges. They are the first of the season's very first crop: a harbinger of winter. Yet they have a taste, not of hard times and leafless landscapes, but of holidays and sunshine, the bright sweet taste of being alive.

Appendixes

Entremeses*

꧁ ꧂

Dichos Culinarios

Most languages have a number of expressions relating to food. English has, to quote just the first few that come into my head, "to be worth its salt," "our daily bread," "bringing home the bacon," "to sit there like a lemon," "salad days" (well, this is from Shakespeare, so it may not count). Spanish is no exception, and there is something about the sheer quantity of food-related dichos (sayings) and refranes (proverbs) in the language that gives one pause. Whole anthologies have been published of Spanish culinary proverbs. Most of them have fallen out of use, but many remain. They are a product of a society which until the 1970s was overwhelmingly rural, and for which the rural world was still the major source of simile and metaphor. The rich legacy of Spanish phrases allows us to glimpse a society that is still able to see human life as a manifestation of nature. De higos a brevas—from figs to early figs—refers to the fact that figs are in season during late summer and autumn, whereas early figs appear in June; and so it means in English "very occasionally." When you don't care a fig for something, the Spanish don't care a cucumber. Estar en un berenjenal, literally "to be in an eggplant field," means to be beset with intractable problems.

---

*Entremés (cul.): hors d'oeuvre. The term "Entremeses" was also used by Miguel de Cervantes to describe the short plays he wrote in the last year of his life. These "interludes" are lighthearted pieces which Cervantes is said to have "chuckled as he wrote."

Why the eggplant should have been chosen to represent hardship and complexity may seem mysterious at first; except that, as anyone who has ever grown eggplants will know, there are often terrible spines around the base of the fruit, so that walking in a field of them might become a prickly and difficult business.

Spanish proverbs relating to cookery mine a rich vein of comedy and color. Someone who is putting his best foot forward, or making an all-or-nothing effort, is said to be "putting all the meat in the roaster." When it comes to cooking utensils we have coger la sartén por el mango—to "grasp the frying pan by the handle," that is, to get serious about something, or to take the bull by the horns. Se le va la olla—roughly, "He's overcooked the pot"—means "He's lost it" or "He's gone crazy." Se me pasa el arroz—"I've overcooked the rice"—is the comically rueful phrase a Spanish woman might utter when she thinks she's now too old to get pregnant by traditional means.

My favorite sayings are the ones that yoke together metaphorically sexual desire, or passionate love, with the act of eating. There is an earthiness about these expressions that to English ears sounds faintly embarrassing and possibly in bad taste. You might say of a sexually appealing person, Está como un queso: "He (or she) is like a cheese." (It would have to be a ripe, oozingly delicious cheese, possibly a torta del casar, into which you dip crisp slices of toast or sticks of raw vegetables in the manner of a fondue.)

If to the Spanish imagination cheese represents lust, bread stands for everything that is reliable, virtuous, and genuine. You often hear it said of people or things that they are más bueno que el pan ("better than bread"). And if you want to describe a thoroughly good, thoroughly well-behaved person, you might say un pedazo de pan—"a hunk of bread."

I remember clearly the first time I heard a man say to his daughter that he found her so "delicious" that he could "eat her up whole." Estás más rica . . . ite voy a comer entera! It was said with a lip-smacking sensuality that my latent Protestantism found shocking; and only when I thought about it carefully did I begin to see the equation of hunger and love, the two great overriding human needs, as something not only poetically appropriate, but also hiding an important psychological truth. It may be a Latin thing, but there is sometimes a fierce intensity about a parent's love for his or her children that, in actual fact, is very well expressed by the metaphor of hunger for a home-made morsel of juicy, meaty, substantial, delicious food.

La Cocina Española
(The Spanish Kitchen)

The Spanish kitchen—in other words, the place where Spanish cooking goes on—sometimes has a rather spartan look about it: decoration and clutter are normally at a minimum, this being essentially a place for work, not leisure. It might be thought underequipped by Anglo-Saxon standards; in reality, of course, it corresponds perfectly to the kinds of dishes to be prepared in it. Especially in rural areas, Spanish kitchens aren't filled with electric toasters, sandwich makers, ice crushers, or the dozens of other gizmos that increasingly clutter western urban life—with the exception of the pressure cooker and the handheld mixer, which is much used for soups and purees. English visitors are often surprised by the absence of electric kettles, which play such a crucial role in the making of our national lifeblood, tea. There is still no proper word in Spanish to describe this device (la tetera is sometimes used, though it really means teapot). When tea is prepared in a Spanish kitchen, the water is boiled, and the tea often made, in a small metal saucepan called el cazo.

Premodern societies have an inherent sense of measure, of economy, which, as postmoderns, we vainly struggle to recapture. The need to reuse oil for frying gave rise to a special pot into which the hot oil was poured, while the bits were strained out at the same time. The giant fridge obscenely groaning with food has only recently made its appearance in the Spanish kitchen—for obvious reasons. Spanish cooks never relied very much on perishable items that needed to be kept cold: they shopped in the market on a daily basis, and many of their ingredients were preserved by other means than chilling, whether dried, smoked, salted, put up in brine, or canned.

If there are things Spanish kitchens lack, by the same token there are kitchen things in Spain that we might regard as oddities. Cooking Spanish dishes in an English kitchen, for instance, can be a frustrating business, because the customary implements are simply not there, and you are forced to improvise. Most of all I miss the stacks of terra-cotta dishes without which many Spanish foods simply don't taste the same. The mortar and pestle, whether made of wood or ceramic, is an essential element of any kitchen however basic, and is especially prominent in Catalonia, where pounded mixtures of nuts and herbs (the picada) are used in any number of ways. Equally, the perforated metal skimmer or espumadera, present in even the humblest Spanish kitchen, is the perfect tool for a nation that loves to fry, and can be applied to all aspects of the task, from basting and stirring to straining off the hot oil. After fifteen years of using it almost daily, I can't imagine frying with anything else.

Globalization and the powerful influence of American habits are rapidly smoothing away the rough edges of our differences—more's the pity. But there is, still, no accounting for taste. Generally speaking—and it's an odd fact, considering their centuries of cohabitation with the culinary cultures of the Middle East—the Spanish are no great lovers of spice or heat in food. It follows that you won't find mustard in most Spanish larders, or bottled hot sauces, or anything pronouncedly piquant, with the exception of those long green Basque chilies in jars, and perhaps a string of little dried red peppers to be added, cautiously, one at a time, in such dishes as prawns al ajillo and salt cod al pil-pil. Even black peppercorns are not common; and the pepper mill, such a staple of life in Italy and France, is still a comparative rarity. (Grind too much into a dish, and you will hear protesting voices: ¡Cómo pica! "It's so hot!") The spices these people love are not so much piquant-hot as generous and warming. Near the stove, where it can be easily reached, you're bound to find a can of pimentón. In a rack on the wall there may be pungent saffron, or else its inadmissible, frankly unbearable substitute, orange food coloring. There will almost certainly be cumin seed and aniseed. And cinnamon—for a good arroz con leche, a leche merengada, a nice wobbly flan, and a creamy natillas are all unthinkable without the warm glow of cinnamon.

Almuerzo

Almuerzo is actually the correct Spanish word for lunch. In the population at large it has been almost entirely superseded by the catchall term comida—food. It still lingers in two particular senses, or maybe three. El almuerzo is a business lunch, a no-nonsense, hard-talking lunch where to discuss the food on the table, for example, would be to betray a certain feebleness of mind. The only other regular use of the word happens at the opposite end of the social scale, when workers who get up at the crack of dawn, such as laborers or builders, stop work at mid-morning and have something to eat. They can often be seen, at ten or eleven in the morning, sitting in the cab of the tractor with the engine off, or squatting in a line on a concrete beam, taking their bocadillos out of aluminum foil, washing down their almuerzo with a can of beer. As lunchtime in Spain seems to slide inexorably toward the trough of the afternoon, there are times when I rather envy the early lunchtime of the working class, and wouldn't mind at all replacing the plodding, ineluctable comida with a quick bocadillo and a beer before getting back to work.

Merienda

Merienda is a gerund, a something fit to be somethinged. Objectively it falls somewhere between snack, picnic, and tea as in the English meal (rather than the drink). Yet, as is often the case with Spanish eating habits, the word takes its true meaning rather more from an attitude, an understanding of the circumstances involved, than from a rigorous set of conventions. The custom of la merienda is most commonly observed by children when they get out of school in the early afternoon. In the past, Spanish mothers, waiting at the gates, might hand their offspring a hunk of bread with a slab of chocolate (like the French *pain au chocolat*), or a bocadillo of jamón York, cheese, or both, wrapped in aluminum foil. Alternatively the merienda might be served at home, especially on a cold day, with hot chocolate or Cola Cao (*the* Spanish childhood drink, bar none) and biscuits, or toast sprinkled with olive oil and sugar.

But there is another sense to merienda: it is the kind of impromptu meal you might take with you on a country walk: a juicy tortilla de patatas, a length of chorizo, and perhaps a Galician empanada stuffed with tuna and red peppers. It therefore becomes a movable feast, something nourishing and robust that will boost your blood sugar level at just the moment when it most needs boosting. To me it suggests not just a stopgap measure, a bite of something to keep you going till dinner, but also something special that falls outside the general scheme of things: a treat.

Comilona

"Big meal" doesn't quite capture it. Neither does *grande bouffe* or "pig-out." To my mind, what comilona implies is a get-together of family and friends around a table on a Saturday or Sunday at lunchtime, or at Christmas or Easter, a long celebration based on some festive food. That food could be a rice dish such as paella, a roast lamb or piglet, a whole baked fish, or a proper cocido with all the trimmings, the soup with the fideos followed by the chickpeas and meats on one big platter and the endless vegetables heaped up on another. Postres (desserts) are a matter of course, as are cheese, fruit, and copious wine. If the meal is held at Christmas it will necessarily wind up with sweets, chocolate truffles, almond turrón, and powdery polvorones that stick to the roof of your mouth. The meal may begin decorously enough, but may well end in shouting and laughter, with children running riot around the table and their elders drinking shots of ice-cold aguardiente and homemade pacharán.

Hoy me toca la comilona con la familia. "Today I've got the big meal with the family." I sometimes fancy I hear a bat's squeak of resentment in the word, as if to imply an obligation that, though enjoyable enough, a part of you would rather like to wriggle out of.

Sobremesa

Portuguese-speakers are often confused by the term sobremesa, because in their language it means simply "dessert." The literal meaning is "over table." In Spanish, however, it refers to what happens after a meal, or more precisely, after the main part of the meal, when the dishes have been cleared away and it's time to relax, to digest, and—most important—to talk. More than anything else, the sobremesa is an opportunity to indulge in freewheeling, lighthearted, pleasurable conversation. The smell of coffee drifts in from the kitchen. There may be digestivos: icy-cold shot glasses of aguardiente, or balloon glasses of brandy, anis, or whisky. Those Spaniards who still smoke—as I write, estimated at just under a quarter—will find this the moment to bring out their cigarettes, their rolling tobacco, or a nice little cheroot from a tin.

La sobremesa encapsulates what for many people is the defining characteristic of the Spanish lifestyle: an emphasis on informality, lack of stress, and unhurried enjoyment of the moment. The ballerina Tamara Rojo, who has become a star of the Royal Ballet in London, was once interviewed by a Spanish newspaper about her life in Britain. She told the journalist, "Aquí no hay sobremesas"—"There are no sobremesas here." It was a neat way of implying in a few words that in London people lived a hurried, purposeful life, which didn't allow for the casual Spanish attitude toward passing time. Rojo seems to have meant no disapproval by her remark: for her, it was just a fact.

The sobremesa varies in length, depending on the meal in question. At lunch on a workday, it might last just a few minutes, half an hour, or more. On special occasions, it might stretch out languidly long into the afternoon, with the dishwasher going in the background and the coffeepot empty on the heater, until the guests drift away from the table and the sobremesa eventually gives way to another fine traditional custom: the siesta.

Siesta

The custom of sleeping after lunch exists in all Mediterranean countries, though nowhere is it such an institution, such a pastime, or such an art form as in Spain.

The word comes from the latin *sexta,* meaning the hours from noon until three in the afternoon. Quite how it began, as a custom, no one really knows; it seems to have been around forever. But it is certainly on the decline: and most Spaniards say they don't take the traditional nap after lunch, at least not during most of the year. The custom has largely retreated into particular times of year, especially hot summer days, when there is no alternative; and holidays, when there's nothing to stop you.

An interesting thing about the siesta is the variety of forms it can take. For some people, it's a ten-minute shut-eye in a chair. Others, like me, actually get into bed, under the covers, and go into REM sleep for as long as the body requires. Some might lie down with a book.

Others might slump on the sofa with the afternoon movie. (Movies on Spanish television in the afternoons are generally unchallenging, fluffy stuff, third-rate Hollywood or 1960s Spanish films that won't interfere too much with a good snooze and might, indeed, encourage one.)

Traditionally, the Spanish had a cheerfully functional and uncomplicated view of the business of sleep. My impression is that, generally speaking, people in this country have tended to sleep soundly, without much insomniac tossing and turning or recourse to sleeping pills and herbal tisanes.

With Spain's entry into the club of the rich and worried, everything has changed. But still, it seems to me, Spanish culture does not make a fetish of sleep in the way other cultures do. The act of sleeping is not surrounded by a universe of products and practices, the pajamas, bathrobes, and buckwheat pillows, and breakfast in bed that the Anglo-Saxon world enjoys. (The idea of eating in bed doesn't sound to the Spanish mind like much of a pleasure.) Sleep is a commodity the body needs more or less of, like water or vitamin C, which is not to say it can't be cheerfully forgone if an all-night fiesta, a long philosophical discussion, or a moonlit walk in the park with the kids should happen to present itself. Lorca wrote that there's a moment just before dawn, when the first light is nothing but a dull glow on the horizon, which was the best moment, he believed, for human beings to go to sleep.

A friend's grandmother, a great conveyor of ancestral wisdom, had a favorite saying: La comida reposada y la cena paseada. It means something like, "Rest after lunch and walk off your dinner." The saying reflects, in part, a widespread conviction among Spaniards that one should not go to bed on a full stomach. This woman's grandchildren, including my friend, were at the age when Spaniards believe they must go out every night, all night. They believed the saying too, but only because it gave them ammunition when the time came to plead with their mother to let them out of the house for some nighttime adventures.

When I worked in offices I could never understand how at two o'clock sharp, after the universal hourlong lunch break, one was expected to continue work in the same alert and intellectually cogent manner as before. For at least an hour after eating, I would often feel faint and woozy, and my colleagues got used to the sight of me snoozing at my desk, head resting on folded arms.

So I took to the siesta like a duck to water.

Think back, think back. It was the start of the summer vacation, early August. A lunch of homegrown suckling pig, roasted on a rack of bay twigs. We sat, a group of adults and children, in a hot kitchen with the summer sun pouring through the open window, sweating slightly as we gorged on the sweet oily meat with its heavenly fragrance of bay leaf and garlic, swigging down red wine from glasses smeared with greasy fingerprints. But the conversation, oddly, was not so much about the excellence of the food, as about the monumental siesta we were all going to have afterward.

There were peaches, a little cheese, coffee, cigarettes. The kids disappeared, clattering their chairs, to play with dolls and dump trucks. A little glass of pacharan, brandy, or aguardiente? Why not? We're on vacation. There was a little more torpid chat while the dishes were removed and the congealing pork fat was scraped from the pan. And then, one by one, we did that Spanish thing: we sloped off to our beds, our sofas, our hammocks, our easy chairs, like animals after a feed, sloping off to their caves. I've known Spanish people to check out the siesta possibilities of a given situation—a nice shady spot under a fig tree, a mattress on the floor of a bodega—well before the big meal begins.

"What a hell of a siesta I'm about to have," muttered Enrique, groping his way toward his chosen site—a sofa just under the window where a faint breeze came in from the sea.

Then came the siestón: the big siesta. This time it was a two- or three-hour sleep, an excessive, baroque, holiday siesta. After a siesta like this you wake not quite knowing where you are, who you are, or what day of the week it is. There are pillow marks on your cheeks. The street outside is slowly coming back to life. There's a disconcerting morning feeling. You sit at the kitchen table dazedly, coming to your senses, drinking black coffee, as if it were breakfast all over again. And, in a way, it is. The second part of the day is grinding into gear—to be lived, if at all possible, as maximally and pleasurably as the first.

Glossary

Cat. = Catalan   Basq. = Basque   Gal. = Gallego

A

a la plancha: cooked on a metal hotplate

a la romana: battered and deep-fried, usually squid rings or hake

aceite: oil

aceituna: olive

acelga: Swiss chard

adafina: Sephardic dish from which cocido derives

adobo: "marinade," cazón en adobo: chunks of fish (cazón belongs to the shark family) marinated in vinegar and spices, then deep-fried. Popular dish in Andalusia

aguardiente: firewater, alcohol

ajoarriero: cf. bacalao al ajoarriero, Navarrese dish of salt cod with garlic

ajoblanco: cold almond soup from Andalusia, often served with grapes

albóndigas: meatballs

alboronía: Andalusian summer-vegetable dish similar to pisto *aliño*: dressing

allioli (Cat.): i.e., *"all í oli,"* "garlic and oil," powerful emulsion sauce made in a mortar and pestle, common accompaniment on Spanish Mediterranean coast to fish, meat, and rice dishes

almazara: olive oil mill

almorta: pulse similar to the lupine seed

alta cocina: haute cuisine

alubias: beans grown for drying, can be white, red, or black

aperitivo: aperitif, snacks served with preprandial drinks

aplec (Cat.): celebration, festival

arros a banda (Cat.): rice "on the side," cooked in a strong fish stock in the paella

arroz a la cubana: plain rice served with fried egg, fried banana, and tomato sauce

artesa: flat-based, long wooden container for kneading bread, mixing sausage meat, etc.

asador: "roaster," grill restaurant

azafrán: saffron

B

bacalao, bacallà (Cat.): salt cod

barra (de pan): long, flattish white loaf (of bread)

barrio: district, neighborhood

berenjena: eggplant

bocadillo: Spanish sandwich, usually made from length of barra (see above)

borraja: borage

broa: maize bread

bullit de peix (Cat.): mixed fish soup-stew (Ibiza)

C

café con leche: coffee with milk

café cortado: black coffee with a dash of milk

café solo: strong black coffee

cala: rocky bay, cove

calabacín: zucchini

calabaza: pumpkin, squash

calamares: squid

calçot/calçotada (Cat.): spring onion (scallion) and its related food event

caldereta: casserole, most often based on lamb or kid (Extremadura) and lobster (Menorca)

caldero: heavy iron pot, by association, fish and rice dish made in this pot (caldero murciano)

caldo: stock, consommé

canelones: "cannelloni," pasta tubes stuffed with minced meats and béchamel sauce

caña: small serving of (draft) beer

caracol: snail

casa de comida: eating house

casquería: variety meats, offal

cecina: dry-cured beef, served in thin slices, a speciality of León

cerdo ibérico: traditional breed of black pig

cervecería: beer bar

chilindrón: sauce of tomato, pepper, onion, and ham, most commonly applied to chicken and lamb, typical of Aragon

chipirones: baby squid, chipirones en su tinta: cooked in their own ink

chiringuito: beach bar/shack

chocos: small cuttlefish

chorizo: cured Spanish slicing sausage made with lean meat, garlic, and pimentón

churro: deep-fried tube of batter, often eaten with thick drinking chocolate

coca: bread-based tart, related to pizza

cochinillo: suckling pig

cocido: long simmered stew based on chickpeas or other pulses, also including vegetables, meats, and embutidos, e.g., cocido madrileño

cogollo: lettuce heart, also dwarf lettuce

comedor: dining room

compangu: refers to meats and embutidos used in fabada asturiana

cordero: lamb

cortijo: country house, farmhouse, esp. in Andalusia

costilla: spare rib

crema catalana: custard with a caramel crust, similar to crème brûlée, national dessert of Catalonia

croquetas: breaded croquettes filled with a thick béchamel, incorporating chopped ham, boiled egg, chicken, etc. Traditionally made with leftover meats from the cocido

D

de autor: "authorial," implies a style of cooking based around the creativity of a particular chef

denominación de origen (D.O.): "denomination of origin," official system controlling and protecting various speciality products and wines

dorada: gilthead bream

dulce (n. and adj.): sweet

E

embutidos: generic term for sausages, from verb embutir, to stuff

empanada: in Spain, a flat, thin pie with a variety of possible fillings, most commonly tuna with pepper and tomato. Originally from Galicia

empanadilla: small turnover stuffed with tuna, minced meat, spinach, and raisins, etc.

encebollado: cooked with fried onion, especially liver or tuna

encina: holm oak

escabeche: mild pickle of vinegar, herbs, and garlic, most commonly applied to rabbit or other small game, or sardines. The ingredient to be prepared en escabeche is previously roasted or fried

escalivada (Cat.): salad of charcoal-grilled vegetables

escanciar: method of serving cider, pouring it from a height into a flat-bottomed glass in order to oxygenate the cider

escudella: Catalan cocido of pulses, meats, and vegetables

estofado: meat stew, usually of beef

F

faba, pl. *fabes*: large dried bean used in fabada asturiana

fideo: thin macaroni-like pasta

fideuà (Cat.): pasta-based dish made in the paella, originated in the town of Gandía (Alicante)

fino: abbr. form of "Jerez fino," pale crisp white sherry of around 15 percent alcohol, the traditional Andalusian accompaniment to appetizers, tapas, and seafood

flauta: thin, crisp, baguette-style loaf

fonda: lodging house, from Arabic *fonduk*. In Catalonia, also implies restaurant

freiduría: fried fish shop

fricandó: traditional Catalan beef stew

G

gachas: savory porridge with fried tocino, panceta, etc.

gallego (n. and adj.): native of Galicia, language spoken there, etc.

gallina: hen, gallina en pepitoria, traditional dish of hen with almonds and saffron

gamba: prawn, shrimp

garbanzo: chickpea

garrofó (Cat.): large flat white bean, used in paella

gazpacho: 1) raw vegetable soup, served cold; 2) gazpacho manchego, rich game-based stew cooked with crushed dry flatbread

granizado: water ice

guiso (n.)/*guisado* (adj.): terms used to describe any dish made by boiling or simmering ingredients (as opposed to roasting or frying)

H

habas: broad beans

herboristería: shop specializing in herbs, natural remedies, etc.

horchata: sweet milky drink made from ground earth nuts (chufas), common in Valencia

hórreo: stone drying shed for maize (Asturias and Galicia)

huerto/huerta: vegetable garden. Also collective term, e.g., La Huerta de Murcia, vegetable-producing area close to the city

hueva: cured and pressed roe, normally tuna or grey mullet

huevos estrellados: fried egg and potato hash, as served at Casa Lucio in Madrid

I

ijar, atún de: tuna preserved in oil

J

jamón serrano: air-cured "mountain" ham

K

kokotxa (Basq.): gelatinous "cheeks" of hake, cod, etc.

L

lacón: salt-cured sweet ham, common in Galicia and Asturias

lampuga: common dolphin fish

latifundio: large country estate

lentejas: lentils

lomo: loin, lomo embuchado: whole cured pork loin

longaniza/llonganissa (Cat.): a variety of thin embutido

M

majado, majao: pounded mixture of spices, herbs, etc., often added to a dish in its final stages of cooking

manchego: of La Mancha, as in sheep's cheese, queso manchego

manteca: pork fat

mantecado: sweet biscuit made with ground almonds and pork fat. Also called polvorón

manzanilla: 1) type of Jerez fino produced in Sanlúcar de Barrameda; 2) chamomile for infusions; 3) variety of olive

mar i muntanya (Cat.): "sea and mountain," any dish combining seafood and meat

marinera: general term for seafood cookery, as in cocina marinera

marisco: shellfish

marmitako (Basq.): tuna and potato casserole

matancera: female expert in the art of the matanza

matanza: traditional pig slaughter and processing

mazapán: marzipan

mejillón: mussel

membrillo: quince, dulce de membrillo: quince paste, typically served with cheese

menestra: vegetable dish made mostly in the spring, originally from Navarre. The menestra may also contain lamb or chicken

menú degustación: tasting menu

merendero: picnic site, snack bar (see Entremeses, "Merienda")

merluza: hake, merluza en salsa verde: in a sauce with clams, parsley, and garlic

michirones: murciano dish made from dried broad beans

miel: honey, miel de caña: sugarcane syrup

migas: fried bread crumbs with garlic, chopped panceta, tocino, red pepper, etc.

milhojas: mille-feuille pastry. Also called hojaldre

mojama: salted cured fish, esp. tuna

mojo: sauce, esp. in Canary Islands, e.g., mojo picón (spicy), mojo verde (with coriander)

mona: Easter speciality in Catalonia. Originally a rich brioche, now more often chocolate cake or figure

mongetes (Cat.): white beans, mongetes amb butifarra (with grilled sausage, popular dish in Catalonia)

morcilla: blood sausage

morros: snout, "face" meat, usually of pork or beef

mortadela: similar to Italian *mortadella,* fine-ground pork slicing sausage used in sandwiches, in Spain stuffing often includes olives

N

níscalo (Cast.)/*rovelló* (Cat.): wild mushroom *Lactarius deliciosus* (saffron milk cap)

Ñ

ñora: round dried pepper, mildly spicy, used in cooking of southeastern Spain

O

olla podrida: substantial cocido-type stew typical of Burgos

P

pa amb tomàquet: Catalan snack, bread or toast rubbed with olive oil and tomato

paella: 1) shallow iron pan with handles; 2) rice dish cooked in this pan, originally from Valencia

panceta: cured pork belly

panellets (Cat.): almond macaroons, often encrusted with pine nuts or other nuts, made in Catalonia for the feast of Epiphany

pargo: porgy fish, common sea bream

pastelería/pastisseria (Cat.): pastry shop

pata negra: "black foot." The term refers to the Iberian pig, to the hams produced from it, and by association to anything of superlative quality

patatas bravas: fried potato pieces with spicy sauce

percebes: goose barnacles

perdiz: partridge

perrunilla: sugary biscuit, made with pork fat

pescaíto frito: an Andalusian favorite, small fish and/or fish chunks, dredged with special flour and deep-fried

picada: pounded mixture of herbs, spices, garlic, bread, biscuits, etc., characteristic of Catalan cooking

picante: piquant, hot

pil-pil: rich olive oil and garlic emulsion sauce, most often applied to salt cod, for one of Basque cuisine's most famous dishes, bacalao al pil-pil

pimentón: finely ground dried red pepper, used as a condiment

pimiento de Padrón: baby green pepper from Galicia, served fried, whose heat is notoriously unpredictable

pimiento de piquillo: variety of small, red, pointy-ended peppers, often stuffed with fish or meat

pintxo (Basq.): variant of tapas, find their highest expression in Bilbao and San Sebastián

piperrada: Basque dish of peppers (capsicum), tomato, onion, etc.

pisto: Spanish summer dish of eggplant, tomato, pepper, onion, etc., originally from La Mancha

pitu de caleya: free-range cockerel (Asturias)

pocha: white bean, picked between fresh and dry

porra: 1) thick churro; 2) porra antequerana, smooth gazpacho from the town of Antequera

porrusalda: leek and potato soup/stew

postre: dessert

potaje: soup/stew, generally with vegetables

pote: cabbage, bean, and meat stew typical of Western Asturias

pringá: kind of pâté made from the finely chopped fatty meats left over from the puchero

prueba: "proof," "trial," sample of sausage mixture fried up for testing at the matanza, now has become a dish in its own right

puchero: cooking pot, also Andalusian one-pot stew, related to cocido

pulpeiras (Gal.): octopus cooks, also refers to places serving octopus (pulpería in Castilian)

pulpo a feira: Gallego specialty, boiled and sliced octopus with cooked potato, olive oil, pimentón, and sea salt, served on a wooden plate

R

rabo de toro: bull's tail

ración: "serving," larger version of a tapa

rape: monkfish

rehogado: technique of sautéing previously cooked vegetables in olive oil

revuelto: scrambled eggs

ribeiro: Galician white wine

romesco: sauce of pounded almonds, hazelnuts, garlic, tomato, olive oil, etc., also refers to a fish dish typical of Tarragona

ropa vieja: chopped mixed leftovers from the cocido, sautéed in olive oil and garlic

rosca/rosco/roscón: varieties of baked goods

S

sagardotegia (Basq.): cider house

salazón: applied to any food preserved in salt, en salazón

salchichón: Spanish salami

salpicón: cold (seafood) salad

samfaina: Catalan base sauce of peppers, eggplant, onion, and tomato

serrano (adj.): "of the mountain," e.g., jamón serrano

setas: (wild) mushrooms

sidra: cider. Principally made (and consumed) in the communities of Asturias, Cantabria, and the Basque country

sobrassada (Cat.): pork sausage from the Balearic Islands, of a spreading consistency, cured with large amounts of pimentón

socarrat (Cat.): highly valued by connoisseurs of paella, the rice at the center of the pan's base, which becomes caramelized or lightly burned during cooking

sofrit pagès (Cat.): (Ibiza) dish of boiled and sautéed meats and vegetables

sofrito/sofregit: sauce base, a sauté of onions and other finely chopped vegetables

solomillo: sirloin

T

tinto de verano: "summer red," red wine with lemonade or fizzy soda and lots of ice

tocinillo de cielo: "heavenly bacon," a sweet made of egg yolks and sugar

tocino: fatty bacon

torta: 1) flatbread; 2) type of rich unctuous sheep's cheese, e.g., torta del casar

tortilla de patatas: Spanish potato omelet

tortillita de camarón: shrimp fritters, made with a thin batter and sizzled a la plancha

turrón: honey and almond nougat, eaten at Christmas. There are two basic types: turrón de Alicante (hard) and turrón de Jijona (soft)

txakoli (Basq): acidic white wine from Basque country

txistorra (Basq.): long thin sausage sold in coils, of Basque/Navarrese origin

txoko (Basq.): gastronomic society

U

urta: fish common on the coast of Cádiz, most often prepared a la roteña (in the style of Rota) with peppers, tomato, and potato

V

venta: roadside locale combining elements of restaurant, shop, bar, and gas station, common in the south of Spain

vi d'agulla (Cat.)/*vino de aguja*: acidic white "needle wine," slightly sparkling

vi ranci (Cat.): maderized wine made from the Garnatxa grape, commonly used in cooking

vieiras (Gal.): scallops

vinagreta: Spanish sauce, similar to French vinaigrette, traditionally includes finely chopped onion, parsley, and boiled egg

vuelta y vuelta: "turn and turn," anything briefly cooked on both sides

Y

yema: egg yolk, also refers to the convent sweet made of it

Z

zorongollo: murciano dish of zucchini, onion, and egg

zurrukutuna (Basq.): salt cod, pepper, and egg soup

Restaurants:
A Personal Selection

Andalusia

Café de Paris
C/Vélez-Málaga 8
Málaga (La Malagueta)
tel. 952 225043
www.rcafedeparis.com

El Faro del Puerto
Avenida de Fuentebravia s/n, km
 0.500
El Puerto de Santa María (Cádiz)
tel. 956 870952
www.elfarodelpuerto.com

Calima
Hotel Gran Meliá Don Pepe
C/José Meliá s/n
Marbella
tel. 952 764252
www.restaurantecalima.com

El Campero
Avenida de la Constitución 5C
Barbate (Cádiz)
tel. 956 432300

Asturias

Casa Marcelo
La Salgar 1
Arriondas
tel. 985 840991
e-mail: restaurant@casamarcelo.net

Casa Gerardo
Crta AS-19, km 9
Prendes
tel. 985 887797
www.casa-gerardo.com

Basque Country

Akelarre
Paseo Padre Orcolaga 56
 (Barrio Igueldo)
San Sebastián (Guipúzcoa)
tel. 943 311209
www.akelarre.net

Gaminiz
Parque Tecnológico Zamudio 212
Zamudio (Vizcaya)
tel. 94 431 7025
www.gaminiz.com

Arzak
Avenida Alcalde Elosegui 273
San Sebastián (Guipúzcoa)
tel. 943 285593
www.arzak.es

Guggenheim Bilbao
Abandoibarra Etorbidea 2
Bilbao (Vizcaya)
tel. 94 423 9333

Mugaritz
Caserio Otzazulueta
Aldura Aldea 20
Errenteria-Rentería (Guipúzcoa)
tel. 943 522455
www.mugaritz.com

Martín Berasategui
C/Loidi 4, Lasarte-Oria
 (Guipúzcoa)
tel. 943 366471
www.martinberasategui.com

Arbola-Gaña
Museo de Bellas Artes
Alameda Conde Arreche s/n
 corner of Plaza Eduardo Chillida
Bilbao (Vizcaya)
tel. 94 442 4657

Castile–La Mancha

Las Rejas
C/General Borrero 49
Las Pedroñeras (Cuenca)
tel. 967 161089
www.lasrejas.net

El Bohío
Avenida Castilla–La Mancha
 s/n 81
Illescas (Toledo)
tel. 925 511126
www.elbohio.com

Catalonia

Can Jubany
Crta Sant Hilari s/n
Calldetenes (Barcelona)
tel. 93 889 1023
www.canjubany.com

Sant Pau
Carrer Nou 10
Sant Pol de Mar (Barcelona)
tel. 937 600662
www.ruscalleda.com

El Celler de Can Roca
Crta Taialà 40
Girona
tel. 972 222157
www.cellercanroca.com

El Bulli
Cala Montjoi
Roses (Girona)
tel. 972 150457
www.elbulli.com

Les Cols
Mas Les Cols
Crta de la Canya s/n
Olot (Girona)
tel. 972 269209
www.lescols.com

La Xicra
Carrer Estret 17
Palafrugell (Girona)
tel. 972 305630

Bonay
Plaça de les Voltes 13
Peratallada (Girona)
tel. 972 634034
www.bonay.com

Cal Campaner
C/Mossen Carles Feliu 2
Roses (Girona)
tel. 972 256954

Abac
C/Rec 79–89
Barcelona
tel. 93 319 6600
www.restaurantabac.com

Restaurant Ot
C/Córcega 537
Barcelona
tel. 93 435 8048
www.otrestaurant.net

Comerç 24
C/Comerç 24
Barcelona
tel. 93 319 2102
www.comerc24.com

Ca l'Isidre
C/Les Flors 12
Barcelona
tel. 93 441 1139
www.calisidre.com

Comunidad Valencia

Casa Salvador
Estany de Cullera s/n
Cullera (Valencia)
tel. 961 720136
www.casasalvador.com

La Rosa
Paseo Neptuno 70
Playa de las Arenas (Valencia)
tel. 963 712076

Ca' Sento
C/Méndez Núñez 17
Valencia
tel. 963 301775

El Poblet
Ctra Les Marines, km 3
Dénia (Alicante)
tel. 965 784179
www.elpoblet.com

Casa Carmina
C/Embarcadero 4
El Saler (Valencia)
tel. 961 830254

Paco
C/San Francisco 2
Pinoso (Alicante)
tel. 965 478023

Casa Pepa
C/Partida Pamis 7–30
Ondara (Alicante)
tel. 965 766606

Extremadura

Atrio
Avenida de España 30
Cáceres
tel. 927 242928
www.restauranteatrio.com

Il Cigno
Avenida de Extremadura 4
Hoyos (Cáceres)
tel. 927 514413

Galicia

Toñi Vicente
Avenida Rosalía de Castro 24
Santiago de Compostela
   (La Coruña)
tel. 981 594100
www.tonivicente.com

Casa Marcelo
Rúa das Hortas 1
Santiago de Compostela
   (La Coruña)
tel. 981 558580
www.casamarcelo.net

Galicia (cont'd)

Dorna
Rúa Castelao 150
O Grove (Pontevedra)
tel. 986 731842

La Rioja

El Portal de Echaurren
C/Héroes de Alcázar 2
Ezcaray
tel. 941 354047
www.echaurren.com

Madrid

Santceloni
Hotel Hesperia
Paseo de la Castellana 57
Madrid
tel. 91 210 8840
www.restaurantsantceloni.com

La Broche
Hotel Miguel Angel
C/Miguel Angel 29
Madrid
tel. 91 399 3437
www.labroche.com

Príncipe de Viana
C/Manuel de Falla 5
Madrid
tel. 91 457 1549

La Terraza del Casino
Casino de Madrid
C/Alcalá 15
Madrid
tel. 91 521 8700
www.casinodemadrid.es

El Chaflán
Avenida Pío XII 34
Madrid
tel: 91 350 6193
www.elchaflan.com

Navarre

Maher
C/Ribera 19
Cintruénigo
tel. 948 811150
www.hotelmaher.com

Bibliography

Spanish Food, General

Adrià, Ferran, *Los Secretos de El Bulli* (Barcelona: Altaya, 1997).

Almodóvar, Miguel Angel, *Rutas con Sabor* (Barcelona: RBA, 2001).

Anson, Rafael, *La Gastronomía Española* (León: Everest, 2000).

Bienzobas, Águeda, *Recetas Tradicionales* (Barcelona: Zendrera, 1999).

Camba, Julio, *La Casa de Lúpulo o el Arte de Comer* (Madrid: Espasa Calpe, 1968).

Capel, José Carlos, *Homenaje a la Tortilla de Patata* (Barcelona: Planeta, 2003).

La Cocina Monacal: Secretos Culinarios de las Clarisas (Barcelona: Planeta, 1999).

Davidson, Alan, *The Tío Pepe Guide to the Seafood of Spain and Portugal* (London: Anness Publishing, 1992).

Doménech, Ignasi, *Guía del Gastrónomo (Vademécum Culinario)* (Barcelona: Quintilla y Cardona, 1968).

———, *Ayunos y Abstinencias: Cocina de Cuaresma* (Barcelona: Alta Fulla, 1982).

Domingo, Xavier, *Cuando Solo Nos Queda la Comida* (Barcelona: Tusquets, 1980).

García, Abraham, *El Placer de Comer* (Madrid: Síntesis, 2004).

García, Jacinto, *Un Convento de Aromas* (Junta de Comunidades de Castilla–La Mancha, 2002).

García Santos, Rafael, *Lo Mejor de la Gastronomía* (Barcelona: Destino, 2004).

Herrera, Ana María, *Manual Clásico de Cocina* (Madrid: El País Aguilar, 2000).

Luján, Nestor, and Perucho, Juan, *El Libro de la Cocina Española* (Barcelona: Tusquets, 2005).

Martínez, Francisco, *Arte de Cocina, Pastelería, Vizcochería y Conservería* (Barcelona: Imprenta de María Angela Martí, 1763).

Menús Familiares (Madrid: Ministerio de Comercio, 1974).

Muñoz Redón, Josep, *La Cocina del Pensamiento* (Barcelona: RBA, 2005).

Muro, Ángel, *El Practicón* (Madrid: Poniente, 1982).

Ortega, Simone, *Mil Ochenta Recetas de Cocina* (Madrid: Alianza, 1972).

Pérez, Dionisio, *La Cocina Clásica Española* (Huesca: La Val de Onsera, 1994).

―――, *Guía del Buen Comer Español* (Madrid: Rivadeneyra, 1929).

Puga y Parga, Manuel María, *La Cocina Práctica* (Santiago de Compostela: Galí, 1972).

Vázquez Montalbán, Manuel, *Contra los Gourmets* (Barcelona: Mondadori, 1997).

―――, *Saber o No Saber* (Barcelona: Ediciones B, 2002).

―――, *Segundo Libro de Cocina* (Barcelona: Muchnik, 1982).

Vega, Luis Antonio de, *Viaje por la Cocina Española* (Madrid: Salvat, 1969).

Regional Spanish Cuisines

Amate, Pablo, *Gastronomía Granadina* (Ayuntamiento de Granada, 1996).

Barcelona Served: Cuina Catalana Contemporània (Ajuntament de Barcelona, 2005).

Bennison, Vicky, *The Taste of a Place: Andalucía* (London: Chakula Press, 2005).

Carpinell (viuda de), Elàdia, *Carmencita o la Buena Cocinera* (Barcelona: Librería Universitaria, 2001).

Castro, Xavier, *Ayunos y Yantares* (Madrid: Nivola, 2001).

Chela, José H., et al., *Cincuenta Recetas Fundamentales de la Cocina Canaria* (Santa Cruz de Tenerife: Cabildo de Tenerife, 2004).

Cofradía Extremeña de Gastronomía, *Nuevo Recetario de Cocina Extremeña* (Mérida: Caja Rural de Extremadura, 2001).

Delgado, Carlos, *Comer en Madrid* (Madrid: Penthalon, 1981).

Doménech, Ignasi, *La Teca* (Barcelona: Març 80, 1994).

Iglesias, Pepe, *Asturias Gastronómica* (Posada de Llanera (Asturias): AG Ediciones, 2004).

Lladonosa i Giró, Josep, *La Cuina que Torna* (Barcelona: Empúries, 1997).

Núñez, Elisa, *Cocina Charra* (Madrid: Alianza, 2002).

Osona Terra de Cuina (Osona Cuina, 2001).

Osorio, Carlos, *Tabernas y Tapas de Madrid* (Madrid: Ediciones La Librería, 2004).

Parellada, Ramón, *El Llibre de les Picades* (Barcelona: La Magrana, 2000).

Pla, Josep, *El Que Hem Menjat* (I and II) (Barcelona: Destino, 1992).

Richardson, Paul, *Williams-Sonoma Barcelona: Authentic Recipes Celebrating the Foods of the World* (San Francisco: Oxmoor House, 2005).

Suárez Granda, Juan Luis, *La Fabada* (Gijón: Trea, 2001).

Taibo, Paco Ignacio, *Breviario de la Fabada* (Barcelona: Mondadori, 1988).

Thibaut i Comalada, Eliana, *La Cuina dels Països Catalans* (Barcelona: Pòrtic, 2001).

Vergara, Antonio, *Anuario Gastronómico de la Comunidad Valenciana* (Valencia: Gratacels, 2004).

Zarzalejos, María de, *Cocina del Camino de Santiago* (Madrid: Alianza, 1993).

History

Almodóvar, Miguel Angel, *El Hambre en España* (Madrid: Oberón, 2003).

Altimiras, Juan, *Nuevo Arte de Cocina* (De la Luna, 2001).

Cunqueiro, Álvaro, *La Cocina Cristiana de Occidente* (Barcelona: Tusquets, 1991).

Díaz, Lorenzo, *Cocina del Quijote* (Madrid: Alianza, 1979).

———, *Cocina del Barroco: La Gastronomía del Siglo de Oro* (Madrid: Alianza, 2003).

Domingo, Xavier, *De la Olla al Mole* (Madrid: Cultura Hispánica, 1984).

Espinet, Miguel, *El Espacio Culinario: De la Taberna Romana a la Cocina Profesional y Doméstica del Siglo XX* (Barcelona: Tusquets, 1984).

Fausto Rodríguez de Sanabria, Luis, *Recetas para Después de una Guerra* (Madrid: Aguilar, 2000).

Fernández-Armesto, Felipe, *Historia de la Comida* (Barcelona: Tusquets, 2004).

Gutiérrez Rueda, Carmen and Laura, *El Hambre en el Madrid de la Guerra Civil* (Madrid: Ediciones La Librería, 2003).

Huici, Ambrosio, *Cocina Hispano-Magrebí durante la Epoca Almohade* (Gijón: Trea, 2005).

Martínez Llopis, Manuel, *Historia de la Gastronomía Española* (Madrid: Alianza, 1989).

Nola, Ruperto de, *Libro de Guisados, Manjares y Potajes, Intitulado Libro de Cozina* (facsimile) (Barcelona: Espasa Calpe, 1992).

Núñez Florencio, Rafael, *Con la Salsa de su Hambre* (Madrid: Alianza, 2004).

Redon, Odile, *Delicias de la Gastronomía Medieval* (Madrid: Anaya y Mario Muchnik, 1996).

Revel, Jean-François, *Un Festín en Palabras: Historia de la Sensibilidad Gastronómica* (Barcelona: Tusquets, 1996).

Rodinson, Maxine, et al., *Medieval Arab Cookery* (Totnes: Prospect Books, 2001).

Sánchez Jiménez, José, *La Vida Rural en la España del Siglo XX* (Barcelona: Planeta, 1975).

Other Works Consulted

Altman, Donald, *Del Cielo a la Mesa* (Barcelona: Integral, 2000).

Berger, John, *Pig Earth* (London: Vintage, 1992).

Ford, Richard, *Handbook for Travellers in Spain and Readers at Home* (Arundel: Centaur Press, 1966).

Lee, Laurie, *As I Walked Out One Midsummer Morning* (London: Penguin, 1979).

Lewis, Norman, *Voices of the Old Sea* (London: Picador, 1996).

Martínez, Angel, *De Techo y Olla: Alojamiento y Cocina en los Libros de Viaje* (Madrid: Miraguano, 2002).

Sen, Miguel, *Un Artículo de Encargo* (Barcelona: RBA, 2004).

Acknowledgments

TO THANK EVERYONE individually who has contributed to the existence of this book would take up more space than is either reasonable or practical. But there are certain debts that need declaring. I am permanently grateful to my mother—who was, after all, the first person to put food on my table—and to my father, brother, sister, and sister-in-law. On the Spanish side, my thanks go out the extended Trives family, whose loyalty and love have been a constant in my chaotic expatriate life.

A heartfelt gracias to all the chefs and cooks, farmers and fishermen who gave freely of their time and expertise—especially to those whose names appear in the text, but also to Javier Oyarbide, Serxio Ces, Sergi Arola, Francis Paniego, Carme Ruscalleda, Angel León, Dani García, Abraham García—and to all those friends, contacts, and acquaintances who have added in small or large measure to my vision of the country and its way of eating. Just a few of these people are: Piluca Molina, Vicente, and all my friends in Valencia; Ana Valls in Madrid; the Arribas family in Plasencia and Bilbao; the Pousa family in O Grove; Wulf and Edwina Taeger in Riudarenes; María Fernández in Granada; Shelagh Vanderpool in Barcelona; Caridad Hernández, Claudio and Cesarea, Antonio, and little Jara; Eva Rincón; Jesús Ladero and Petri García; Antonio Navarro and Luigina diMeo; Mikel and Miren; Miguel Muriel and Nazaret Téllez; Pepa Miranda and her parents; Paloma Rozalen; Caco and Torro; Loli and Siro, María Vázquez, José and Mencía, and all our good neighbors in the Sierra. Special love and thanks, though she is sadly not around to receive them, to the late

Sally Stein. Not forgetting those friends in the UK who are still on my virtual Christmas-card list despite the distances in time and space, including Katie Owen, Katy Emck, Neil Crombie and David Brooke, Sacha Schoenfeld, Alex Willcock, Adam and Emma Barker, Carol Downie, Catherine Heard and Carla Pinto, Marlena Spieler, John and Antonia Price, Ruth Afzali, Jason Lowe and Lori de Mori, Colin Spencer and Claire Clifton.

On a professional note, I would like to offer my gratitude to Maria José Sevilla, who unwittingly kick-started my adventures in Spanish food, and to Sarah Spankie and Sarah Miller at *Condé Nast Traveller,* whose commissions for the magazine have formed the basis of my knowledge of modern Spanish restaurant cooking. Thanks, too, to my agent Julian Alexander for his many years of loyal support, to my editor in the U.S. Alexis Gargagliano for her great enthusiasm and efficiency, and to copy editor Susan Gamer for a job meticulously done.

About the Author

Paul Richardson has lived for more than fifteen years in Spain, where he has a small farm with a vineyard and olive groves. He is the author of several books published by Little, Brown UK: *Our Lady of the Sewers and Other Adventures in Deep Spain*; *Cornucopia: A Gastronomic Tour of Britain*; and *Indulgence: One Man's Selfless Search for the Best Chocolate in the World*, as well as *Williams-Sonoma Barcelona: Authentic Recipes Celebrating the Foods of the World*, which was published in the United States.